LITURGY AND POWER

LITURGY AND POWER

Brian P. Flanagan and Johann M. Vento
Editors

**THE ANNUAL PUBLICATION
OF THE COLLEGE THEOLOGY SOCIETY
2016
VOLUME 62**

ORBIS BOOKS
Maryknoll, New York 10545

ORBIS BOOKS
Maryknoll, New York 10545

Fathers and Brothers
MARYKNOLL™

Founded in 1970, Orbis Books endeavors to publish works that enlighten the mind, nourish the spirit, and challenge the conscience. The publishing arm of the Maryknoll Fathers and Brothers, Orbis seeks to explore the global dimensions of the Christian faith and mission, to invite dialogue with diverse cultures and religious traditions, and to serve the cause of reconciliation and peace. The books published reflect the views of their authors and do not represent the official position of the Maryknoll Society. To learn more about Maryknoll and Orbis Books, please visit our website at www.maryknollsociety.org.

Library of Congress Cataloging-in-Publication Data

Names: College Theology Society. Annual Meeting (2016 : Rockhurst University)
 | Flanagan, Brian P., editor.
Title: Liturgy and power / Brian P. Flanagan and Johann M. Vento, editors.
Description: Maryknoll : Orbis Books, 2017. | Series: The annual publication
 of the College Theology Society ; VOLUME 62
Identifiers: LCCN 2016050196 (print) | LCCN 2017006590 (ebook) | ISBN
 9781626982178 (pbk.) | ISBN 9781608336821 (e-book)
Subjects: LCSH: Catholic Church—Liturgy—Congresses.
Classification: LCC BX1970 .C654 2016 (print) | LCC BX1970 (ebook) |
DDC
 230/.2—dc23
LC record available at https://lccn.loc.gov/2016050196

Contents

v

Part III
Liturgy and Power in Lived Religion

Introduction

Brian P. Flanagan and Johann M. Vento

In *Sacrosanctum Concilium*, the Second Vatican Council declared that "the liturgy is the summit toward which the activity of the Church is directed; at the same time it is the font from which all her power flows" (§10). The liturgy is a crucial location of praxis and theological reflection, and in its various forms it also raises numerous questions about power, human and divine, in the Christian life. The 2016 Annual Meeting of the College Theology Society at Rockhurst University in Kansas City, Missouri, focused upon these two complex, multifaceted realities and their interaction: the ritual and symbolic practices of the Christian tradition, and forms of power—positive and negative, human and divine, coercive and non-competitive—that are encountered in and through the liturgy. The conference, and the essays in this volume, take their starting point from the conciliar insight into the liturgy as the "source and summit" of the life of the Church. Through attention to power, weakness, and lived practice, these authors explore the liturgy's slopes and plumb its depths to provide signposts for further exploration of this primary source of Christian life and thought.

The late twentieth and early twenty-first centuries have seen a flourishing of scholarly study of both liturgy and power. Built upon the foundations of the liturgical movement and the postconciliar reform of the liturgy in the Roman Catholic Church, theological reflection on the liturgy and liturgical theology taking the lived ritual practice of the church as *theologia prima* have matured and grown in the past five decades. In addition to an ever-growing corpus of critical historical studies of the past forms of the liturgy, attention to ritual studies, theories of embodiment, and ethnographic and other anthropological methodologies have allowed for new and increasingly sophisticated theologies of and from the liturgy.

At the same time, growth in the study of the nature and contours of power has been a key aspect of developments in philosophy and critical theory in the past decades. Scholars in these fields have worked to highlight the complex relations between power, knowledge, and the structures of human activity. Further, scholarly attention across a variety of disciplines came to focus upon the diversity of forms of power, including forms of agency exercised by marginalized or "subaltern" communities and voices, as well as powers of resistance exercised in struggles for liberation.

While the topic and plenary speakers for our Annual Meeting were chosen well in advance, our gathering was marked by attention within and without our sessions to the complex realities of power in the United States in the year 2016. It has been a time marked by violence and threats of violence, particularly against young African American men, by the demonization of immigrants and refugees, and by the rituals of a presidential election season suffused with the rhetoric of power and weakness. At the same time, religious leaders and theologians pushed back against "the powers" of racism, xenophobia, and hatred. The 2016 meeting, and the essays in this volume, therefore, were not formulated in an abstract zone of scholarly indifference, but are rooted in the particularly ambiguous context of life in our country in an unsettled time.

This volume provides some sense of the richness of the conversation at the 2016 Annual Meeting. While the particularities of these essays overlap in ways that defy easy categorization, we have organized them into three broad parts, each anchored by one of the meeting's plenary addresses. Part I, "Liturgy and Power, Human and Divine" looks broadly at the nature of power and liturgy within the structures and practices of the Christian church, as related to the way the power of God can be seen at work in the liturgy, beginning with Bruce Morrill's attention to the ambiguities of power in a particular liturgical experience. Part II, "Liturgy and the World: Weakness and Power," looks at power of and in the liturgy as this functions in relationship to the world. Susan Ross's essay situates this part's particular focus upon the ambiguous, paradoxical power of weakness and the use of power in the service of liberation. Part III, "Liturgy and Power in Lived Religion," focuses upon the phenomena of power in particular liturgical and paraliturgical practices; while all three parts attend to the interplay of theory and praxis, this third part starts from what Ricky Manalo outlines in his essay as the "liturgy of life." The essays in each part explore these dynamics by engaging the topic of liturgy and power in relation to violence and trauma, environmental, racial, and gender justice, spiritual practice, family life, religious life, and ecumenism. As is the case with any collected volume, this collection might be better compared to a quilt stitched together from multiple swatches or, perhaps more appropriately for a theological volume, of an abstract stained glass window composed of multiple unique pieces of colored glass. Yet it is our hope that the reader will appreciate, as we have, the light shed upon liturgy and power in and through these particular authors' voices.

Liturgy and Power, Human and Divine

Bruce Morrill's plenary address, "Sacramental Liturgy as Negotiation of Power, Human and Divine," opens up a horizon of inquiry for the entire volume by outlining a theoretical approach to the reality of human and divine power in sacramental-liturgical experience and its analysis, and by exemplifying some of the contours of such analysis in his treatment of a particular liturgical event. The first part of the text draws on a history of liturgical-sacramental theology and on the thought of Louis-Marie Chauvet and Bernard Cooke to argue that any analysis of the power of sacraments and liturgy must begin with attention to liturgy as an activity, and therefore to concrete, particular experiences of liturgy, if theology is to understand the dynamics of human and divine power therein. In the second part of his text, Morrill exemplifies this inductive approach to liturgical analysis and theology in narrating an experience of an Ash Wednesday liturgy particularly marked by cross-currents of power, human and divine. This narrative leads to his further analysis on the ambiguous symbolic power of Ash Wednesday, in the particular related experience and beyond. Morrill concludes with an emphasis, echoed throughout the following papers in this part, on the paradoxical divine-human power of the paschal mystery that can best, or even only, be studied through attention to the particularities of the activity of the liturgy. The essays that follow in this part further highlight the ambiguity of power in the experience and study of the liturgy.

In her essay, "The Power of Memory and Witnessing: A Trauma-Informed Analysis of *Anamnesis* in the Roman Catholic Mass," Annie Selak weaves together a treatment of memory in trauma theory and in liturgical theology. She suggests ways in which the understanding of memory pursued in trauma studies might inform and reform theologians' conception of *anamnesis* in the Eucharist. Using the notions of "memory" and "witnessing," Selak suggests that trauma theory might helpfully contribute to an understanding of how the particular remembering of liturgical *anamnesis* has the power it does in the life of the Christian community.

Paul Schutz highlights the shortcomings of the treatment of the Eucharist in Pope Francis's encyclical *Laudato Si'* in his essay "'All Creation Sings': The Ecological Crisis, *Laudato Si'*, and an Orthodoxy of Praise." Drawing on the work of Aidan Kavanaugh, Schutz argues that the "magisterial model" of the Eucharist, in which liturgy is domesticated from a powerful encounter with God to a discourse about God, is operative in *Laudato Si'*'s sparse references to the Eucharist as a source for addressing the deformations of our common home. Schutz then suggests ways in which a deeper praxis of the Eucharist as act would allow the Eucharist to "manifest its full power as an impetus to ecological conversion," and better support the call to conversion to which Pope Francis is calling the church and all women and men of good will.

"Liturgy as Power-Sharing: Synergy for Solidarity," Marcus Mescher's contribution to the volume, uses the category of "synergy" to discuss the invitation to share power and relationship with God and with each other in the liturgy, and at the reasons why such synergy for solidarity fails to occur. He names three possible obstacles: the inequalities and divisions that mark life within and without the church today; a "sacramental optimism" that discusses efficacy of the sacraments without reference to the more ambiguous, wounded locations in which they are celebrated; and a "sacramental consumerism" in which the liturgy is experienced primarily as an object of spiritual consumption rather than as invitation to active participation. He concludes with some strategies for addressing these obstacles in the life of the church.

Liturgy and the World: Weakness and Power

"Power and Weakness: Liturgy, Justice, and the World," Susan Ross's contribution to this volume, similarly begins with narrative attention to particular events, academic and sacramental, and especially to a dangerous memory of power in weakness that exemplifies the paradox named in her title. She continues in the first part of her essay by outlining, with the help of John Caputo, Sarah Coakley, and other philosophers and theologians, a theology of the "weak power" of God, and of the possible reception of that weak power by humans in and through the God-given weakness of our bodies. She then turns to the ambiguity of the exercise of power in the liturgy, looking at both the liturgy's own weak power, and at the liturgy's vulnerability to other exercises of power, weak and strong, through continuing narrative attention to some of her experiences. She then concludes by exploring the relation of liturgy, power, and justice, attending to the danger and the promise of the weak power of self-gift, particularly in the lives of women for whom disempowerment has been an ecclesial reality and with whom the language of self-gift must be used with deep caution. And yet she concludes by pointing to particular liturgical acts, including but not limited to the Eucharist, in which the weak power of God, of the liturgy, and of the marginalized can be a source of transformative resistance and encounter with God. The papers that follow in this part highlight this capacity of liturgy as a "weak" response to suffering at the hands of "naked" power and the interplay of liturgical power and weakness in the service of struggles for justice in the world.

In response to Pope Francis's call in *Laudato Si'* for the cultivation of "sound virtues" needed "to make a selfless ecological commitment," Anne Clifford's essay, "The Power of Liturgical Lament to Evoke Ecological Virtues," proposes and constructs a communal para-liturgical day of prayer designed, through the use of lament as well as reflection on the cardinal virtues, to lead its participants to greater capacity for virtuous action in the face of ecological destruction.

Krista Stevens recalls the intrinsic connection between liturgy and ethics as she describes the deep embeddedness of concern for social justice in the African American liturgical renewal movement. Her essay, "Recovering Liturgy: African American Catholic Liturgical Revivalism," explores two examples of this connection, the Interracial Sundays which defied segregation to bring together black and white Catholic college students for worship, breakfast, and theological reflection in the Jim Crow South, and the work of Fr. Clarence R. J. Rivers in the African American liturgical renewal rooted in the call to meet the concrete needs of the people for hope and justice.

Todd Whitmore's essay "Traditional Devotion, Radical Witness: Insights from Fieldwork in Conflict Northern Uganda'" calls into question the supposed divide between liberal and conservative Catholics, sometimes characterized as "social justice" versus "right to life" Catholics. Using testimony from Catholic nuns in Northern Uganda about their activities during a recent period of violent conflict, in conversation with the work of anthropologist James George Frazer, Whitmore makes the case that traditional devotional practices normally associated with a conservative form of Catholicism empower the Little Sisters of Mary Immaculate of Gulu to radical, life-risking witness to peace and justice.

Arising out of a panel offered at the annual meeting entitled "Women's Silent Suffering: Constructive Theological and Liturgical Responses," Cynthia Cameron's and Susan Bigelow Reynolds's essays give voice to two often-silenced experiences of women's bodies, self-injury and prenatal loss, and in their constructive proposals suggest ways in which the liturgy can further give voice and make manifest Christ's love for women who suffer in silence. In her study of women, particularly young women, who self-injure in "Hidden Self-Injury and Public Liturgy," Cameron argues for strategies in addition to the Anointing of the Sick that would not reinforce the hiddenness often conjoined to forms of self-harm. She suggests that the Eucharist and other forms of public prayer are untapped locations for the church's pastoral care of women who self-injure. Reynolds, in "Catholic Liturgy and Prenatal Loss: Ritual, Ambiguity, and the Miscarrying Body," similarly argues for ways in which the church's liturgy, particularly a liturgy more open to the agency and leadership of women, is necessary to bring experiences of miscarriage out of the shadows of the church community. Doing so, she suggests, would lead not only to better pastoral care for women in the church, but also to new insights into bodily relationality and sacramental theology. Both authors draw upon Susan Ross's understanding of the ambiguity of the sacraments and of women's bodies, and so it is fitting that her response to these theologians' engagement with her thought is included here.

Liturgy and Power in Lived Religion

"The Liturgy of Life: The Eucharist, Power, and Lived Religion," the third plenary address of the meeting, explores the relationship between Eucharistic liturgy and worship practices that occur in everyday life. Ricky Manalo argues that liturgical studies must take into consideration the interrelations between the Sunday Eucharist and the ways in which the religious lives of Catholics are expressed in unofficial worship practices. He reviews the work of Peter Phan in characterizing unofficial worship practices of everyday life and the Eucharist as one movement of worship. Manalo then puts into dialogue the insights of sociologists of religion and his own ethnographic research to argue for "the dynamic interrelationship between Sunday Eucharist and other worshipful practices that occur in everyday life." The following three papers in this part take up the theme of the relationship of the "official" liturgy to everyday life in a variety of ways.

In "Words Uttered by God: Reformulating 'Source and Summit' Language with Karl Rahner," Michael Rubbelke contributes to the discussion of the apparent disconnect between the liturgy as summit and source of the church's life with the everyday lives of Christians in the world. Drawing on Rahner's understanding of prayer, Rubbelke suggests an alternate formulation whereby the *Word* of God, Christ, is the summit and source of the liturgy, which in turn empowers the call of Christians to become *words* of God in the world.

Anne McGowan, in "The Power to Bless: The Negotiation of Ecclesial Authority and Christian Identity in Roman Catholic Liturgical Blessings of Parents and Children," explores ambiguity about clerical and lay power embedded in norms about the use of liturgical blessings of children. Her work argues that blessings by parents of children that take place outside of church, in the context of family life, are themselves liturgical. She also analyzes the texts of blessings of children and parents, surfacing power dynamics implicit in the blessings revealing limiting assumptions about the value of childhood for Christian life and hierarchies of gender with regard to blessings of parents.

The essay "The Power of Virtual Space" arises out of a panel presented at the Consultation of Evangelical Catholics and Catholic Evangelicals at the annual convention. The theme of the consultation this year was liturgy and contemporary social and communications media. Derek C. Hatch and Katherine G. Schmidt offer an ecumenical conversation about the potential power of virtuality. The first part of the essay argues for a broad understanding of virtuality that encompasses ancient Christian notions of mediation and sacramentality. Here, Schmidt argues for taking virtuality seriously for its capacity to proliferate new extra-liturgical spaces, ancillary to the eucharistic assembly, to replace the older such groups that are on the wane in our current suburbanized Christianity. The second part takes up the theme of the potential of virtuality in supporting a broadly democratic ecumenical movement which transgresses traditional confessional boundaries in open theological and liturgical sharing. Through the power of virtuality, both authors observe the increasing power of the laity to extend liturgical action into the everyday lives of Christians to bring about a "renewed vision of the fullness of the church catholic."

Final Insights

There is a longstanding, and usually unfair, joke in some circles about the difficulty of negotiating with a liturgical specialist.[1] But one insight that comes to the fore in these essays is the centrality of serious, faithful, and often improvised negotiation of power among individuals, communities, and God in and through the practices of liturgical prayer. In a chapter on ritual and power in his pneumatological study *Power and the Spirit of God*, the late Bernard Cooke writes, "Religious ritual is meant to be the external enacting in bodily 'dance' of the inner, never resolved dialectic between God's loving and human freedom—a special kind of 'conflict' upon which man's other 'powers' impinge, a conflict that is not oppressive but lovingly welcomed."[2] The essays in this volume provide vivid examples of the negotiation of human and divine power in and through the liturgy, and together an exemplar of the complex, ambiguous, and never resolved theological task of studying the paschal dance between God and humanity. Our hope is that this volume will contribute to further practical and theoretical appropriation of liturgy and power.

Acknowledgments

We would like to take the opportunity to thank the many individuals who made this volume possible. In the first place, we would like to thank the authors whose work appears here, particularly our three plenary speakers, Bruce Morrill, Susan Ross, and Ricky Manalo. We also want to thank all those who submitted contributions for the Annual Volume, and the nearly 80 members of the society who served as reviewers of those submissions, assisting us in our task of evaluating the many excellent essays we received, some of which, sadly, we were unable to include. We thank those who made the 2016 Annual Meeting such a rich and fruitful meeting, including the section conveners; our hosts at Rockhurst University, especially local coordinator Glenn Young; and the Society's Director of Conventions, David Gentry-Akin. The careful attention of the Society's Director of Publications, Bill Collinge, was indispensable to the clarity and precision of the finished text. Finally, Jim Keane of Orbis Books has been a patient and gentle guide through the entire publishing process.

Notes

[1]"What's the difference between a liturgist and a terrorist?" "You can negotiate with a terrorist."

[2]Bernard Cooke, *Power and the Spirit of God* (New York: Oxford University Press, 2004), 155.

PART I

LITURGY AND POWER,
HUMAN AND DIVINE

Sacramental Liturgy as Negotiation of Power, Human and Divine

Bruce T. Morrill, SJ

Please allow me to begin by saying that I found myself honored and privileged to lead off the CTS annual meeting, to be entrusted with addressing the meeting's theme, "Liturgy and Power," in such a way, I presumed and could only hope, as to be informative, perhaps insightful, and even motivational for the panoply of presentations, panels, and discussions that took place. That decision about and action on the theme on the part of the convention chairs and society board was already an exercise of power—albeit not, I trust, in the form of despotic, authoritarian command to you, the members: "You *will* engage the topic of liturgy and power, and you *will* enjoy it!" That would, of course, amount to the power of force and its constant complement, fear, which, frankly, I rather doubt these individuals can affect.

My little (attempt at a) joke here intends to indicate the complexity, but also the theoretical generativity, of the term "power," a concept that, as we all know, has over the past several decades gained broad currency as an analytical tool in the social sciences and humanities. Without bogging down in a comprehensive literature review, I would just note the influential contribution of Michel Foucault, who argued that theoretical reifications of power, that is, thinking about or promoting power as if "it" were a substantive entity, constitute a fundamental category mistake. Power is not a "thing" to be possessed or deployed but, rather, an activity situated in a social body, a web of relationships, wherein people act with and/or upon others so as to direct their activity (what they think and do with their lives). For this reason, ritual theorist Catherine

Bell explains, Foucault argued in terms not of a theory of power (for that would only aid and abet a substantive understanding of power) but rather of an "analytics of power." This approach Bell finds analogous to Clifford Geertz's "poetics of power," whereby power cannot be conceived as "something external to its social workings."[1] Building on those philosophical and social-scientific insights, as well as those of others, such as Pierre Bourdieu, Bell made her contribution to analyzing rituals by likewise arguing in terms of ritualization and ritual bodies, that is, for approaching rituals always as specific activities wherein the bodies performing them maintain or become the persons they are within that body of social relations.

If we return, then, to my opening words for this essay, the joke lay in my misrepresenting the sort of social body the College Theology Society functionally is and, thus, the type of power the membership affords its officers to practice in relation to them and the Society's purpose and goals. But prior to that little zinger (and therefore probably already forgotten in its wake) I began by laying out what I saw to be the power invested in me and my role or activity in the opening plenary ritual at CTS, namely, the power of conveying knowledge, the power of exercising imagination, and the power of motivating this social body in its activity for several days.

I speak here of Bell, of course, due to her work's relevance to my own field of sacramental-liturgical theology. That hyphenated term is the clumsy effort at indicating that sacraments, like all rituals, are not things but, rather, symbolic activities performed by and for ritual bodies. The Christian term for such activity is liturgy, and so yoking the terms "sacramental" and "liturgical" is the strategy many of us in my field have adopted in order to indicate—to symbolize—the irreducibly praxiological, bodily practical, nature of our subject matter. The sacraments and other rites of the church only exist in performance by its members, which are clergy and laity. And they are powerful . . . or not. That last tag, however, points to the disquiet the turn to social-scientific theory has caused (if I may speak in generalities) among the Radical Orthodox movement and, in various ways, for some other dogmatic and systematic theologians. Is this not dragging the sublime offer of grace down, reducing humans to power struggles rather than elevating their thoughts to the divine power and offer of grace?

Do we not make a different category mistake by analyzing the rites of the church in those terms rather than primarily (if not in some cases, exclusively) thinking of the sacraments metaphysically and ontologically? After all, Christians believe that the unseen, incorporeal God is acting in the church's sacramental signs for the sanctification of people, in some cases even effecting ontological change in the recipients of those signs (think baptism, confirmation, holy orders) or in the signs themselves (think Eucharist).

Aquinas knew how to think such power, and did so with undeniable brilliance and reverence. If so disposed, that is, if one's faith yearns for understanding *and* if one understands at least the rudiments of Platonic and Aristotelian philosophy, the reader enters a beautiful "world" in the *Summa Theologiae* wherein, as Mark Jordan persuasively demonstrates,[2] the closing Treatise on the Sacraments functions as the teleological lens for understanding all that has unfolded voluminously before. The sacraments are not some extra add-on to the fundamental theology, anthropology, ethics, and Christology Aquinas has worked out philosophically; rather, they are the means whereby God's grace achieves the very end for which humans are created, namely, body-and-soul participation in the very life of God. Aquinas explains how sacraments are thus effective in terms of powers—the principal cause of grace which is God, the divine power in Christ's Passion operative through his humanity, the powers of human body, intellect, and will created so as to be receptive to the healing (justifying) and sanctifying grace in the sacraments, with the Holy Spirit working through them to make believers active members of the body of Christ. That fellowship, activated and sustained through the instrumental power of the sacraments, gives a veritable share in divine charity and goodness that empowers Christians to enact the virtues of faith, hope, and above all love in their lives.

As we know, Aquinas produced his understanding of the sacraments on the basis of both the writings of Church Fathers before him and the elements of the rites as they were practiced in the medieval church of his day. As I already mentioned, if one enters into his text with a dynamic sense of God's movement (grace) in one's life and the world around one, as well as a fervent and informed participation in and regular exposure to the rites in practice, then study of the *Summa* can indeed prove very powerful. But the problem in seminaries and catechisms was (and, I'm afraid, often still is) that God remained distant, some*body* faraway some*place* (heaven). Unless one finds a way to make the constantly invoked term "charity" affectively connect with experiential knowledge of love,[3] then this can all go very dry very quickly.

Understanding does empower faith. The problem historically was Scholasticism's apologetic reduction of such dynamic and sophisticated thought as that of Aquinas into questions and answers about "things"—God, grace, virtues, etc. Seminary education in post-Tridentine Catholicism came to treat the sacraments as a mere unit in dogmatic theology and canon law. Sacraments were surely upheld as powerful, but within a teach-and-tell seminary context forming the ritual bodies of a teach-and-tell clerical culture, in which deferential loyalty and obedience are the key practical, moral, and political virtues. That system persists and has over the past dozen years or so realized a modest but significant resurgence in new members: seminarians taught and told concepts through ritualization in classrooms and chapels forming them as men sent to teach and tell a laity from whom, in turn, obedience is the ideal expectation.

That such a teaching, sanctifying, and governing model of church was rapidly losing its power on the popular, ground level of European societies by the second half of the twentieth century had become obvious to the redoubtable pastoral intellectuals among the French Dominicans,[4] as well as such Jesuits as Henri de Lubac and Karl Rahner. With his modification of Thomism through a fundamental anthropology of the supernatural existential Rahner produced a steady stream of essays phenomenologically connecting the church's traditional sacraments (as well as popular pious practices called sacramentals) to everyday human experience. Rahner was striving to help fellow believers—clergy, vowed religious, and laity—to tap into the divine power immanent in the spectrum of ritualization across everyday human life and ecclesial traditions.[5] With remarkable efficiency and lucidity Edward Schillebeeckx in his now classic book *Christ, the Sacrament of the Encounter with God* consolidated the achievements of the renewed pastoral-theological scholarship in Patristics and Transcendental Thomism to help the faithful understand and desire the divine meaning to be experienced in the rites and shared in their human lives.[6] Translating the genius of Rahner and Schillebeeckx in a developmental-psychological idiom, Bernard Cooke, in a still widely used textbook, established the deeply traditional principle underlying such phenomenological understanding of the purpose and significance of celebrating the rites by invoking the centuries-old adage: *sacramenta pro populo*.[7] Sacraments are for the benefit of people and only achieve their purpose, let alone "exist" in any real sense, in people's practices of them as integral to their lives of faith and, thus, their lives in the world. The efforts of sacramental theologians, then, have been to renew and augment the power of the rites by making them (more) meaningful for the faithful.

I could, as you might well imagine, rehearse a litany of other major contemporary thinkers of liturgy and sacraments, all of whom have striven to connect liturgy and life, to rescue theological reflection and inspiration for sacramental-liturgical practice from banality and irrelevance for late-modern Catholics (and other Christians).[8] Louis-Marie Chauvet, recognizing that urgency, is a standout with his exhaustive semiotic treatment of sacraments as one pole (along with word and ethics) in the symbolic network of the faith of the church. One extended quote from the French priest-theologian's 550-page tome may serve to convey the theoretical approach and pastoral passion of his project:

> Just as empirical writing is the phenomenal manifestation of an arch-writing that constitutes language as the place where the human subject comes into being, so the sacraments can be appreciated as the empirical manifestation of the *'arch-sacramentality' that constitutes the language of faith*, which is the place where the believing subject comes into being. This arch-sacramentality is a *transcendental condition for Christian existence*. It indicates that *there is no faith unless somewhere inscribed, inscribed in a body*—a body from a specific culture, a body with a concrete history, a body of desire. Baptism, the first sacrament of the faith, shows this well: the plunge into water, together with this 'precipitate' of the Christian Scriptures, which is the mention of the names of the Father and the Son and the Holy Spirit, is a metaphor for being plunged into the body of signifiers—material, institutional, cultural, and traditional—of the Church: assembly, ordained minister, sign of the cross on the forehead, book of the Scriptures, confession of faith, remembrance of Jesus Christ and invocation of the Spirit, paschal candle. . . . . All

these are symbolic elements that are inscribed on the body of every baptized person, his or her *scriptural* body on which they are bestowed as a testament. *One becomes a Christian only by entering an institution and in letting this institution stamp its 'trademark,' its 'character,' on one's body.*

The faith thus appears to us as *'sacramental' in its constitution,* and not simply by derivation. Our existence is Christian insofar as it is always-already structured by sacramentality, better still, as it is *always-already inscribed in the order of the sacramental.* It is thus impossible to conceive of the faith outside of the body.[9]

Chauvet's is, as Lieven Boeve points out,[10] a hermeneutical project in dialogue with philosophy and the social sciences with the intention of interpreting the traditional elements of the faith such that it might still be incarnated in history, be lived and professed as meaningful and empowering in the person-bodies of postmodern Christians. His detailed philosophical and social-scientific analyses of the liturgical rites, attuned to history and tradition, Chauvet always carries out with a view to reviving and/or augmenting their pastoral effectiveness, what Tridentine doctrine called their fruitfulness. But that is just another way of saying, to unleash their potential power. The ultimate power source of the liturgy, indeed, is the Spirit of the Risen Crucified One, a participation in the very life of God. Chauvet does treat of this in the latter part of his major book. Still, the burden of the work is not speculative theology but theoretical, critical understanding to renew the relevance and viability of the faith, to motivate its practice, both ritual and ethical.

Relevance is power. Motivation is power. Knowledge is power. My thinking about and parsing the notion of power along these lines is further influenced by Cooke. Whereas his sacramental theology, both in his writing and tireless teaching in college and pastoral ministry classrooms, comprised exercises in getting people to reflect on how they construct meaning through their life-experiences, in his final writing years Cooke situated symbolic activity, including Christians' sacramental ritualizing, within the larger question of power, divine and human. This he did through essaying an "Experience-Based Pneumatology," the subtitle of his final scholarly book, *Power and the Spirit of God.* Spirit as the power of divine Word is the theological principle for Cooke's sacramental anthropology, an anthropology irreducibly entailing individual human personhood, interpersonal friendship, and social, communitarian life. For this reason, Cooke argues, Christianity is not meant narrowly to be a religion but, rather, a way of being human, a new creation sacramentally realizing divine love in human sharing.[11] That creativity comes by the power of God's Spirit, yet only in prophetic tension with the whole range of ways humans exercise power. Cooke organized the book as a series of thematically grouped chapters along a trajectory starting with the forms of human power he argues are most alienating from the divine (force and fear), through a number with varied potential (office, law, fame, wealth, nature, imagination, and creativity), to the types of human power most amenable to the divine power revealed in scripture and tradition (symbol, word, thought, and ritual). That latter symbolic cluster is particularly amenable to mediating the divine Word in creation and as salvation, with the Word's power being the love that is God's Spirit. Insofar as power ultimately entails the ability to motivate and achieve a particular goal, Cooke argues, Christian theological reflection arrives at love as "the affective movement toward 'the good' . . . the ultimate exercise of power, that is, the motivations that lead humans to action."[12] For Christians that love is definitively revealed in Christ Jesus, especially through word and sacrament. Still, these do not happen in a vacuum, but rather as part of larger communal and societal bodies, including the institutional life of the church, from the local to Vatican levels.

The conclusion and motivation I draw at the end of this first half of my text is that the relationship between liturgy and power must attend to particular experiences of liturgy, particular exercises of the symbolic ritual that nonetheless are always contextual within the whole range of other human forms of power Cooke has identified, such as office and law, creativity and imagination, but also force and fear. For addressing my assigned topic at the moment, I take God's power (grace, the love of the Spirit) in and through the pastoral activity of the church as a theological given, the topic that sacramental theology has covered. The more specifically liturgical-theological questions, on the other hand, necessarily deal with the primary practice of the church's theology, namely, actual people in communities carrying out the rites. If academic, that is to say, second-order theology, is to get at the experience, then I have found, at least for my own methodology, that I can do so only by means of narrative. For this second half of my text, then, I shall now offer an exercise in my inductive approach to liturgical theology, whereby I first recount in some detail a pastoral narrative that I then analyze on the basis of theological resources and with a view toward making normative theological claims. In this case, the analysis is in terms of the types of power, divine and human, at work and being negotiated in a liturgical event. The goal is to think about the liturgical experience such that thought might motivate, renew, or advance practice, so that thought might, to invoke Paul Ricoeur, return to the symbol.

Description and Analysis of a Liturgical Event: Ash Wednesday

About a decade ago while on faculty at a certain Catholic university I was part of a team providing the Sunday evening liturgy on one of the university's undergraduate campuses. Two full-time lay campus ministers, two part-time graduate-student ministers, and three priests made up the team, with the latter presiding and preaching on a rotating basis. As the start of the Lenten Season approached that year, I recall our having a conversation about what to do for the Ash Wednesday liturgy. That this service would take place at the same hour as the Sunday Mass—9 p.m., which in undergrad time, as we know, is roughly midafternoon—was immediately agreed. The other two priests each begged off involvement, saying they would already have helped at a local parish or on another campus that day. All heads turned to me, who asked whether we needed to be working from the assumption that the service should be a Mass, and if not, whether a priest presiding and preaching in this context would be pastorally optimal. I opined that Ash Wednesday is not a "holy day of obligation" and, therefore, did not necessitate a Mass, and that I believed it presented a prime opportunity for the lay chaplains to preside over a Service of the Word with Distribution of Ashes, during which one or even two of them could give homiletic reflections. I was aware that these lay ministers very much desired such opportunities, that the hierarchy's reinforced restriction of the Mass's homily to ordained clergy made awkward the insertion of lay preaching ("reflections") at the beginning or conclusion of Mass (we Catholics are, like all human beings, creatures of habit-memory[13]), and that, in contrast, the order of service for Ash Wednesday would afford the students to hear a word from these ministers at the time to which they were so attuned, namely, after the proclamation of the Gospel. Implied in my argument, of course, was the conviction that, in part, the "medium was the message," that is, that hearing about the call to repentance and conversion from a lay man and woman (rather than a clergyman) could well affect the young people in ways both conscious and subconscious. Such affecting, I note here, can be powerful. I explained that we would not be inventing anything, that the Sacramentary (the missal) provided the complete service, which included all the important ritual components of the Liturgy of the Word (communal song, collect prayer, biblical readings and psalmody, homily, prayers of intercession, but with the distribution of ashes inserted between the latter two). Everybody expressed delight at the idea, and plans began accordingly.

A few days later I received a call from one of the lay chaplains who explained that when she relayed our plan to the priest-director of the Office of Campus Ministry (her boss), he was displeased and insisted that a Mass be celebrated on Ash Wednesday evening. My recollection is that I was a bit surprised that she had to run the plans by him for his approval, but on the other hand I found myself not completely surprised that a priest was insistent that ashes be ministered during Mass. You see, just a few years before, during my last year of doctoral studies when I was earning my room and board in residence at a local parish, the pastor had in similar fashion inextricably tied conferring ashes to celebrating Mass, for which there would be the normal two early morning weekday Masses, a noon Mass (which he asked me to take, saying it would be standing room only, with loads of people from nearby office parks), plus an early evening Mass. I had the temerity (of youth, I'd like to suppose) of asking why all these Masses on a day not requiring them and, more to the point, whether the people coming from the workplaces at midday could afford the time for an entire Mass. He said that, unfortunately, some would show up late and leave early, but that did not detract from the necessity of Mass, which he asserted as obvious (and final!). For my part that noon, seeing the packed house before me, I explained in the opening rite that the church requires that ashes be distributed in conjunction with the proclamation of God's word, but that remaining for the Liturgy of the Eucharist, while warmly encouraged, was nonetheless optional. People either pressed for time or not disposed to receiving Holy Communion, I advised, should not feel guilty about departing at the conclusion of the Liturgy of the Word. A palpable sigh of relief (variably expressed) quietly rose and subsided. Later, probably a third of the people left before the Liturgy of the Eucharist began. I believed I had met the pastor's directive while also meeting the pastoral needs of the people.

Such is my little tale, but it is loaded with theological implications, the extent of which well exceed what I can address. Here I shall only attempt an initial overview of the sorts of power evident in the scenarios, which will then lead to a more extended consideration of the symbolism of Ash Wednesday itself. In thinking how to break down the whole into parts I take as a heuristic guide the Constitution on the Sacred Liturgy's description of the multiple ways Christ is present in the enactment of the Church's rites.[14] Surely this divine-human presence implies power, the means through which, in the power of the Holy Spirit (the Constitution teaches) God is glorified and the people sanctified. The modes of presence include the sacramental minister, the symbols of the sacrament being celebrated (with that presence being unique in the case of Eucharistic elements), the proclamation of word in Scripture, and the people themselves gathered in prayer and song.

- The exercise of various types of power in ministerial leadership is evident not only on the obvious point that each scenario entailed a Mass and, thus, the priestly office and charism, per the Roman Catholic Church, lo these many centuries. But in each case the exercise of pastoral authority by the campus ministry director and the pastor were likewise in play. And part of the drama in the situations had to do with the difference in how I understood the pastoral-theological-liturgical situation in contrast to those two men. On the primary theological terrain of actual Catholic communities we are very much still in what no doubt will be an extended period of varying interpretations of the general instructions of the official rites and the other doctrinal and procedural directives on divine worship coming from the Vatican and local bishops—even as these rites and their introductions are in processes of revision all over again. These touch on every facet of theology (Christology, pneumatology, ecclesiology, anthropology, biblical revelation, and interpretation). The Vatican has, in addition, given directives on the possibilities and limits of lay pastoral and liturgical ministries. Such instruction arises occasionally, occasioned by contestation over emergent local practices judged by the bishops to need regulation or prohibition. Myself, I find the 2004 Vatican instruction *Redemptionis Sacramentum* breathtaking in its scope and detail (enumerating multiple abuses to be abrogated).[15] Then, obviously, arises consideration here of the entire notion of priesthood in relation to the clerical caste and how it is circumscribed. Not only have many of the issues been polarizing, some have alienated people—laity, especially women, but also many of the ordained.

- To note, then, briefly the laity: The liturgical assembly, formed by a multitude or few, perhaps especially in all diversities, is a powerful symbol indeed. In fact, the assembly is the basic symbol upon which all the rites depend. I shall say a bit more about the theological characteristics of assembling in prayer and song a bit later, but here I would just note the uncontested assumption by all in both scenarios that liturgical assembling is essential to the celebration (the ritual performance) of Ash Wednesday. Why is that? Why not just have people drop in for ashes at a drive-through window or street corner (per scattered practices of Episcopal and Protestant churches), as has been gleefully reported in the press in recent years?[16] One last note in relation to the assembly: Surely the kind of moral and even religious authority people accord the clergy covers a spectrum, with people quietly but openly doing their own thing in ways previously unimagined.

- Of monumental importance and impact in the liturgical reform Vatican II set in motion was the augmentation of the Liturgy of the Word in the Mass, as well as the prescription that all the rites of the church include the proclamation of Scripture. This, to my mind, has unleashed powers of revelation beyond human measure. What *can* be measurably observed is the amount of time and care now widely devoted to the celebration of the word, most extensively in the Mass (with the bountiful lectionary cycles, expanded numbers of readings, psalmody, *and* the liturgical homily). Ours is a very different Mass now from that of 1962. And over the decades the impact has been widespread: People hear a full range of the gospels and, however poor the preaching may be, they hear *in the midst of the assembly* and the context of their personal lives stories, for example, about Jesus feeding multitudes, befriending and dining with sinners (social outcasts), etc., leading them to pose serious questions about Roman liturgical law's restrictions on who may or may not receive Holy Communion and in what venues. But that is just one notably contested example. With regard to these Ash Wednesday scenarios, my own priority for the day's liturgy was about high quality proclamation and response to the word, leading into the procession (the people's corporate movement together) and reception of the ashes (the word written on the body, per Chauvet). Whether I was (or am) right or wrong on this point, I do think the symbolic impact of doing this sacramental gesture alone (that is, without the further celebration of the sacrament of the Eucharist) would enhance the power of the ritual. This, again, is a complex idea, not least due to the question of whether the Mass (or Eucharist), while the apex of the church's liturgical life, may not have evolved into a de facto requirement for the celebration of *any* rite to be experienced as divinely powerful.

Fearful that the above run-through of power issues has been so cursory and suggestive as to disappoint, I want nevertheless to use the time remaining to consider, then, the symbol of Ash Wednesday itself, doing this as an exercise in pastoral-liturgical theology.

We would do well not to underestimate the power of the symbol of Ash Wednesday. If we think liturgy in this case first of all in terms of the liturgical calendar, the church year, then Ash Wednesday ranks among the top three in North American Catholicism, across the spectrum of ethnicities. While not dismissing festival days highly important (because so richly celebrated) within particular ethnic groups, such as Our Lady of Guadalupe, I am arguing here in terms of liturgical days universally observed on the popular level. Easter and Christmas are big, for sure, but just as with those holidays, Ash Wednesday is a day that Catholics who do not attend Sunday Mass regularly (let alone weekly) nonetheless take note of and participate in. The secular press and now wider social media are annually abuzz when the day arrives, and this is no small thing, this attentiveness to the event, given the fact that the particular date on the calendar changes annually. Media outlets "get" that this day is a powerfully defining one in the "social imaginary" of Roman Catholics and many other Christians. I am, of course, employing Charles Taylor's concept for the pre-theoretical shared images, stories, symbols whereby a group or society shape their common understanding and practices, lending them their legitimacy.[17] The media—exercising so much power in relation to fame, wealth, office (politics), word, and image—they "get" Ash Wednesday because believers "do" it in such visible numbers (and one must ponder how the secular media thereby empowers the Christian symbol). The practice is widely described as the beginning of the most holy season of the Christian year, and the season as forty days of fasting and prayerful reflection (but not, at least to my attentive eyes and ears, of almsgiving). Yet few Catholics literally, actually fast—that is, cut their food consumption to one meal and two small snacks per day—for forty days or even on the two days that church law mandates such bodily ritual observance by healthy adults—Ash Wednesday and Good Friday. Larger numbers may abstain from meat (with a nod to Mary Douglas and her affection for the Bog Irish[18]) on Ash Wednesday and Lenten Fridays, but to my observation even this has trailed off among the younger generations. I bring this up not to decry laxity but to keep a sharp eye on what motivates Catholic and other Christians in actual practice and, thereby, what one can reasonably deduce is powerful about their faith for their identity, for their personal, interpersonal, and social agency.

"Did you get your ashes?" I recall some years ago how a twenty-something friend, a youth social worker living and serving a severely troubled South Boston (think poverty, low educational attainment, high suicide rates), became so agitated over how everybody around her on Ash Wednesday, young and old, kept asking that question of each other. She hated what she, as nearly the only person of her or the next older generation present weekly at Sunday Mass, saw as hypocrisy. I think it is fair to say that she saw the fuss over getting to a church for a smudge of ashes on the forehead as an empty, inauthentic symbol. Ah, but therein lies the rub (pardon the pun!). To think the power of ritual and symbol, with Bell and the theorists she enlists, in terms of activity within a social body, creating and sustaining and gradually morphing the identity and agency of the members *by their very participation therein*, is to resist the modern temptation to prioritize thought over action, mind over body, supposedly autonomous individual over social institutions. The enthusiasm for Ash Wednesday participation, past and present, for so many includes, often primarily entails, a profound sense of belonging, of Catholic self and mutual identification through performance. Canon Law and doctrinal instruction concerning Sunday Mass attendance or fasting and abstinence or confessing serious sin in sacramental penance before receiving Holy Communion—the accurate comprehension and careful following of these do not, it would seem, carry nearly as much weight in popular practice of Catholicism, in the ritual bodies of Catholics, as does the inscription of ashes on foreheads one wintry Wednesday per year.

As another team of social scientists have put it, modernity in all its sectors—academic, institutional, popular—has been mistaken in assuming the extent to which precision of thought governs people's lives. Adam Seligman and associates place *ritual* (broadly conceived) at one end of the human continuum for "framing experience, action, and understanding," while at the other end—and in ongoing tension—is what they call *sincerity*, which values individual decision and the exercise of the will, the workings of which "are singular, unique, discursive, and indicative to the highest degree."[19] Human ritual negotiates ambiguity without completely resolving it, as would, in contrast, a discursive (that is, sincere) explanation. Indeed, the ambiguity that haunts all boundaries in life—physical, social, traditional—is the very reason for ritualizing.[20] To quote Seligman and associates a bit more: "Ritual's repeated, performative, and antidiscursive nature . . . provides a critical way of dealing with, rather than overcoming, the eternal contradiction and ambiguity of human existence."[21] Ritual is the way we humans hold the many irresolvable ambivalences of life in a *both-and* tension that orients and, with repetition, reorients people's identity and agency amidst the ambiguities of interpersonal, social, and cosmic relations as well as through the changes in the individual life cycle—with death always looming around the edges. Attention to such human activity does not lend itself well to the pursuit of certitude through pure argument, nor to apodictic assertions about the singular proper execution of a given rite and its meaning.

In light of this line of theorizing, the symbolic power of Ash Wednesday for Roman Catholics and many other Christians becomes quite evident. The day with its primary symbol all but revels in the ambiguity of human life (for which the theological symbols are sin and death), inscribing it on the body—on the face, no less. The standard Catholic ritual prior to the post-Vatican II reform was for a priest simply to be standing in front of the sanctuary for posted hours at a time, with individuals coming down the aisle to have him perfunctorily press a thumb of ashes to one's forehead while solemnly proclaiming, "Remember, man, that thou art dust and unto dust thou shall return." I think it's fair to say that the conceptual and imaginal input the ritual offered the individual was quite minimal. *Memoria mortis*, indeed, and in light of that mortality take stock of one's life. In one sense there is not much explicitly Christian in such a symbolic gesture, unless one takes into further account the bodily sensation of walking down the aisle of the church, the sacred Catholic space, with the pews all empty, to place oneself in the hand of the Christ-bearing priest. And those surely are no small factors. Be that as it may, the historical fact is that the Second Vatican Council's mandated reform and renewal of the liturgy included making proclamation of the word of God integral to the celebration of every and all rites. Priority was likewise to be given to the corporate, communal nature of the church in its assembled members, among whom full, conscious, and active participation is to be fostered. These, as well as a clergy educated in and imbued with the "spirit and power"[22] of the liturgy constituted the fundamental components of liturgical practice that could produce a reformed and renewed Catholic social imaginary, and this as needed amidst a rapidly changing, pluralistic world.

Hence the change in how the ritual conferring of ashes is to take place on Ash Wednesday. A genuine liturgy, that is, a work of service by and for the benefit of the people of God, is for Roman Catholicism now the only ordinary way for celebrating the first day of Lent, including the conferral of ashes. Why this need for assembling? This is the sign that people do not go it alone but, rather, live as members of Christ's body, responsible to and for one another. The power in numbers, even just two or three gathered in Christ's name, cannot be gainsaid. One way to look at the need for such assembling is the changing context, the pluralistic and rapidly secularizing world in which believers strive to live the faith. Assembling in symbolically significant sacred space, synchronizing individual person-bodies into a common, shared range of bodily vibration by means of music (heard but, for even greater effect, sung), falling together into habituated patterns of corporate silence and listening and vocal prayer,[23] by doing all of this the people are not producing something external to themselves but rather, to follow Bell's persuasive theory, they are producing (or performing) themselves as the body of Christ, in his many members.

This must not, nonetheless, be sectarian, that is, a community closed in upon itself. Paul, the apostolic author responsible for the symbolism of the church as Christ's body, himself had to convert the social imaginaries of the wealthier Christians in Corinth to recognize economic-class enclaves had no legitimacy in the local church body. Each local assembly, furthermore, needed to develop a sense of itself, in its very ritual bodies sharing in the sacred mysteries, as symbolic of the universal church. Liturgical practice with those present, closest to them, through ritual word and deed was to broaden their vision toward and solidarity (communion) with those physically afar. Paul's taking up the collection for the struggling Jerusalem community, making his appeal not only in person but through his letters being read in the liturgically assembled community, is indicative of the symbolic power the ritualization of word, water bath, anointing, meal, and intercessory prayer could have for motivating love of one another and the wider others. Within the social and political conditions under which they lived, those earliest Christians were in their liturgy, to borrow a phrase from the liturgical theologian Aidan Kavanagh, "doing the world" as God intended it.[24] The post-Vatican II reformed emphasis on the active participation of all the liturgical assembly seeks to foster a similarly powerful social imaginary for contemporary believers. The readings for Ash Wednesday's liturgy of the word seek to reorient the community, with Paul exhorting the Corinthians to be reconciled to one another as Christ has reconciled humanity with God (2 Cor 5:20-6:2), and then Jesus instructing on practices of prayer, fasting, and almsgiving to be done without drawing attention (Mt 6:1-6, 16-18).

Neither did the early Christians nor do we today ever "do the world" in the liturgy perfectly. Theological reflection on this human fact of ritualizing, I would propose, resides in the scandal of the crucified and risen Christ, of the God revealed therein, whose ways are such as to place the baptized in an ongoing eschatologically tense life, rife with ambiguities and, yes, longings, founded on the promises born of God's having taken into glory the humanity of the executed Nazarene. Irenaeus and other ancient pastors, when faced with the ambiguities of evil and suffering, wrote of God as long-suffering which, to my mind, invites deep personal and communal reflection. But there also at the church's origins is the apocalyptic cry, as J. B. Metz paraphrases the close to the Book of Revelation, "God, what are you waiting for? Come, and soon!"[25] The theology in the documents of Vatican II centers on the paradoxical divine-human power of the paschal mystery. I close by asserting that to be the hermeneutical key for theologically interpreting the liturgy's power in all the ambiguities of its performances and contexts.

Notes

[1]Catherine Bell, *Ritual Theory, Ritual Practice* (New York: Oxford University Press, 1992), 200.

[2]While my general reference to Jordan's latest work on Aquinas is based on my having had the honor of responding to his Henry Luce III Fellowship project in 2012, I am happy to note the publication of the fruits of his labors. See Mark D. Jordan, *Teaching Bodies: Moral Formation in the Summa of Thomas Aquinas* (New York: Fordham University Press, 2016).

[3]For arguments for how Eucharistic celebration is meant to elevate human friendship into the theological virtue of friendship, see Bernard Cooke and Bruce T. Morrill, *The Essential Writings of Bernard Cooke: A Narrative Theology of Church, Sacrament, and Ministry* (New York: Paulist Press, 2016), ch. 3, pts. 3 and 5. Kimberly Hope Belcher has proved insightful commentary on this theme in Cooke's work in a blog post, "Sacramentality and Foundational Experience: A Reflection on Bruce Morrill's *The Essential Writings of Bernard Cooke*," Pray Tell: Worship, Wit & Wisdom. Accessed on 11 August 2016, at http://www.praytellblog.com/.

[4]For a captivating, if not inspirational, account, see Thomas F. O'Meara and Paul Philibert, *Scanning the Signs of the Times: French Dominicans in the Twentieth Century* (Adelaide: ATF Press, 2013).

[5]Every one of the more than two dozen volumes of Rahner's *Theological Investigations* includes essays addressing various sacraments, sacramentals, and other practices. Notable monographs include his *The Church and the*

Sacraments, trans. W. J. O'Hara (New York: Herder and Herder, 1963).

[6]See Edward Schillebeeckx, *Christ, the Sacrament of the Encounter with God,* trans. Paul Barrett, ed. Mark Schoof and Laurence Bright (New York: Sheed and Ward, 1963).

[7]Bernard Cooke, *Sacraments and Sacramentality* (Mystic: Twenty-Third Publications, 1994), 7.

[8]Lest this problem of banal explanations and growing irrelevance of the sacraments be assumed as an exclusively "first" or "developed" world phenomenon, I would direct the reader to similar ecclesial and social challenges now widespread in Catholic India, reported in Francis Gonsalves, S.J., *Feet Rooted, Hearts Radiant, Minds Raised: Living Sacraments in India* (Anand: Gujarat Sahitya Prakash, 2015).

[9]Louis-Marie Chauvet, *Symbol and Sacrament: A Sacramental Reinterpretation of Christian Existence,* trans. Patrick Madigan and Madeleine Beaumont (Collegeville: Liturgical Press, 1995), 154-155.

[10]See Lieven Boeve, "Theology in a Postmodern Context and the Hermeneutical Project of Louis-Marie Chauvet," in *Sacraments: Revelation of the Humanity of God: Engaging the Fundamental Theology of Louis-Marie Chauvet,* ed. Philippe Bordeyne and Bruce T. Morrill (Collegeville: Liturgical Press, 2008), 5-24.

[11]See Bernard Cooke, *Power and the Spirit of God: Toward an Experience-Based Pneumatology* (New York: Oxford University Press, 2004), 27.

[12]Ibid., 168, 176.

[13]See Paul Connerton, *How Societies Remember,* Themes in the Social Sciences (Cambridge: Cambridge University Press, 1989), 22-29, 36, 84, 88.

[14]See Constitution on the Sacred Liturgy: *Sacrosanctum Concilium,* in Austin Flannery, ed., *Vatican Council II: Volume 1: The Conciliar and Postconciliar Documents,* rev. ed. (Northport, NY: Costello Publishing, 1996), nos. 7, 33.

[15]See Congregation for Divine Worship and the Discipline of the Sacraments, *Redemptionis Sacramentum: On Certain Matters to Be Observed or to Be Avoided Regarding the Most Holy Eucharist* (2004). Accessed at: http://www.vatican.va/roman_curia/congregations/ccdds/documents/rc_con_ccdds_doc_20040423_redemptionis-sacramentum_en.html.

[16]It turns out there now exists a website, "Ashes To Go: Taking Worship to the Streets," providing information for obtaining ashes at street locations (as well as train platforms, and outside supermarkets, and coffee shops) in some 31 U.S. states and the District of Columbia. Accessed at: http://ashestogo.org.

[17]See Charles Taylor, *A Secular Age* (Cambridge: Belknap/Harvard University Press, 2007), 171-172.

[18]See Mary Douglas, *Natural Symbols,* 2nd ed. (New York: Routledge, 1970/1996), 39-56.

[19]Adam B. Seligman et al., *Ritual and Its Consequences: An Essay on the Limits of Sincerity* (New York: Oxford University Press, 2008), 7, 118.

[20]Ibid., 41-47.

[21]Ibid., 129-30.

[22]See Constitution on the Sacred Liturgy, no. 14.

[23]See Bruce T. Morrill, with Andrea Goodrich, "Liturgical Music: Bodies Proclaiming and Responding to the Word of God," in *Bodies of Worship:*

Explorations in Theory and Practice, ed. Bruce T. Morrill (Collegeville: Liturgical Press, 1999), 157-172.

[24]See Aidan Kavanagh, *On Liturgical Theology* (Collegeville: Pueblo Books/Liturgical Press, 1984/1990), 52-71.

[25]See Johann Baptist Metz, *A Passion for God: The Mystical-Political Dimension of Christianity*, trans. J. Matthew Ashley (New York: Paulist Press, 1998), 58, 71, 84.

The Power of Memory and Witnessing

A Trauma-Informed Analysis of *Anamnesis* in the Roman Catholic Mass

Annie Selak

Situating Trauma Theory and *Anamnesis*

The straightforward account of memory as recollection is one that is commonly held in our society—and one that both trauma theory and liturgy problematize. Trauma studies resituates our understandings of time, language, and bodies; liturgy holds these aspects together in contradictory yet coherent ways. A central point in the Roman Catholic celebration of Mass is *anamnesis*, a process of remembering that makes the past and future come together in the present. How are we to think of *anamnesis* from a trauma-informed approach? This theoretical lens[1] disrupts what we think of as time and memory. However, this does not implicate liturgy, for the Mass has the power to hold these disruptions.

Trauma theory, while an overarching system of thought applicable to a variety of events, is best illustrated and understood in specific examples of trauma. A prevalent experience of trauma on college campuses is sexual assault.[2] Consider the following case study as an example to ground the interaction of trauma and liturgy:

At 9:55 pm, the dorm chapel is overflowing with students. It is the final mass of the semester, known as the "senior mass." Jillian, a college sophomore, settles into her pew. Once an active participant in mass, Jillian abruptly stopped attending mass during the fall semester. Most of the community assumes she was overwhelmed by her Organic Chemistry lab reports, due every Monday morning, and stopped attending mass so that she could instead focus on her pre-med studies. Only her three roommates know that on Halloween weekend, she was sexually assaulted. Jillian tries to push this experience aside, attempting to minimize its impact on her life through not speaking of it. In fact, she does not intentionally recall this experience, hoping to move on from it and never think of it again. She did not intentionally stop attending mass, but found herself avoiding the chapel each week, afraid on some level that it would remind her of experiences she wanted so desperately to forget. She hesitantly attends this final mass of the year, hoping that she has effectively put the experience of being sexually assaulted behind her and wanting to be a part of this important event of saying goodbye to her community. As mass begins, she finds the Liturgy of the Word to be comforting. This feeling shifts during the liturgy of the Eucharist. As the presider intones, "Take this, all of you, and eat of it: For this is my body which will be given up for you," her body begins to tense up. She grabs her best friend's hand, hoping that will calm her down. Her best friend responds with a comforting look and gently squeezes her hand. Instead of feeling reassured, Jillian panics. Moments from Halloween night begin filling her mind in fragmentary pieces. As she hears, "Do this in memory of me," Jillian feels simultaneously present in the chapel, yet back in the room of the party on Halloween night. She rushes out of the chapel, followed by her roommates. Back in her room, she reveals details of that night to her roommates, details previously unshared, even unknown to herself.[3]

Throughout this essay, I will refer to Jillian's experience in order to highlight the many ways that our understanding of memory, time, and witnessing are nuanced and complicated by trauma studies and liturgy. Remembering the human dimension of trauma grounds this study in the lived reality of trauma and resists the temptation to understand trauma and liturgy strictly at the level of theory.

This examination focuses upon inaccessibility, belatedness, disruption, and witnessing as key concepts in trauma theory. Trauma, originating from the Greek term for "wound," has grown into a field extending much beyond Sigmund Freud and psychoanalysis.[4] This study is predicated on the notion that trauma is not an event located in the past, but rather, a disruption of the present. Simply put, "trauma is what does not go away,"[5] as theologian Shelly Rambo describes. But why does trauma persist, or not go away? Cathy Caruth, an eminent scholar in trauma theory, describes the structure of trauma, stating, "Trauma is not locatable in the simple violent or original event in an individual's past, but rather in the way that its very unassimilated nature—the way it was precisely *not known* in the first instance—returns to haunt the survivor later on."[6] In a paradox of belatedness, trauma becomes known after the event. The importance of witnessing is crucial, for this process brings out a new knowledge of trauma. In listening to trauma, the witness hears both the experience of the event as well as the departure from it.[7]

This essay proceeds in three parts. First, I look to the role of memory in trauma theory and the eucharistic celebration of Mass. Next, I lift up witnessing as a central aspect of trauma theory that enhances our understanding of *anamnesis*. Finally, I look to the power of liturgy that is highlighted through a trauma-informed approach. This study seeks to problematize our notions of memory, liturgy, and time in a way that leads to a richer understanding of *anamnesis*. I contend that a trauma-informed approach to memory and witnessing draws out important aspects of *anamnesis*. In examining the themes of memory and witnessing, I seek to weave trauma theory and liturgical theology together in order to display their resonances and engage the movements of presence and absence, accessibility and inaccessibility of trauma.

An Examination of Memory

Memory is a central aspect of the entire Christian experience. Theologian Bruce Morrill underscores the importance of memory in the project of Christianity, asserting, "Memory has an essential role in Christianity, not only on the part of the faithful but also on the part of God."[8] At first glace, liturgy in the Roman Catholic Church might appear to promote a concept of time and history as chronological and linear, as the liturgical calendar is methodically punctuated by colors and feast days, and readings for Sunday Masses are organized by a three-year cycle. However, the celebration of the Eucharist operates according to an elasticity of time, allowing past and future to commingle in the present. Liturgy is an alternative form of experience and knowledge, creating an opening for the unknowable. Philip Sheldrake captures the intimate relationship of Eucharist and memory, commenting, "Eucharistic place is very much a landscape of memory—not least of ambiguous and conflicting memories. Beyond the immediate participants, there are wider and deeper narrative currents in any Eucharistic celebration."[9] This richness in memory and community is fertile ground for an examination through a trauma lens.

While the entire eucharistic celebration involves memory, the anamnetic rubric in the Eucharistic Prayer is a poignant moment that draws upon memory in a particular way.[10] As the community prepares to receive the Body and Blood of Christ, we communally enter into an act of remembrance that makes the past present in this very moment, while also incorporating the eschatological future. In this particular act, chronological time is superseded by the mingling of past, present, and future. This act of memory is more than recall, a point that both sacramental theology and trauma theory underscore. Andrea Bieler and Luise Schottroff emphasize the importance of this distinction: "If it was a mere recalling it would be nostalgic or fetishistic memory, disconnected from the promise of resurrection. It would transform neither our present nor our future."[11] Yet the Eucharist is meant to transform the present and the future through making the past truly present in Mass, rather than an intellectual activity that summons to mind the past.

Trauma complicates our notions of temporality, as "trauma and traumatic memory alters the linearity of historical, narrativized time."[12] The belatedness of traumatic memory is one example of the troubling of chronology and history, for it tells of a "history that literally has no place, neither in the past, in which it was not fully experienced, nor in the present, in which its precise images and enactments are not fully understood."[13] How are we to understand history when it occurred in the past but is not confined to the past? This is a question that trauma studies poses, and one that resonates with the liturgy. Given that *anamnesis* brings together past, present, and future, the Last Supper and Jesus's passion, death, and resurrection cannot be confined strictly to the past, for the past erupts into the present through *anamnesis*. Yet this does not negate the fact that there was indeed a gathering of Jesus and his disciples at a specific historical moment. A trauma lens creates space to enter into the ambiguous temporality that comes with trauma and liturgy. *Anamnesis* nuances the repetition of this event by emphasizing that our remembrance is not a reenactment, but rather a continued participation and communal remembrance.

While *anamnesis* and traumatic memory share common ground in their understanding of the past commingling with the present, anamnetic memory also incorporates the eschatological future. Bieler and Schottroff explain, "Eschatological *anamnesis* in the context of the Eucharist means practicing resurrection hope by connecting the remembrance of God's saving works, in Israel's history and in the Christ event, with our lives."[14] Our remembering is intimately connected to a forward-looking dimension of the Reign of God. This is an area where liturgical studies can offer much to trauma theory, for the tradition of holding together the past, present, and future incorporates a sense of forward-direction as well as mystery. Trauma studies would be well served by this contribution.

Another example of trauma troubling the linear understanding of time is found in disruptions. Theologian Dirk Lange examines the many ways that trauma and liturgy both disrupt traditional forms of remembrance and knowledge. He explains, "This disruption, however, does not mean that we cannot 'know' history . . . Rather, knowing itself is redefined. There is a blurring of the distinction between knowing the (traumatic) event and the way in which that event is remembered."[15] The role of disruption in problematizing our understanding of time and history can be extended to examine *anamnesis*. Looking to *anamnesis* as a disruption calls attention to the many ways that the act of remembering in liturgy not only conjures memories of the past, but also makes demands on the present and future. *Anamnesis* leads us beyond common understandings of chronology, for "the act of praying breaks open the pattern of linear time."[16] Disruption brings connotations of action, emphasizing the potential of the liturgy to be a driving force in our lives.

The notion of disruption raises the issue of accessibility of traumatic memory, a central question in trauma studies. In exploring this question, Caruth emphasizes the connection of repetition with the inaccessibility of the trauma event: "The historical power of trauma is not just that the experience is repeated after its forgetting, but that it is only in and through its inherent forgetting that it is first experienced at all."[17] Jillian's experience of disruption, inaccessibility, and witnessing displays the connection of these elements. This pattern of blurring remembering and knowing is seen acutely in the celebration of the Eucharist. *Anamnesis* makes present the past. More than a memorial, the past is connected with the present in a way that defies chronological ordering of history. Further, the Mass is intended to be repeated by a community, evoking the repetitive pattern of trauma. In this way, it mirrors the pattern of trauma theory troubling our understanding of temporality.

An important gift of trauma theory to liturgy is a shift in focus that leads to a wider space that can hold inaccessible experiences.[18] Trauma theory moves the question from the traditional phrasing of "what *exactly* happened?" to recognizing that precision in description is not the goal. Rather, we are called to bear witness to an inaccessible experience. Instead of focusing upon how exactly the past and future come together in the present, trauma theory prompts us to take up the posture of a wider, softer gaze. The focus shifts from explanation to creating space for holding the inaccessible. A wider, softer gaze resists the temptation to organize events in a linear fashion by holding together tensions in a communal space. This allows for disruptions, silences, ambiguity, and contradictions to mingle together. When applied to the opening case study, a wider, softer gaze resists searching for a precise explanation for how and why the Eucharistic Prayer led to Jillian's reaction, but rather, acknowledges and respects the mystery of the connection. In turn, this posture promotes a reverence for the mystery of God and the connection of the community. At its core, is this not what the celebration of the Eucharist is all about? Just as sacraments call attention to the grace of God that is already present (opposed to making present what is absent), this broader focus of trauma theory fosters reverence for what is already occurring.

Anamnesis in the celebration of the Eucharist creates space for this traumatic re-ordering of time and history. When the richness of *anamnesis* is embraced, liturgy can be the context that holds an openness for traumatic complications of memory. We now turn to the role of witnessing in trauma in order to explore how *anamnesis*, liturgy, and trauma are further enriched when examined together.

The Role of Witnessing

A key component of Jillian's experience was the role of her roommates as witnesses. Through recounting her story to them, she uncovered aspects of the traumatic event that were unknown to her. In looking to the inaccessibility and belatedness inherent in trauma, Caruth asserts that trauma "defies and demands witness."[19] Witnessing springs forth from the inaccessibility and belatedness of the traumatic event, for "it is in the event of this incomprehension and in our departure from sense and understanding that our own witnessing may indeed begin to take place."[20] This seemingly contradictory phenomenon—defying and demanding witness—is at the core of this examination of witnessing.

Trauma theory addresses the concept of witnessing on many levels. Dori Laub identifies three positions of witnessing as "the level of being a witness to oneself within the experience; the level of being a witness to the testimonies of others; and the level of being a witness to the process of witnessing itself."[21] While each of these three positions of witnessing has potential to shed light upon *anamnesis*, this study will focus upon bearing witness to the testimony of others, given the communal dimension of Eucharist. This act of witnessing is inherent in the inaccessible structure of trauma, for "the speaking subject constantly bears witness to a truth that nonetheless continues to escape him, a truth that is, essentially, *not available* to its own speaker."[22] It is important to nuance this truth-claim, lest we attempt to possess the truth of another. Drawing on Freud's works surrounding the inaccessible,[23] Shoshana Felman states, "One does not have to *possess*, or *own* the truth, in order to effectively *bear witness* to it."[24] Thus, trauma studies lifts up the seemingly contradictory aspects of witnessing as accessible and inaccessible, truth and possession, communal and individual, and holds all of these together in tension. Jillian's roommates did not possess her truth, but through the act of witnessing they were able to accompany her through the process of sharing her story. One can imagine Jillian's roommates later attending Mass with her and engaging in a new form of witnessing as Jillian encounters moments of disruption and moments of consolation.

The paradox of trauma defying and demanding a witness elicits the question of how *anamnesis* in the celebration of the Eucharist defies and demands a witness. It breaks open the question of how in celebrating the Eucharist as a community and through the living memorial of *anamnesis*, we witness to trauma in others in ways that demand our witness, but remain inaccessible. A trauma lens lifts up the tension of presence and absence, accessibility and inaccessibility, death and survival,[25] community and solitary prayer that *anamnesis* also evokes. Trauma theory allows us to name these movements that are already present and hold them together in liturgy.

More than just naming and holding these tensions, trauma studies opens up the role of the witness in liturgy. Given that the "experiencing of the traumatic event is not only belated; it often involves another person, a listener, to whom the trauma can be recounted,"[26] we must further examine the role of the witness from this perspective. One way to look at witnessing is through the role of listener, a position that Laub examines. He states, "The testimony to the trauma thus includes its hearer, who is, so to speak, the blank screen on which the event comes to be inscribed for the first time."[27] Yet the role of the listener goes beyond that of a blank slate.[28] Laub continues: "The listener, therefore, is a party to the creation of knowledge *de novo*."[29] Looking at this from the viewpoint of *anamnesis*, one can see the creation of new knowledge that springs forth from the Eucharist. *Anamnesis* opens the door to all memory, including traumatic memory, and through the role of witnessing, new knowledge can be born.

Witnessing in liturgy is not simply an isolated or solitary act, though there may be moments where it takes an individualized form. Rather, there is a movement of communal witnessing: "It is a position in which one acts as a member of a collectivity or culture."[30] *Anamnesis* may have intimate components, yet the communal context is a defining feature of the eucharistic celebration. *Anamnesis* creates the space in liturgy to hold a new knowledge that is born from communal witnessing. The question becomes how the new knowledge that springs forth from communal witnessing is to be received. This is a central question concerning the power of liturgy, for it is not enough to simply name the power occurring, but one must look to the ways that communities receive and act with this power. For example, Jillian's liturgical community should not remain the same in light of her experience. While there may be many in the community that remain unaware of her experience, the witnessing of her roommates and her own experience transform the community. There must be room in the liturgy to respond to this change and the many other experiences of the community. As a result, reading liturgy through a trauma-lens creates demands for liturgy to which theologians and ministers alike must respond.

The Power to Send Forth

Examining witnessing through the lens of trauma studies reveals that witnessing is not a passive activity, but demands action. Witnessing makes an ethical demand on us. E. Ann Kaplan argues, "Witnessing in the ethical sense has to address not just the individual but the social collectivity as well. It involves taking responsibility for injustices in the past and . . . preventing future human-based catastrophe."[31] So too, does the Mass make an ethical demand on the collective body. We must remember that Mass derives from *missa*, meaning "to send forth." Therefore, at its core, the Mass is an exercise of sending forth. As we examine the power of liturgy, the ethical demand that springs forth from witnessing is a key component of that power. Communal witnessing compels the body to go forth into the world, take responsibility for past injustice and work to create a more just world.

Trauma studies and *anamnesis* both lift up the significance of long-lasting impact that cannot be precisely measured. Just as the resurrected Christ appeared to the disciples as a wounded figure, the wounds of trauma continue to have impact far beyond the initial occurrence. As a result, trauma studies and the Gospel both reinforce the fact that wounds do not disappear, but continue to shape the individual and community. In discussing the connection of trauma, memory, and eucharistic solidarity, M. Shawn Copeland concludes, "Our daily living out, and out of, the dangerous memory of the torture and abuse, death and resurrection of Jesus Christ constitutes us as his own body raised up and made visible in the world."[32] Trauma studies and liturgy both draw out the ways that the wounded body becomes the Body of Christ in the world in a way that "re-orders us, restores us, and makes us one."[33] The ambiguous re-ordering of time and experience associated with trauma theory encourages the liturgical community to allow for a more just reordering of the community. Thus, the community can be restored to more fully embody and bring about the justice of the Reign of God. As the re-ordered, restored, united, and wounded Body of Christ, the church community is challenged to bear witness to one another and the wounded in the world in a way that works to create a more just world.

Utilizing a trauma lens to examine *anamnesis* in liturgy reveals the sending power of liturgy. At the same time, the wider, softer gaze of trauma theory prompts the liturgical community to hold together the disruptions, silences, presence, and absence that accompany the traumatic.[34] Liturgy is not implicated by an analysis through a trauma lens, for it has the capacity to hold together these complex, powerful forces. Trauma theory and Eucharistic meanings of memory each diverge from traditional notions of temporality, thus creating a space that holds and reverences the mystery of trauma, liturgy, and their connection. Trauma theory highlights the irruption of the past into the present that is experienced in *anamnesis,* allowing for a renewed understanding of *anamnesis.* A trauma lens reminds us that the Eucharist continues to shape and make demands on our community. At the same time, *anamnesis* sheds light upon trauma theory, asking how the eschatological future commingles with the past in the present. By complicating notions of time, memory, and the role of witness, trauma theory highlights powerful elements already present in the celebration of the Eucharist. The community is compelled to go forth, preaching the Gospel and witnessing with their lives.

Notes

[1]In describing the "lens of trauma," Shelly Rambo explains, "Reading through this shattered lens, we discover things we had not noticed before— things that have been, and continue to be, covered over" (*Spirit and Trauma: A Theology of Remaining* [Louisville, KY: Westminster John Knox Press, 2010], 11).

[2]Data reports that one in four women will experience sexual violence in her lifetime and one in five women will experience sexual violence while in college (Christopher P. Krebs, Christine H. Lindquist, Tara D. Warner, Bonnie S. Fisher, Sandra L. Martin, *The Campus Sexual Assault Study* [Washington, DC: U.S. Department of Justice, December 2007], xii-xiii, https://www.ncjrs.gov/pdffiles1/nij/grants/221153.pdf).

[3]This case study is a composite experience drawn from the experience of many undergraduate students.

[4]Shelly Rambo, "Refiguring Wounds in the Afterlife (of Trauma)," in *Carnal Hermeneutics*, ed. Richard Kearney and Brian Treanor (New York: Fordham University Press, 2015), 264.

[5]Rambo, *Spirit and Trauma*, 2.

[6]Cathy Caruth, *Unclaimed Experience: Trauma, Narrative, and History* (Baltimore: Johns Hopkins University Press, 1996), 4.

[7]Cathy Caruth, *Trauma: Explorations in Memory* (Baltimore: Johns Hopkins University Press, 1995), 10.

[8]Bruce T. Morrill, *Anamnesis as Dangerous Memory: Political and Liturgical Theology in Dialogue* (Collegeville, MN: Liturgical Press, 2000), 163.

[9]Philip Sheldrake, *Spaces for the Sacred: Place, Memory, and Identity* (Baltimore: Johns Hopkins University Press, 2001), 80.

[10]I use the term *anamnesis* as both a general term referring to the remembrance quality of eucharistic liturgies corresponding to the originating event of the Last Supper, as well as a specific component of the Rite. For a detailed description, consult David William Austin Gregg, *Anamnesis in the Eucharist*, Grove Liturgical Study, No. 5 (Bramcote, Nottinghamshire, UK: Grove Books, 1976), 3.

[11]Andrea Bieler and Luise Schottroff, *The Eucharist: Bodies, Bread, & Resurrection* (Minneapolis: Fortress Press, 2007), 166.

[12]Jenny Edkins, "Forget Trauma? Responses to September 11," *International Relations* 16, no. 2 (2002): 246.

[13]Caruth, *Trauma: Explorations in Memory*, 153.

[14]Bieler and Schottroff, *The Eucharist*, 162.

[15]Dirk Lange, *Trauma Recalled: Liturgy, Disruption, and Theology* (Minneapolis: Fortress, 2009), 6.

[16]Bieler and Schottroff, *The Eucharist*, 27.

[17]Caruth, *Unclaimed Experience*, 17.

[18]Lange, *Trauma Recalled*, 8.

[19]Caruth, *Unclaimed Experience*, 5.

[20]Ibid., 56.

[21]Shoshana Felman and Dori Laub, *Testimony: Crises of Witnessing in Literature, Psychoanalysis, and History* (New York: Routledge, 1992), 75.

[22]Shoshana Felman, "Education and Crisis, or the Vicissitudes of Teaching," in *Trauma: Explorations in Memory*, ed. Cathy Caruth (Baltimore: Johns Hopkins University Press, 1995), 24.

[23]For further explanation of Freud's work on inaccessibility, see Sigmund Freud, "Remembering, Repeating and Working-Through," 1914, 147–56; Sigmund Freud, *Beyond the Pleasure Principle*, ed. Todd Dufresne, Gregory C. Richter, and Gregory C. Richter, Broadview Editions (Buffalo, NY: Broadview Press, 2011).

[24]Felman, "Education and Crisis, or the Vicissitudes of Teaching," 24.

[25]Lange describes the question of survival in trauma: "The traumatic event is experienced as a shock of survival—why did I survive? The shock of survival is the shock that 'death' was encountered and missed. Something in the event

was missed and is continually experienced, *after* the event, as something inaccessible, as something that haunts" (Lange, *Trauma Recalled*, 8).

[26]Edkins, "Forget Trauma? Responses to September 11," 246.

[27]Felman and Laub, *Testimony*, 57.

[28]There is also a movement within the witness. Laub describes this process: "By extension, the listener to trauma comes to be a participant and a co-owner of the traumatic event: through his very listening, he comes to partially experience trauma in himself. The listener, therefore, has to be at the same time a witness to the trauma witness and a witness to himself" (ibid., 57–58).

[29]Ibid., 57.

[30]E. Ann Kaplan, "Trauma Studies Moving Forward," *Journal of Dramatic Theory and Criticism* 27, no. 2 (Spring 2013): 54.

[31]Ibid.

[32]M. Shawn Copeland, *Enfleshing Freedom: Body, Race, and Being* (Minneapolis: Fortress Press, 2010), 126–127.

[33]Ibid., 128.

[34]The notion of lingering as related to trauma theory was further explored by Kimberly Humphrey in her paper, "The Haunting of the Holy Ghost: Reading Epiclesis Through a Trauma Lens" (presented at College Theology Society Annual Convention, Kansas City, MO, June 3, 2016).

"All Creation Sings"

The Ecological Crisis, *Laudato Si'*, and an Orthodoxy of Praise

Paul J. Schutz

Laudato Si' and the Eucharist

"Praise be to you, my Lord!"[1] So begins Pope Francis's 2015 encyclical *Laudato Si': On Care for Our Common Home*, a document whose expansion of the church's commitment to justice for all the natural world blazes new trails for theology and Christian life amid unprecedented ecological distress. In addressing the challenges presented by the contemporary ecological crisis, Francis situates his argument around two main themes. To develop the first theme—*praise*[2]—he invokes the image of all things praising God in Francis of Assisi's *Canticle of the Creatures*[3] and in Psalm 148[4] to connect the act of praise *by* all things with the dignity *of* all things before their Creator God. He writes, "By their mere existence they bless him and give him glory,"[5] such that "we are called to recognize that other living beings have a value of their own in God's eyes."[6] This shared act of praise points toward a second theme—*relationality*[7]—which Francis develops in terms of interdependence. He writes, "God wills the interdependence of creatures. The sun and the moon, the cedar and the little flower, the eagle and the sparrow: the spectacle of their countless diversities and inequalities tells us that no creature is self-sufficient. Creatures exist only in dependence on each other, to complete each other, in the service of each other."[8] Recognizing this relationality is the foundation of the ecological conversion *Laudato Si'* seeks. As

Francis puts it, "Because all creatures are connected, each must be cherished with love and respect, for all of us as living creatures are dependent on one another."[9]

This thematic survey is not only intended as an introduction to *Laudato Si'*. It also reveals what I believe is the most significant shortcoming of this wonderful encyclical. For, given Francis's desire for an "integral ecology lived out joyfully and authentically,"[10] it is striking that the Eucharist—the church's primary locus of *praise, relationality*, and *conversion*—receives but one brief paragraph in *Laudato Si'*. Admittedly, this is not that surprising. Benedictine liturgical theologian Aidan Kavanagh bemoans the ambiguous, often inferior, status granted the Eucharist in contemporary magisterial and academic discourse.[11] Be that as it may, the meager treatment of the Eucharist in *Laudato Si'* demands that we consider in depth the relationship between the church's concrete, embodied eucharistic praxis and the power of the Eucharist to serve as an impetus to "conversion to the Earth,"[12] to use Elizabeth Johnson's pithy phrase. This paper will argue that if Francis's statements on the Eucharist in *Laudato Si'* are to function powerfully, as more than theological platitudes, the church must reclaim the eucharistic liturgy as a primary theological locus and concern and reclaim an understanding of orthodoxy as "right praise."

Domesticating the Eucharist? Magisterial Theology and the Eucharist "From Above"

In paragraph 236—its only extended treatment in *Laudato Si'*—Francis names the Eucharist the "greatest exaltation" of creation, the "culmination of the Incarnation."[13] Drawing on John Paul II's words, he continues, "Even when it is celebrated on the humble altar of a country church, the Eucharist is always in some way celebrated on the altar of the world,"[14] such that "the whole cosmos gives thanks to God" in "an act of cosmic love" that "joins heaven and earth."[15] Indeed, as Kevin Irwin explains in *Models of the Eucharist*, the prayers for the consecration of the bread and wine manifest cosmic significance as prayers for the sanctification of all things.[16] In Francis's words, "[The Lord . . . reaches] our intimate depths through a fragment of matter . . . that we might find [God] in this world of ours. In the Eucharist, fullness is *already* achieved; it is the living center of the universe, the overflowing core of love and of inexhaustible life."[17] On this basis, Francis names the Eucharist "a source of light and motivation for our concerns for the environment, directing us to be stewards of all creation."[18]

In addition to its brevity, it is noteworthy that while paragraph 236 speaks about "the Eucharist," the words "Mass" and "liturgy" are entirely absent from *Laudato Si'*, and "celebration" appears only once, in a heading. When Francis uses the verb "celebrate," it appears only in the passive voice, as "is celebrated," without an active subject. As a negative norm, this indicates that when Francis says "the Eucharist," he does not appear to mean the eucharistic liturgy. Given all this, what does Francis mean by "the Eucharist"?

On the basis of the words, images, and grammar he employs—words like "exaltation," "culmination," "fullness"; images like "food" and "a fragment of matter"; and the passive voice "is celebrated" and "is already achieved"—Francis appears to employ the standard, "magisterial" conception of the Eucharist—the meaning most often found in magisterial documents. What are the characteristics of this "magisterial" approach? To use Kavanagh's term, the "magisterial" approach begins "from above";[19] it moves from the abstract, doctrinal, spiritual meaning conveyed by the eucharistic species to the liturgical act.

This approach generates several critical confusions about the Eucharist. First, it emphasizes the eschatological "already"—the "exaltation" and "fullness . . . already achieved"[20]—at the expense of the "blessed mess"[21] of eucharistic worship—the "not-yet" *praise* enacted by the assembly as it stands with all its concerns before the living God. In so doing, the 'magisterial' approach implicitly characterizes the Eucharist as an object, or a commodity to be received, or a symbol to be understood, rather than as an *act* of celebration.[22] This confusion seems especially problematic in light of *Laudato Si*'s strong critiques of consumerism, commodification, individualism, and anthropocentrism. Second, the "magisterial" approach implies that the grace and meaning of the Eucharist are *pre*-determined, *already*-accomplished, *self*-evident—*ex opere operato*, "from the work worked"—independent of the assembly's disposition (not to mention its participation!) in the eucharistic act. This is the *ex opere operantis*, "from the doer's work." This emphasis on the "already" makes it difficult to take seriously the challenges of the "not-yet," of which our ecological crisis is a prime example. Kavanagh says this approach "tends to exploit meaning in such raw and aggressive quantity that congregations often are reduced to passivity, seated in pews with texts before them in order to give their full attention to the meaning purveyed in the service."[23] In sum, these confusions render the Eucharist more an abstract spiritual reality to be understood and received than an embodied act to be done and—truncating its transformative power—reduce the encounter with the living God sacramentally enacted in the liturgy to an encounter with disembodied doctrines and lofty ideas.

Orthodoxy: The Loss of "Right Praise" and the Rise of "Right Belief"

This is what Kavanagh means when he says the liturgy has shifted from being "of God"—centered on encounter—to being "about God."[24] In Kavanagh's view, this shift is one result of a historical shift in the meaning of *orthodoxy*, which "reached its high point after the Reformation," when "secondary theology" was

> officially defined as "correct" now determining rather than interpreting liturgical text and form. This step was momentous because it confirmed many on both sides of the schism in a notion of *orthodoxia* not as a sustained life of "right worship," but as "correct doctrine" to be maintained by centralized ecclesiastical authority.[25]

He continues,

> Worship provided the prime occasion during the week at which this literate effort could be exercised. . . . And the power of communal activity built up and magnified in a shared tradition over generations mutated into the power of individual concepts enunciated by major scholars, composers . . . and authoritative ecclesiastical bureaucracies such as Sacred Congregations and societies for the promotion of Christian this or that.[26]

In sum, "*Orthodoxia*, right worship . . . has become *orthopistis*, right believing, or *orthodidascalia*, right teaching, and both are by the context centered upon church officials. . . . Praxis and belief have grown apart,"[27] and the power of the liturgy has been subsumed within a set of words and actions to be impeccably executed by an officially appointed minister of the church.

Here, it is crucial to note that although the eucharistic liturgy is orthodoxy's source, when Kavanagh speaks of "right praise," he does not intend something limited to the liturgy itself. For Kavanagh, "right praise" is the posture of life proper to a Christian at all times and in all seasons; "right belief" subsists within a life of "right praise." Kavanagh's approach thus renders belief a dynamic function of praise—an expression of the church's identity as it stands, held by the Spirit, before the living God. Assuming this posture of praise within the eucharistic liturgy places the church in a posture of continual discernment that teaches Christians how to live their belief—which is surely Francis's aim. Kavanagh illustrates this point with a powerful example from the eucharistic celebrations of ancient Rome, in which the people's participation in processions through the city sacramentally signified the sanctification of the world and formed the faithful in a vision of the cosmos replete with God's glory, made holy in their act of praise.[28]

This is the essence of the Eucharist understood "from below," and it constitutes the core of Kavanagh's argument, expressed succinctly in Prosper of Aquitaine's axiom, *"Lex supplicandi legem statuat credendi"*—let the law of prayer constitute the law of belief. According to Kavanagh, the "magisterial" approach effectively reverses the power dynamic implicit in Prosper's axiom, replacing the liturgy's power over the church with the church's power over the liturgy. Kavanagh writes, "The liturgical assembly, which has been meeting under God fifty-two times a year for the past 2,000, now must be regarded as a theological cipher drawing whatever theological awareness it has not from its own response to its graced encounter with the living God, but from sources found in ecclesiastical bureaucracies and within the walls of academe."[29]

To borrow a term from William Placher's book *The Domestication of Transcendence*,[30] the confusions wrought by the shift from "right praise" to "right belief" "domesticate" the Eucharist. They eclipse the radical *encounter* with the living God sacramentally enacted in the eucharistic celebration—the primary locus of *praise, relationality*, and *conversion*—in favor of a eucharistic *theology* neatly packaged in a wafer and, perhaps, some wine.

True, the assembly stands before God, but it is more God precisely *as symbolized*, God subject to ecclesial "house rules," rather than the ineffable mystery of the living God. And liturgy—the people's work—emerges from this milieu a spectator sport, with a priest guarding the goal. In Kavanagh's words,

> The notion that this privatized and vicarious act, done entirely in one place before a seated audience, has any implications for or connection with the human City in which it occurs, or that it has any roots in or effect upon the *res publica* of Church and World, is hard to take seriously. The pastoral and theological results of so severe a constriction of experience, reflection, stimulation, imagination, and enactment upon the awareness of Christian communities and individuals are as far-reaching as they should be disturbing.[31]

Kavanagh goes so far as to compare this "constriction" to a "stroke," or "cerebral hemorrhage," which inhibits the church's ability to function in the world.[32]

To be clear, raising these issues does not intend to challenge the doctrinal or theological content of the "magisterial" approach or the *ex opere operato* power of the Eucharist. Nor does it intend to reify the distinction between eucharistic worship "from below" and "from above." To speak of the Eucharist is always to speak of the eucharistic *act*. That said, these critical confusions matter deeply in discussions of the practical power of the Eucharist to effect conversion in Christian life, insofar as they shape the subjective dispositions of the members of the assembly and their conceptions of what the Eucharist is before they gather for Mass Sunday after Sunday. This is what the *Catechism* means when it says, "the fruits of the sacraments also depend on the disposition of the one who receives them,"[33] what Aquinas intends in his discussions of spiritual disposition,[34] and what *Sacrosanctum Concilium* means when it states that "full and active participation by all the people . . . internally and externally, taking into account their age and condition, their way of life, and standard of religious culture" is "the aim to be considered before all else, for it is the primary and indispensable source from which the faithful are to derive the true Christian spirit."[35]

This passage clearly aims to refocus attention on the relationship between the *active practice of the eucharistic celebration* and "the true Christian spirit"—the Christian's way of living in the world—which is ultimately what *Laudato Si'* is all about. To put it briefly, in light of the pressing concerns of the Anthropocene—and given Francis's emphasis on *praise, relationality*, and *conversion*—the "magisterial" conception of the Eucharist simply cannot bear the weight of his concerns. And so, we must say "Yes, and . . . " to Francis and move beyond the conception of orthodoxy as "right belief" implicit in the "magisterial" approach.

All Creation Sings: "Orthodoxy of Praise" as an Alternative Paradigm

Before sketching what this "Yes, and . . . " might look like, it is important to note that despite the issues surrounding his discussion of the Eucharist, Francis shares an intuition with Kavanagh about the relationship between belief and praxis that is implicit in the distinction between "right belief" and "right praise." He writes,

> A commitment this lofty cannot be sustained by doctrine alone, without a spirituality capable of inspiring us . . . . Admittedly, Christians have not always appropriated and developed the spiritual treasures bestowed by God upon the Church, where the life of the spirit is not dissociated from the body or from nature or from worldly realities, but lived in and with them, in communion with all that surrounds us.[36]

But how might the church reclaim the Eucharist as a primary theological locus and rediscover orthodoxy as a sustained life of "right praise"? To begin to answer this question, I sought an image to counter Placher's "domestication"—and emerged with the image of *wilderness*.

Biblically and theologically speaking, wilderness is the place of encounter and possibility. It is the place where Moses meets God in the Burning Bush and the land through which the Israelites wander. In the Gospels, it is the place where Jesus asserts himself against great temptation. As Catherine Keller explains, it is the space of "unformed . . . potentiality," the "mysterious and fecund" primordial chaos from which Creation emerges.[37] Wilderness is the dwelling place of Mystery, a place that defies our knowledge, desires, and expectations—the ineffable and unknown.[38] Ecotheologically, wilderness represents nature as yet untouched—nature that stands, so untouched, in uninhibited praise of its Creator. In this way, the image of wilderness poses an implicit challenge to the anthropocentrism in which the Anthropocene has its roots. But what does the image of wilderness have to offer the eucharistic concerns this paper has raised? Kavanagh makes the connection clear. Citing Urban Holmes's image of the liturgy as the "edge of chaos," he writes,

> Good liturgy borders on the vulgar. . . . Liturgy leads regularly to the edge of chaos, and from this regular flirt with doom comes a theology different from any other. . . . It seems that what results in the first instance from such an experience is deep change in the very lives of those who participate in the liturgical act. And deep change will affect their next liturgical act, howsoever slightly.[39]

The eucharistic liturgy is, then, the church's wilderness, its place of encounter with the God who calls it toward a sustained life of praise. Likewise, imagining the liturgy as the "edge of chaos" renders it radically *theocentric*. It allows for no unchecked anthropocentricism or assertion of creaturely power. It demands humility. By letting the power of the liturgy *be*, it reveals new avenues of growth and conversion. As such, it offers a framework for achieving the vision articulated in *Laudato Si'* in and through the church's primary act of praise. As Kavanagh puts it, "A Church that lives close up to the icon of the Gospel by faith . . . is the central workshop of the human City, a City which under grace has already begun to mutate by fits and starts into the City-of-God-in-the-making, the focal point of a World made new in Christ Jesus."[40]

First Steps into the Wilderness

In summary, if it is to manifest its full power as an impetus to ecological conversion, the Eucharist must be understood as *act* rather than *object*—as something done by an assembly before the living God. Over and against assertions of power rooted in ecclesiastical structures and doctrines, the church must be willing to journey into the wilderness to meet the God who has, throughout history, called it to new ways of living in the messy but beautiful world it inhabits. Reclaiming this sense of the Eucharist as relational *act* can move the church toward recognizing its own relationality and provide a concrete context for comprehending the praise rendered by all creatures. As Francis puts it, "A great cultural, spiritual and educational challenge stands before us, and it will demand that we set out on the long path of renewal."[41]

Building on an insight implicit in Elizabeth Johnson's famous maxim, "The symbol of God functions," that is, the language of faith affects the practice of faith,[42] I have argued in this essay that if we want to change what the church believes, we must change how it prays. It has worked to show that renewal begins from full participation in the Eucharist, from which it extends to all dimensions of the church's life in the world. But such renewal is contingent upon the renewal of the liturgy itself—on a journey into the wilderness. And so, to conclude, let us take two first steps into this wilderness.

First, confronting Kavanagh's claim that "theology remains impervious to pastoral impregnation while the pastoral arts sink further into the strategic infecundity of clinicalism, educationalism, and personal idiosyncrasy,"[43] theologians and those who minister in the church must engage concretely with the strengths and shortcomings of the church's liturgical life and interrogate how the liturgy functions and fails to function in relation to their theological and pastoral concerns. For example, in light of Francis's emphasis on *praise* and *relationality*, we might ask how practices of hospitality and inclusion in the eucharistic liturgy support or inhibit the doxological and relational vision he promotes. We might ask how the individualism, inactivity, and inertia of many liturgical assemblies inhibits our ability to relate to and to recognize the praise of our fellow humans and of otherkind. Above all, we cannot forget that the Sunday Eucharist offers the only exposure to theology most Catholics ever have.

Second, the church must reclaim a vision of orthodoxy as a sustained life of "right praise." This will not happen on its own, nor is it something that lies within anyone's power. It is a sort of chicken-egg problem: reclaiming this sense of "right praise" will only happen through sustained attention to how—both by what means and in what manner—the church prays. No redefinition of the term can *make* this shift take place. As a fundamentally theocentric posture, only praying at the "edge of chaos," in the wilderness of discernment, will reveal what a life of praise means for the church today. Kavanagh puts it poetically,

> We might stumble onto the road out of suburbia, a road best traveled not in a tour bus but on foot so that we could stop when we wished in cold woods, with laughing flesh, to admire ladies in silk dresses and their beaux, and even get ourselves swept up into a rowdy mob on its way downtown to do the world now and then, there perhaps to encounter a new possibility leaning into the wind.[44]

In sum, if the church is to achieve the vision articulated in *Laudato Si'*, it must renew its commitment to the vision of full, conscious, and active participation articulated in *Sacrosanctum Concilium*. Like Rahner, Kavanagh, and many others, I do not think the church has succeeded on this front.[45] But if Prosper's axiom holds, the Eucharist is indeed the foundation of "conversion to the earth"—one aspect of the inestimable power of the sustained life of praise Kavanagh so passionately seeks. On that note, let us conclude with a few words from Kavanagh that unite the doxological, relational, and ecological, very much in the spirit of *Laudato Si'*. He writes, "Along with the blood-bought right of Christian *orthodoxia* to celebrate creation root and branch, there goes an obligation to exorcise continually its human inmates' lust to do their own thing no matter what, especially as doing their own thing blinds them to the risks, duties, and nobility of being creatures of creation's Source and friends of creation's Redeemer."[46]

Notes

[1] Pope Francis, *Laudato Si'* [hereafter LS], 1.

[2] As indicated by the title, '*Laudato Si'*. See LS 1, 11-12, 72, 87, 91, 235-237, and 245.

[3] *Canticle of the Creatures*, in *Francis of Assisi – the Saint: Early Documents*, vol. 1, ed. Regis J. Armstrong (New York: New City Press, 1999), 113-114, cited in LS 1 and 87.

[4] It is disheartening that Psalm 148 only appears in the lectionary on Wednesday of the 6th Week of Easter and on Monday of the 19th week in Ordinary Time. More disheartening is the fact that verses 3-10, in which na-

ture gives praise to God, are edited out of the lectionary, which jumps from the angels (vs. 2), to humans (vs. 11), silencing Otherkind's praise. The same goes for the 12th chapter of Job, which gives the title to Elizabeth Johnson's *Ask the Beasts.* Given that Sunday Mass is the only formation many Catholics receive, if the Eucharist is to function as a source of environmental concern, the magisterium must critically consider which texts are used and not used in the liturgy—not to mention the potential impact of its editorial choices.

[5] *Catechism of the Catholic Church* [hereafter CCC], 2416, cited in LS 69.

[6] LS 69.

[7] As indicated by the phrase "our common home." See LS 1, 15-16, 20, 47, 65-71, 81-82, 85-86, esp. 115-121, 141-144.

[8] CCC 340, cited in LS 86.

[9] LS 42.

[10] Ibid., 10.

[11] Aidan Kavanagh, O.S.B., *On Liturgical Theology* (Collegeville: Liturgical Press, 1984), 7-8. "Liturgical tradition is not merely one theological source among others. . . . Rather, [I regard] liturgical tradition . . . as the dynamic condition within which theological reflection is done, within which the Word of God is appropriately understood." Cf. 75.

[12] Elizabeth A. Johnson, CSJ, *Ask the Beasts: Darwin and the God of Love* (London: Bloomsbury, 2014), 258.

[13] LS 236.

[14] Pope John Paul II, *Ecclesia de Eucharistia*, 8, cited in *LS* 236.

[15] LS 236.

[16] Kevin Irwin, *Models of the Eucharist* (New York: Paulist, 2005), esp. ch. 1.

[17] LS 236, emphasis mine.

[18] Ibid.

[19] Aidan Kavanagh, O.S.B., "Liturgical Needs for Today and Tomorrow," *Worship* 43, no. 8 (October 1969): 495.

[20] LS 236.

[21] Thomas Scirghi, "This Blessed Mess," in *Living Beauty: The Art of Liturgy*, ed. Alejandro Garcia Rivera and Thomas Scirghi (Lanham, MD: Rowman & Littlefield, 2008), 19.

[22] The widespread, perhaps exaggerated, popularity of Eucharistic Adoration and the frequent *en masse* exodus of Catholics from churches after "receiving Communion" may be two unhappy outcomes of this approach. See Nathan Mitchell, OSB, *Cult and Controversy: The Worship of the Eucharist Outside Mass* (Collegeville, MN: Liturgical Press, 1982).

[23] Kavanagh, *On Liturgical Theology*, 4.

[24] Ibid., Chapter 6.

[25] Ibid., 81.

[26] Ibid., 109.

[27] Ibid., 82.

[28] Ibid., Chapter 4, esp. 56-60.

[29] Ibid., 83.

[30] William Placher, *The Domestication of Transcendence* (Louisville: Westminster John Knox, 1996).

[31]Kavanagh, *On Liturgical Theology*, 61.
[32]Ibid., 61-62.
[33]CCC 128.
[34]*Summa Theologiae* III, q. 73-83, esp. q. 80. Cf. Joseph K. Wawrykow, "Aquinas on the Eucharist," in *The Oxford Handbook of Sacramental Theology*, ed. Hans Boersma and Matthew Levering (Oxford: Oxford University Press, 2015), 224-228.
[35]SC 14.
[36]LS 216.
[37]Catherine Keller, "Spirit Wilds: Climate and Theology," in *An Unexpected Wilderness: Christianity and the Natural World*, ed. Colleen Carpenter, The Annual Publication of the College Theology Society, vol. 61 (Maryknoll, NY: Orbis, 2015), 7-8. See the other essays in that volume.
[38]Ibid., 11-12.
[39]Kavanagh, *On Liturgical Theology*, 73-74.
[40]Ibid., 42.
[41]LS 202.
[42]Elizabeth A. Johnson, CSJ, *She Who Is: The Mystery of God in Feminist Discourse*, 10th Anniversary Edition (New York: Crossroad, 2002).
[43]Kavanagh, *On Liturgical Theology*, 19.
[44]Ibid., 69.
[45]Karl Rahner, "The High Point of an Eighty-Year-Old Theologian's Life," in *Faith in a Wintry Season* (New York: Crossroad, 1991), 38-39. When asked about Vatican II, Rahner states, "Actually that ecumenical Council has not really been put into practice in the Church, either according to its letter or according to its spirit."
[46]Kavanagh, *On Liturgical Theology*, 175.

Liturgy as Power-Sharing

Synergy for Solidarity

Marcus Mescher

Liturgy is celebrated to remember the Paschal Mystery, to re-enact God's covenantal bond with humanity, to petition the presence and power of the Holy Spirit, and to give thanks for the foretaste of our eschatological destiny. Also, as the *Catechism* teaches, it "commits us to the poor."[1] It is a sacramental experience that mediates God's sharing of life with God's people through sharing the gifts of creation. The ritual sharing commemorates human and divine synergy, cooperation in grace shared by God with humanity.[2] For this reason, liturgy can be understood as a celebration of vertical and horizontal solidarity, recommitting the participants to right-relationship with God and one another.[3] However, this soaring vision of what liturgy is meant to signify is not widely experienced today. This essay focuses on three obstacles and three possible solutions to more sufficiently live out the vision of liturgy as synergy for solidarity after first reviewing some of the contributions to the long and rich tradition that has developed the connection between the church's celebration of liturgy and its social mission of service and justice. This includes addressing the inequalities and divisions that mark the church and society today, the "sacramental optimism" that ignores these wounds in the Body of Christ, and the "sacramental consumerism" that reduces liturgical participation to reception without responsibility. To adequately respond to these challenges, the church must commit to improved faith formation, more inclusive networks of belonging, and practices that foster broad co-responsibility so that God's presence and power can be shared among a "discipleship of equals."[4]

Gathering for liturgy draws its inspiration from Jesus's inclusive table fellowship. Like his boundary-breaking teaching and healing ministry (e.g., Mk 7:24-30, Lk 10:25-37), Jesus's mode of eating contested social and religious norms that rendered some unclean, unworthy, and thus unwelcome to share a meal together (e.g., Mk 2:13-17, Lk 7:36-50). This inclusivity was so disruptive to the worldview of Jesus's contemporaries that they wanted him dead.[5] Some early Christian communities intentionally remembered and reenacted these practices to honor Jesus's example and strategically forge unity across differences between Jews and Gentiles.[6] The first disciples were Jews who were bound by dietarily restrictions that kept them from eating with non-Jews, so early liturgical *agape* meals consisting of bread, fish, and wine were dietary "neutral" selections for Jewish and Gentile Christians to move from "two menus and two tables" toward the ideal of being "one in Christ" (Gal 3:28).[7] These liturgical meals replicated Jesus's example of abolishing the exclusion of sinners or others considered impure (e.g., Mt 9:10-13, Lk 5:30) and honored his directive to share food and fellowship with the poor (Lk 14:12-14; see also Ja 2:15-16). In this way, the first followers of Jesus became a "new family" across previously enforced boundaries and provided concrete care for one another through mutual sharing and cooperation that included persons who were marginalized or vulnerable.[8]

The connection between liturgy and social justice has been a consistent teaching in church tradition. The link between receiving communion and becoming a communion of inclusive right-relationship has been traced by Paul,[9] early church fathers like John Chrysostom[10] and Augustine,[11] and recent popes including John Paul II,[12] Benedict XVI,[13] and Francis.[14] To describe Eucharist as the "source and summit"[15] of the Christian life and the "sum and summary of our faith"[16] is not to relegate it to the realm of piety alone; liturgy continues to be described as the font of moral responsibility. John Coleman argues this relationship represents a "necessary 'mystical marriage' between the Eucharist and social justice."[17] William Spohn writes, "Every dimension of Christian moral formation flows out from community worship and congregating around the Lord's table."[18] Coleman persuasively states that Eucharist "effects what it signifies: covenant, communion with

God through Christ and with one another; and Christ's real and transforming presence that transfigures us into the body of Christ, making us God's temple and children of God's Holy Spirit."[19]

However, recent survey data and current experience of the prayer, belief, and actions of Christian faith communities do not reflect these claims. 68 percent of Catholics agree with the statement, "I can be a good Catholic without going to Mass," which points to widespread ignorance of or indifference to church teaching about the primacy of the sacramental life celebrated in community as well as the relationship between Eucharist and moral responsibility.[20] Moreover, the church is experienced by the faithful as a body wounded by denigrations and divisions caused by differences in sex and sexual orientation, race and ethnicity, social and economic class, age and marital status, as well as various other status markers, including ordination, denomination, and geographical context. Many Catholics have expressed resentment and anger because some members of the community are deprived of the Eucharist.[21] Not only do some experience Eucharist as a wedge that breaks apart the community, but others see it walling off denominations while debates rage over who is worthy to receive communion.[22] This reinforces other factions experienced in the Body of Christ. In the 48 years since Dr. Martin Luther King declared 11 o'clock on Sunday morning "the most segregated hour of America," faith communities have become only marginally more diverse and inclusive.[23] Despite the fact that just one in five Catholics attends a racially diverse worship service, that is the highest percentage of any faith tradition.[24]

In most geographic contexts, America's faith congregations maintain greater segregation than what is found in most U.S. cities and towns. Much of this has to do with the demographic and geographic history of various waves of Christian immigrants. John McGreevy recounts the history of how Catholic neighborhoods in the urban north were "created, not found," based on ethnic identities.[25] For example, Irish, German, and Italian immigrants chose to live and worship in particular neighborhoods to reinforce a shared-sense of identity distinct from those considered "other." This self-selecting segregation created a culture that resisted integration from the time after WWII through the civil rights era.[26] When some church leaders championed integration (especially after Vatican II), this was met with the rise of the "church shopping" phenomenon, as Catholics sought out a parish "whose liturgy and programs matched their own inclinations."[27] This trend continues today, as parishioners cluster into "enclaves of the likeminded," reinforcing homogeneity, if not by race or ethnicity, then by political and economic ideology.[28]

The wider U.S. socio-cultural context reflects growing distance and inequality between various social groups. As Robert Putnam observes, "Growing class segregation across neighborhoods, schools, marriages (and probably also civic associations, workplaces, and friendship circles) means that rich Americans and poor Americans are living, learning, and raising children in increasingly separate and unequal worlds," which removes not only "the stepping-stones to upward mobility" but even "firsthand knowledge of the lives" of those who are different.[29] Racial divisions are yet another example of a lack of engagement with or understanding across differences. According to one recent study, 91 percent of white Americans' social networks are composed of other whites and 83 percent of black Americans' social networks are composed of other blacks; in fact, 75 percent of white Americans report they don't have a single black friend, and 65 percent of black Americans indicate their social circle is entirely black.[30]

If American life is marked by such alienation and division, how are Christians able to understand those whose reality might be different from their own, much less care about them, much less be in communion with them? In the face of so much brokenness, inequality, and injustice, Gustavo Gutiérrez describes the current celebration of Eucharist as "an exercise in make-believe."[31] How can it be that the liturgy appears so impotent in helping the church resist and transform the misuse of power that causes so much separation and suffering, rendering the Body of Christ "a body of broken bones?"[32]

Part of the problem stems from a "sacramental optimism," the presumption that the church can reform itself from within and that individuals, with the right dispositions and habits, can be transformed.[33] This tendency toward "sacramental optimism" does not adequately take into account the sinfulness and suffering that wound the Body of Christ.[34] Instead, "sacramental realism" acknowledges the church as it really is and generates the language, responsibility, and relationships required to live up to its vocation. Adopting "sacramental realism" means recognizing that the church is a porous social body, not wholly distinct from the world.[35] For example, describing the church as a "spotless spouse of the spotless Lamb" ignores the porosity of the Body of Christ corrupted by vice, such as sexism or racism.[36] It is necessary to use language that reflects the reality of the church in terms of the beliefs and actions of its individual members as well as its corporate practices and structures. As Irenaeus observes, "Our way of thinking is attuned to the Eucharist, and the Eucharist in turn confirms our way of thinking."[37] Liturgy cannot be experienced as the synergy of human and divine power-sharing for inclusive solidarity unless and until those gathered are aware of the reality they are being invited to receive and for which they are expected to take responsibility. Religious formation has failed in this regard: as one recent study of U.S. Catholics found, only 46 percent of the lay faithful are aware of the church's teaching about and believe in the Real Presence of Christ in the Eucharist.[38] Without "sacramental realism," the Eucharist will continue to function as an "exercise in make-believe," incapable of effecting real or lasting change.

Liturgy has been prevented from being experienced as synergy for solidarity through several forms of power-dysfunction. One example is the lack of the laity's "fully active and conscious participation" during liturgy.[39] Other examples include the institutional structure, policies, and practices that perpetuate clericalism and patriarchy, racism and white supremacy, thus preventing a "discipleship of equals."[40] Additional factors include ignorance or indifference, ineffective religious education, incompetent moral formation, or hollow liturgical worship.[41] Some might even blame the rise of secularism, individualization, or any number of personal and collective sins. In the face of all these obstacles to receiving and sharing power, this raises the question: What would it take for Christians to, as Augustine preached so long ago, become what we receive, the Body of Christ?

One approach to these problems is to see them as failures of reception. Beyond this lies the need to recognize that language of reception is itself problematic. Language of reception reinforces a passivity that puts greater emphasis on *receiving* communion than *being* communion. It is truer to describe Eucharist as an activity of reception than an object to be received because Eucharist is an act of consumption by corporeal individuals who constitute the church. The sacrament ought not be indistinguishable from other, more routinely consumed goods or services. In contrast to liturgy functioning (as its etymological roots signify) as "the public work of the people,"[42] a social framework of consumer reception makes Eucharist just another transaction (rendering ordained and lay ministers "service providers" and the lay faithful "service recipients"). This results in what may be called "sacramental consumerism."[43]

"Sacramental consumerism" offers an inadequate response to profound spiritual restlessness. As William Cavanaugh argues, consumerism is characterized not by "attachment to things but detachment. People do not hoard money; they spend it. People do not cling to things; they discard them and buy other things. . . . In consumer culture, dissatisfaction and satisfaction cease to be opposites, for pleasure is not so much in the possession of things as in their pursuit."[44] In a context of "sacramental consumerism," people come to believe that it is sufficient to attend liturgy or receive Eucharist without any corresponding responsibilities to contribute to liturgy or carry out the church's social mission that is meant to be energized by this "source and summit" sacramental experience. Others may also think they can find secular analogs to attending this ritual or receiving communion, especially if they find more nourishing experiences of sharing communion elsewhere (at a gym, coffee shop, or in a walk outdoors, for example). This begins to explain the widespread detachment from Eucharist, taking shape in what may be called an uninterested, disempowered "culture of Catholicism" that results in low attendance and tepid spoken and sung participation during liturgy.[45] Sacraments ritualize the reception and sharing of God's presence and power (also known as grace, the gift of God's self),[46] but in this framework of "sacramental consumerism," power meant to be shared and spread goes untapped.

Sacraments are an invitation to participate, not just to attend or receive. Louis-Marie Chauvet outlines participation in the sacraments as a ternary "symbolic exchange" in contrast to the binary "market exchange." This "symbolic exchange" unfolds as a three-step dynamic: God's gratuitous self-gift implies not only the believer's reception of the gift, but a return-gift, as well.[47] He explains that the reception "of God's grace as grace and not as anything else" requires "the *return-gift* of faith, love, conversion of heart, witness by one's life." In this view, the "gift is received as such only if it elicits the return-gift of gratitude, thanksgiving, increase of love." In other words, the potency or "fecundity" of the sacrament "depends on the believing subject."[48] To receive the gift without making a return-gift is to fail to participate in liturgy as it is intended: a practice of power-sharing partnership with God and one another. This is not Chauvet's original invention in sacramental theology, but reflects the early vision of the church as *koinōnia*.[49] *Koinōnia* is typically translated as "communion," but it refers to holding things in common. Some suggest a more accurate translation might be "partnership," both in the interpersonal sense of building community as well as cooperating with the Holy Spirit, the presence and power of God.[50] The church—most clearly in the liturgy—is the assembly of people gathered together and empowered by the synergy shared between humanity and divinity in this "symbolic exchange" of gift offered, received, and returned.

In this way, the church continues to bear witness to the "joint activity" between human and divine energies revealed in the Incarnation. To describe the liturgy in terms of synergy is to refer to "a classical term in patristic theology" used "to account for the utter newness in the union of God and man in Christ and in the Christian life. For those who live in Christ, every action of the Holy Spirit is in synergy with the action of man."[51] Jesus's entire life, from baptism through his teaching and healing ministry to his death, resurrection, and ascension, can be viewed as a witness to the divine plan for synergy between humanity and divinity.[52] Synergy can also be understood in terms of a contemporary invitation to participate in *theosis* (divinization), found principally in the liturgy.

God's invitation to power-sharing is in the mode of *kenosis* (self-emptying), which implies humility, generosity, and mutuality. This means that synergy occurs through "the meeting of the kenosis of God with the kenosis of man."[53] Synergy reflects the ternary movement of "symbolic exchange," in that it unfolds first through being manifest, then invites participation, and culminates in shared communion, which is reflected in the church community.[54] These three steps are illustrated in the rites of Eucharist: first, Christ is manifest in the Liturgy of the Word, the *anamnesis* (remembering that makes present) of what God has done for God's people in history; second, this inspires the church's prayer of *epiclesis* (petition to the presence and power of the Holy Spirit), through which those gathered receive and become the Body of Christ; third, the church is empowered to become what is done in the liturgy, such that the Spirit "opens us to the liturgy that we are to live out" by becoming communion in the world.[55] If Jesus can be understood as "the sacrament of God's justice in the world,"[56] then the liturgy to be lived out is to be modeled after the sacrament of Jesus's teaching and healing ministry marked by unconditional love and generosity, courage and compassion, and boundary-breaking solidarity.[57] To realize this vision for liturgical participation will require finding ways to replace "sacramental consumerism" with a "sacramental partnership" that implies co-responsibility for not just celebrating liturgy, but living it in the world today.

Emphasizing liturgical co-responsibility underscores the fact that synergy for solidarity depends on the faithful to translate this vision into practice. Sacramental theologians can exhort disciples to participate in *theosis* through *kenosis* in order to become "more and more the body of Christ" by "Christ become increasingly all in all,"[58] but this will only be realized to the extent that individuals and communities invest in the beliefs, practices, and relationships that cultivate power-sharing for ever-more-inclusive solidarity. Historically, liturgy was practiced in part to revitalize the disciples' resistance against the Roman Empire.[59] Today, liturgy should more explicitly adopt the language, symbols, and rituals to resist the toleration of an unjust status quo, especially in the face of a Body of Christ wounded by so many divisions and so much suffering.

As the "public work of the people," liturgy is meant to be a shared gift and task of the whole assembly, not the responsibility of a select few to prepare and provide for the rest. As Nicholas Wolterstorff states,

> The liturgy is not something enacted by the clergy for the purpose of satisfying the needs and desires of the congregants. . . . It's the church that enacts the liturgy. . . . Further, these are not just to be numbered among the many good things that the church does; it was for the performance of such actions that God created the church. When the church assembles for communal worship, she does what she was called into existence to do.[60]

This vision of co-responsibility relies on more of the laity taking leadership roles. Lay leadership defies the norm in the American Catholic experience, with 58 percent of Catholics agreeing that "most priests don't expect the laity to be leaders" and 65 percent saying that most Catholics don't want to take leadership roles in their parish.[61] "Sacramental optimism" and "sacramental consumerism" have combined not just to enervate the laity, but to fracture the church community as a whole. This betrays the meaning of the church as *koinōnia* and prevents believers from encountering Christ who is "revealed as truth not *in* a community, but *as* a community."[62] "Sacramental realism" and "sacramental partnership" are necessary to become attentive and responsive to God's activity to remove all distance between Godself and God's people (e.g., Jn 6:53-56; Jn 15:5; Rom 8:9-11).

Importantly, this means attending to the distance and divisions between God's people that remain between lay and ordained, women and men, LGBTQI and straight cis-gendered individuals and relationships, single, married, divorced, remarried, and widows/widowers, rich and poor, young and old, whites and people of color. Calling for solidarity across these differences implies starting with empathy, and empathy relies on taking up the vantage point of the "other." Empathy begins with encountering people, listening to them, and building networks of belonging that forge unity across difference. In terms of what makes for effective moral formation, belief matters less than belongingness. In other words, individuals and groups are shaped more by their relationships and shared practices than by teaching certain beliefs or values.[63] Insofar as people are transformed through their relationships, liturgy will be transformational in direct proportion to the quality and kind of relationships of those participating in liturgy. The movements of the liturgy, intentionally ordered and exercised to effect change—by first offering God praise in word, gesture, and song, then proclaiming the Word to remind the assembly what God has done and has promised to do for God's people for covenantal right-relationship, next reflecting on and appropriating the Word for our own context, subsequently lifting up the prayer of the faithful, sharing a sign of peace (an act meant to signify reconciliation in preparation for Eucharist), then offering gifts from the people to be taken, blessed, broken, and shared, and finally sending the assembly out in the world in continuation of these words and actions—are meant to invite those gathered to share in and be renewed by the synergy between the Spirit and the church. However, rituals that are so familiar can become desiccated if not domesticated. Moreover, if the rituals are practiced individualistically or as a private devotion more than as inclusively relational and aware of one's context, then they lose their potency. Synergy for solidarity takes root after first cultivating a sacramental contemplation and imagination to become aware of the presence and power of God in our midst who is calling and empowering participants to creatively unleash the possibilities for being who God is in the world: a communion of love, inviting participation in synergy for solidarity with all, especially those on the margins.[64] Sacramental contemplation and imagination lead to action in partnerships that encourage people to invest their time and abilities in meeting the needs of others. This also involves identifying and undoing obstacles to right-relationship, or experiences of "antiliturgy."[65]

Furthermore, these practices have to be combined with greater intentionality about the space where liturgy is celebrated or the places where liturgy is noticeably absent. Just as people are shaped by their relationships and practices, they are also formed by their surroundings. This is true for individuals and the church as a whole. To take seriously the porosity of the Body of Christ is to confront the brokenness of individuals and relationships, neighborhoods and communities, policies and structures that produce a broken, sinful, and suffering church.[66] Since liturgy is celebrated as a parish, parish life is thus "the heart of the matter"[67] for taking up the shared work necessary to identify and practice strategies for accurate and effective language, inclusive relationships of belonging, and meaningful practices that will liberate individuals and communities to more inclusively share in synergy for solidarity.

Given the "broken body of bones" reflected in the church today, individuals and communities need to change their social location, take up a vantage point that is not their own, and forge unity across difference in partnership with those who are marginalized, vulnerable, and excluded. Inclusive power-sharing functions as inclusive co-responsibility. For liturgy to become genuine synergy for solidarity, the celebration of liturgy must become a practice of co-responsibility initiated by radical welcome, reception of God's self-giving presence and power, and a return-gift that uses this presence and power to cultivate inclusive relationships rooted in justice and love. The co-responsibility of the faithful makes this a shared gift and task, a common accountability to emulate Jesus's teaching and healing ministry, including his radically counter-cultural table fellowship. Only then will the church be a true witness of Jesus Christ, experienced as communion. Only then will we more readily become what we receive, the Body of Christ.

Notes

[1] *Catechism of the Catholic Church*, 1397.

[2] This connection between synergy and power-sharing relies on Thomas Aquinas's understanding of grace as cooperation, the person's free response to God's self-gift. See *Summa Theologica* I-II q.111, art. 2, "Of the Division of Grace" *St. Thomas Aquinas Summa Theologica*, trans. Fathers of the English Dominican Province, vol. 2 (Notre Dame, IN: Ave Maria, 1981), 1136-1137.

[3] I use the term "solidarity" in reference to the principle of Catholic social thought that aims to realize the unity of the human family by overcoming the social, economic, and political boundaries that separate and at times subjugate persons. Solidarity traditionally refers to inclusive friendship in "social charity" as well as a just ordering of society (e.g., *Catechism of the Catholic Church*, 1939-1941). I use it to connote identifying with the "other" to initiate unity across difference through shared empowerment for communal right-relationship.

[4] Elisabeth Schüssler Fiorenza, *Discipleship of Equals: A Critical Feminist Ekklesia-logy of Liberation* (New York: Crossroad, 1993), 11-12.

[5] Robert Karris puts it plainly, "Jesus was crucified because of how he ate," in *Luke: Artist & Theologian: Luke's Passion Account as Literature* (Eugene, OR: Wipf and Stock, 1985), 47.

[6] Rodney Stark, *The Rise of Christianity: A Sociologist Reconsiders History* (Princeton, NJ: Princeton University Press, 1996).

[7] On the "sociology of food" for the early church, see Graydon Snyder, *Inculturation of the Jesus Tradition: The Impact of Jesus on Jewish and Roman Cultures* (Harrisburg, PA: Trinity Press International, 1999), 129-174. Snyder writes, "Despite the importance of theology, the death and resurrection of Jesus, and an ethic of caring, the real alteration in Judaism occurred (and Christianity clearly emerged) when table fellowship was not blocked by dietary obligations or the rejection of food dedicated to idols" (155).

[8] Richard Horsley, *Sociology and the Jesus Movement* (New York: Crossroad, 1989), 122-125.

[9] Paul writes to a divided community in Corinth, denouncing the class divisions that resulted in the wealthy eating and drinking to excess while other members of the community went hungry: "Therefore whoever eats the bread or drinks the cup of the Lord unworthily will have to answer for the body and blood of the Lord. A person should examine himself, and so eat the

bread and drink the cup. For anyone who eats and drinks without discerning the body, eats and drinks judgment on himself. That is why many among you are ill and infirm, and a considerable number are dying" (1 Cor 11:23-30).

[10]In his homily on the Gospel of Matthew, John Chrysostom asserts, "The temple of our afflicted neighbor's body is more holy than the altar on which you celebrate the holy offering" (cited in Pope John Paul II, *Sollicitudo Rei Socialis*, 31 [n. 59]). In another homily, he claims, "You dishonor this table when you do not judge worthy of sharing your food someone judged worthy to take part in this meal. . . . God freed you from all your sins and invited you here, but you have not become more merciful" (quoted in *Catechism of the Catholic Church*, 1397).

[11]In Sermon 272, Augustine states, "If you are the body and members of Christ, then it is your sacrament that is placed on the table of the Lord; it is your sacrament that you receive. To that which you are you respond 'Amen' ('yes, it is true!') and by responding to it you assent to it. For you hear the words, 'the Body of Christ' and respond 'Amen.' Be then a member of the Body of Christ that your Amen may be true" (quoted in Michael S. Driscoll, "Eucharist and Justice," in *Sacraments and Justice,* ed. Doris Donnelly [Collegeville, MN: Liturgical Press, 2014], 43). This reflects the spirit of his oft-quoted line from Sermon 227: "you are yourselves what you receive" (the Body of Christ).

[12]The connection between the Eucharist and social justice was a recurrent theme in several documents of Pope John Paul II. For example, John Paul II wrote: "All of us who partake in the Eucharist are called to discover, through this sacrament, the profound meaning of our actions in the world in favor of development and peace; and to receive from it the strength to commit ourselves ever more generously, following the example of Christ, who in this sacrament lays down his life for his friends" (*Sollicitudo Rei Socialis*, 48). See also *Ecclesia de Eucharistia*, 20, and *Mane Nobiscum Domine*, 25.

[13]*Sacramentum Caritatis*, 89. Then-Joseph Cardinal Ratzinger wrote, "we cannot have communion with the Lord if we are not in communion with each other" and "above all the Eucharist must reach out beyond the limits of the church itself in the manifold forms of service to men and to the world" in *God Is Near Us* (San Francisco, CA: Ignatius, 2003), 53, 91.

[14]Francis explains: "The Church is called to be the house of the Father, with doors always wide open. One concrete sign of such openness is that our church doors should always be open, so that if someone, moved by the Spirit, comes there looking for God, he or she will not find a closed door. There are other doors that should not be closed either. Everyone can share in some way in the life of the Church; everyone can be part of the community, nor should the doors of the sacraments be closed for simply any reason. . . . The Eucharist, although it is the fullness of sacramental life, is not a prize for the perfect but a powerful medicine and nourishment for the weak. These convictions have pastoral consequences that we are called to consider with prudence and boldness. Frequently, we act as arbiters of grace rather than its facilitators. But the Church is not a tollhouse; it is the house of the Father, where there is a place for everyone, with all their problems" (*Evangelii Gaudium*, 47).

[15]*Lumen Gentium*, 11.

[16]*Catechism of the Catholic Church*, 1327.

[17]John A. Coleman, "How the Eucharist Proclaims Social Justice (Part Two)," *Church* (Spring 2001): 11.

[18]William C. Spohn, *Go and Do Likewise: Jesus and Ethics* (New York: Continuum, 2006), 113.

[19]John A. Coleman, "How the Eucharist Proclaims Social Justice (Part One)," *Church* (Winter 2000): 9.

[20]Center for Applied Research in the Apostolate, "Sacraments Today: Belief and Practice among U.S. Catholics" (February 2008), http://cara.georgetown. edu. It is worth noting that 61 percent of Catholics agree with the statement, "Sacraments are essential to my faith," compared to 66 percent who agree that "Helping the poor and needy is a moral obligation for Catholics" (96).

[21]In preparation for the 2015 Synod of Bishops on the Family, the USCCB sent out a 46-question *Lineamenta* to inform the bishops about the lived experiences of the lay faithful. The responses they received were filled with frustrations ranging from the role of women to the exclusion of the LGBTQI individuals, the lack of attention given to the elderly (especially widows) and immigrants (particularly Latinos), the stigma associated with divorced and remarried Catholics, and especially for those not welcome to receive the Eucharist. This insight is informed by a research project funded by Xavier University's College of Arts and Sciences in 2015. In reviewing responses to the *Lineamenta* as provided by various diocesan offices (for example: Burlington, Knoxville, Portland, Scranton, St. Petersburg, and Wichita), widespread discontent was evident, not only with the church hierarchy and teaching, but also with the 46-question survey itself, given the number and length of questions as well as the complexity of language used.

[22]See R. Kevin Seasoltz's insightful analysis of Eucharist as God's "gift-giving" of forgiveness, reconciliation, and healing for "broken, sinful individuals" and "a sinful, broken church" in *God's Gift Giving: In Christ Through the Spirit* (New York: Continuum, 2007), 212-231 (at 217).

[23]80 percent of American church-goers attend services where one ethnic or racial group constitutes at least 80 percent of the congregation, although this was true for 85 percent of Americans in 1998 (Michael Lipka, "Many U.S. congregations are still racially segregated but things are changing," *Pew Research Center* (8 December 2014), http://www.pewresearch.org/ fact-tank/2014/12/08/many-u-s-congregations-are-still-racially-segregated-but-things-are-changing-2/).

[24]Compare 21 percent of Catholics who attend a diverse service with 16 percent of Evangelical Protestants, 13 percent of Black Protestants, 9 percent of Mainline Protestants, 6 percent of Mormons, and 4 percent of Jews, as reported by Robert D. Putnam and David E. Campbell, *American Grace: How Religion Divides and Unites Us* (New York: Simon & Schuster, 2010), 292.

[25]John T. McGreevy, *Parish Boundaries: The Catholic Encounter with Race in the Twentieth-Century Urban North* (Chicago: University of Chicago Press, 1999), 20.

[26]For example, McGreevy cites a 1945 survey of a Philadelphia Catholic high school wherein 92 percent of students recognized African Americans as

members of the Body of Christ, but only 67 percent believed that African Americans had a right to attend any Catholic church, and 94 percent of the students supported restricting African Americans to certain areas of the city (ibid.,107).

[27]Ibid., 261.

[28]Vincent J. Miller, "Where Is the Church? Globalization and Catholicity," *Theological Studies* 69, no. 2 (June 2008): 421. As a broader socio-cultural trend, see Bill Bishop, *The Big Sort: Why the Clustering of Like-Minded America is Tearing Us Apart* (Boston, MA: Mariner, 2009).

[29]Robert D. Putnam, *Our Kids: The American Dream in Crisis* (New York: Simon & Schuster, 2015), 41.

[30]Daniel Cox et al., "Race and Americans' Social Networks" *PRRI* (28 August 2014), http://www.prri.org.

[31]Gutiérrez continues, "Clarion calls to Christian unity which do not take into account the deep causes of present conditions and the real prerequisites for building a just society are merely escapist. . . . Unity is not an event accomplished once and for all, but something which is always in the process of becoming, something which is achieved with courage and freedom of spirit" (Gustavo Gutiérrez, *A Theology of Liberation: History, Politics, and Salvation,* tr. Sister Caridad Inda and John Eagleson [Maryknoll, NY: Orbis Books, 1973], 75).

[32]This observation is made by Thomas Merton in *New Seeds of Contemplation* (New York: New Directions, 1961), 70-79. It has been further developed by M. Shawn Copeland, *Enfleshing Freedom: Body, Race, and Being* (Minneapolis: Fortress, 2010), 101-105.

[33]I use this phrase in reference to the work of Katie Grimes, who critiques those who "overestimate the countercultural . . . capacity of the sacraments" with "the belief that the church's practices can, if enacted and understood properly, possess a demonstrable capacity to resist the atomizing individualism of the modern world and thereby enable the church to performatively receive its identity as the body of Christ" (Katie M. Grimes, "Breaking the Body of Christ: The Sacraments of Initiation in a Habitat of White Supremacy," *Political Theology* [2016]: 1-22, at 17, 13).

[34]See, for example, M. Shawn Copeland's chapter, "The Church Is Marked by Suffering," in *The Many Marks of the Church,* ed. William Madges and Michael J. Daley (New London, CT: Twenty-Third, 2006), 212-216.

[35]Grimes contends the church "comprises a corporate body, and bodies, unlike fortresses, cannot be walled off or sealed shut. Possessing an essential porosity, bodies are not divided from the world; they interact with it." She adds, to blame "the divided character of the body of Christ primarily on the atomizing individualism of the modern nation-state" is "like a homeowner who blames rain for a leaky roof" ("Breaking the Body," 17).

[36]*Lumen Gentium,* 6.

[37]Irenaeus, *Against Heresies,* 4.18.5.

[38]William V. D'Antonio, Michele Dillon, and Mary L. Gautier, *American Catholics in Transition* (Lanham, MD: Rowman and Littlefield, 2013), 112-115. 4 percent of Catholics are aware of the teaching and doubt its veracity; 33 percent are unaware and do not believe in the Real Presence; 17 percent

are unaware of the church teaching and yet still believe in the Real Presence.

[39]*Sacrosanctum Concilium*, 14.

[40]Elisabeth Schüssler Fiorenza uses this term to retrieve an "*ekklēsia* as discipleship of equals that can make present the *basileia*, the alternative world of justice and well-being intended by the life-giving power of G-d as reality and vision in the midst of the death-dealing powers of patriarchal oppression and dehumanization," made possible "by gathering people around the table and inviting everyone without exception to it, by feeding the hungry, healing the sick, and liberating the oppressed" (*Discipleship of Equals*, 11-12).

[41]Paul Lakeland, *The Liberation of the Laity: In Search of an Accountable Church* (New York: Continuum, 2002).

[42]John D. Zizioulas, *Being as Communion: Studies in Personhood and the Church* (Crestwood, NY: St. Vladimir's Seminary, 1985), 152.

[43]I borrow this term from Michael Paul Gallagher in his essay, "What Are We Doing When We Do Theology?" *Landas* 28, no.1 (2014): 1-12. Gallagher describes the need for conversion (through religious experience) to produce a "living theology" meant to "overcome a certain sacramental consumerism caused by a distorted theology of sin and grace" (9).

[44]William T. Cavanaugh, *Being Consumed: Economics and Christian Desire* (Grand Rapids, MI: Eerdmans, 2008), 34, 47.

[45]Acknowledging this may be in deference to Catholic piety or reverence, Thomas Day argues this betrays the meaning of liturgy as the shared work of the people in *Why Catholics Can't Sing: The Culture of Catholicism and the Triumph of Bad Taste* (New York: Crossroad, 1990).

[46]Karl Rahner, *Foundations of Christian Faith: An Introduction to the Idea of Christianity,* trans. William V. Dych (New York: Crossroad, 1978), 120.

[47]Louis-Marie Chauvet, *The Sacraments: The Word of God at the Mercy of the Body*, trans. Madeleine Beaumont (Collegeville, MN: Pueblo, 2001), 121-127.

[48]Ibid., 124.

[49]Ephesians 2:19 states that the members of the church "are no longer strangers and sojourners, but fellow citizens with the saints and members of the household of God."

[50]John Koenig explains, "In the great majority of passages where the *koinōnia* words appear, the meaning has to do with human participation in a blessing or task of higher reality that is directed by God." He adds, "The New Testament writers conceive of partnership chiefly as cooperation in a divine project" (John Koenig, *New Testament Hospitality: Partnership with Strangers as Promise and Mission* [Philadelphia: Fortress, 1985], 9). This understanding is shared by other biblical scholars as well; see, for example, J. Paul Sampley, *Pauline Partnership in Christ* (Philadelphia: Fortress, 1980).

[51]Jean Corbon, *The Wellspring of Worship*, trans. Matthew J. O'Connell (San Francisco: Ignatius, 1988), 38 (n. 4). Corbon argues the trajectory of synergy begins with the Annunciation, in which "Mary says 'Yes,' and the Spirit who unites the Word and the Yes, divine energy and human energy, gift and acceptance, comes upon her" (37).

[52]For example, Corbon writes of the resurrection: "On this day of birth the river of life becomes LITURGY as it spreads out from the tomb and reaches

us in the incorruptible body of Christ. Its wellspring is no longer the Father alone but the body of his Son, since this is henceforth wholly permeated by his glory. . . . [T]hese two energies are now joined together forever" (ibid., 54-55).

[53]Corbon adds, "Kenosis is the properly divine way of loving . . . [firstly in] the self-emptying of the Word in the Incarnation, but this is completed in the self-emptying of the Spirit in the Church, while it also reveals the self-emptying of the living God in creation" (ibid., 17-18).

[54]Ibid., 100. To be clear, the church relies on God's initiative: the church "has no energy that is not the energy of her Lord's Spirit" (112).

[55]Ibid., 146.

[56]John Donahue, "Biblical Perspectives on Justice," in *The Faith That Does Justice: Examining the Christian Sources for Social Change* ed. John C. Haughey (1977; repr. Eugene, OR: Wipf and Stock, 2006), 88.

[57]Ada María Isasi-Díaz contends, "Salvation depends on love of neighbor, and because love of neighbor today should be expressed through solidarity, solidarity can and should be considered the *sine qua non* of salvation" ("Solidarity: Love of Neighbor in the 21st Century," in *Lift Every Voice: Constructing Christian Theologies from the Underside,* ed. Susan Brooks Thistlethwaite and Mary Potter Engel [Maryknoll, NY: Orbis Books, 1998], 31).

[58]Corbon, *Wellspring of Worship*, 252.

[59]See, for example, Richard A. Horsley, *Jesus and Empire: The Kingdom of God and the New World Order* (Minneapolis: Fortress, 2002).

[60]Nicholas Wolterstorff, *The God We Worship: An Exploration of Liturgical Theology* (Grand Rapids, MI: Eerdmans, 2015), 11.

[61]D'Antonio, Dillon, and Gautier, *American Catholics in Transition*, 36.

[62]Zizioulas, *Being as Communion*, 115.

[63]Putnam and Campbell, *American Grace*, 444, 468-475. Putnam and Campbell state directly, "Mobilization or exhortations by clergy seem not to be a major factor in explaining good neighborliness," whereas "friends in general have a powerful effect on civic involvement" and even more specifically, "Having close friends at church, discussing religion frequently with your family and friends, and taking part in small groups at church are extremely powerful predictors of the range of generosity, good neighborliness, and civic engagement" (471-472).

[64]As Christopher Pramuk explains, Eucharist aims to teach us "one thing: namely, the art and discipline of contemplation, of seeing God's hidden presence in the world, through eyes of love. The sacred spaces of the religious world—from the ornate cathedrals of Europe to the humblest chapels and hillside shrines of El Salvador—teach us especially to pay attention to silence. . . .The rituals and spaces of formal religious worship can be for us and our children a school of wonder and mystery, a saving alternative to a world flattened out by commerce and technology, emptied of mystery or surprise, emptied of beauty, by the everyday drudge and demands of economic survival, by the ubiquitous drug of entertainment and advertising imagery. Regular immersion in sacred ritual is one way to make contact again with that hidden Mystery who breathes within all things, sustaining us into being with every moment. . . . The phrase 'Do not fear!' appears over three hundred fifty times in Scripture, yet how many of us still struggle with that dread

feeling that I have to get right with God before I walk in the door? Church is, or ought to be, where we go to find welcome and support precisely with our brokenness, relational failures, and moral shortcomings" (*Hope Sings, So Beautiful: Graced Encounters Across the Color Line* [Collegeville, MN: Liturgical, 2013], 144-145).

[65]Copeland explains, "To stand silent before war and death, incarceration and torture, rape and queer-bashing, pain and disease, abuse of power and position is to be complicit with empire's sacrilegious antiliturgy, which dislodges the table of the bread of life. That desiccated antiliturgy hands us all over to consumption by the corrupt body of the market" (*Enfleshing Freedom*, 83).

[66]As Grimes argues, "Human beings do not simply have habits; they are also habituated. This also holds true of the truly embodied body of Christ. In performing its body-shaping practices while residing in sites of white supremacist habituation, the church becomes not only what it does, but also where it lives. Place, I maintain, shapes habits, which in turn sculpt bodies. In order to change the church's white supremacist habits, therefore, we cannot merely change the way we inhabit space; we must also change the character of the places we inhabit. . . . White Christians need to be made to submit to spatial re-habituation. Rather than distinguishing themselves from the world in order to serve and save it, white Christians need to be compelled to inhabit a world not of their making. In particular, white Christians will be re-habituated only when they no longer possess the power to perpetuate white supremacist racial segregation in their neighborhoods and parishes" ("Breaking the Body of Christ," 21-22).

[67]Lakeland, *Liberation of the Laity*, 267.

PART II

LITURGY AND THE WORLD: WEAKNESS AND POWER

Power and Weakness

Liturgy, Justice, and the World

Susan A. Ross

In June of 1982, I had just finished my dissertation and was presenting my first conference paper at the College Theology Society's annual convention. Based on my dissertation, it was on the relationship between sacramental theologies of revelation and theological aesthetics. When I came into the classroom where the session was, Bernard Cooke was sitting in the front row. With fear and trembling, I presented my paper in front of the most significant sacramental theologian in the US, someone whose work had been so important in my own theological development. During the Q and A, Bernard pressed me on my use of von Balthasar, making sure I knew that Balthasar was someone to be very careful with. I assured him that I was well aware of that, and I told him that Balthasar was in my dissertation because my adviser, David Tracy, insisted that if I were dealing with theological aesthetics, I could not ignore his work. Bernard became a mentor and supporter of my own scholarship and a wonderful colleague; I later came to know him much better through a common project we were both involved in during the mid-90s. We are all in his debt, especially for the theme of this convention.

As I prepared this essay, I felt something of the same trepidation I felt 34 years ago, since I was asked to speak on a topic that is related to but also distinct from the field where I feel more comfortable—that is to say that liturgical theology is a somewhat different field than sacramental theology. I came to sacramental theology through systematic theology, and I studied theology and ethics at a school dominated by Protestant theologians (although there were also a few Catholics). My hope, though, is that my 60-plus years of experiences of liturgy, my theological and personal reflections, and the contributions of a number of wise philosophers and theologians can help inform this lecture. In other words, I begin from something of a position of weakness, a theme that I will play variations on in our reflections on power and liturgy today.

My formal remarks today will tell another story, and I will use this story to tease out some of the complex issues that surround discussions of liturgy and power. Putting these two terms side by side raises a number of intriguing and difficult questions. I will by no means be able to answer all of these, but I hope to formulate issues in such a way that we can move beyond some of the obstacles that have closed off further discussion.

So, the story: over twenty years ago, for a time my husband and I regularly worshiped at a Lutheran congregation in the South Loop of Chicago, where we had celebrated our marriage. The reasons for our being there are a whole other story, having to do with my discontent with the Catholic Church, my husband's canonical status, and the relationships that I had developed with the pastor and the community. This Evangelical Lutheran Church in America (ELCA) parish was a "Reconciled in Christ" congregation, meaning that it openly welcomed LGBTQ people at a time when such ecclesial acceptance was far less prevalent than today.[1] Two members of the church, a gay couple who were both ordained Lutheran pastors, were active members, with one being the music director and the other often preaching and presiding at Eucharist. They helped me to greatly appreciate the Lutheran approach to liturgy. They were also good friends of ours. A few weeks before the incident I will relate, David had received the expected news that because of his open committed relationship with Jonathan, he was to be dropped from the ELCA clergy roster. The clergy roster includes a variety of pastoral roles; being dropped from the roster means that one no longer can serve the church in an official capacity.

On this particular Sunday, David presided and preached, and at the end of the liturgy, he announced that, because of the ELCA's action, he would respond by literally divesting himself of his clerical robes and status. He then proceeded to take off, piece by piece, his stole, his alb, his cross, and his clerical collar and shirt.

As he took off these symbols of his pastoral status, he spoke of what they meant to him and his deep grief over this situation. He would no longer be able to do what he felt in his heart that he had been called by God to do. He then stood in front of us in his white undershirt and pants, stripped of his clerical robes as the church had stripped him of his status. He was literally de-frocked. His was an act of submission, of weakness in the face of institutional power. And yet it was also a powerful gesture, one that expressed his confidence and indeed his pride in his identity and his commitment to and love for Jonathan, a pride that, one could say, was supported in some ways by the world and not the institutional church. In a sense, one might say that worldly and churchly power conflicted in his literal and symbolic de-frocking.

Over the last year or so, as I have thought about this lecture and what I might say, this scene came back to me again and again. It would not let me go. It seemed to express to me so many related issues: the power of an institution, the power of a dramatic act, the power of an oppressed minority in speaking truth, the power of liturgy. While David was making his powerlessness as a gay Lutheran pastor the center of his action, at the same time there was an immense power to this action which expressed the power of weakness, but also the power of his identity as a gay man, an identity he refused to hide.

What I would like to do in this essay is, first, to explore the relationship of power and weakness by drawing on the thought of some recent philosophers and theologians who have embraced the idea of weakness, particularly divine weakness. What are we to make of a "weak" God? How does this affect the way we worship and how we as Christians make our way in the world? How do the different roles of power and weakness in the church and in the world interact?

Second, I want to consider the ambiguity and ambivalence of weakness in relation to liturgy. How can divine weakness provide a model for how the church might think about how it exerts power, especially liturgical and sacramental power, in relation to the world? How does weakness also serve negatively to disempower people, both lay people in relation to clerics and those on the margins of society, and to work against the church having an impact on the world? I want to argue that liturgy can and should serve as a counter-narrative to other narratives of naked power and force in the world and to the pain and suffering that challenge our lives in the world. Yet the church is, of course, not without its own narratives of power and the world is not without its own powerful narratives of weakness.

Third, I will consider how we might use power and weakness in liturgy so as to work toward justice in the world. In all of this, I offer not so much a complete and coherent answer to questions of the liturgy's relationship to the (powers of) the world, but rather a series of observations and interruptions. In other words, I offer no powerful metanarrative, but rather fragments of a possibly weak response, but also a response informed by the strength of weakness in relation to structures of power.

Power and Weakness

It is a truism to say that traditional Christian belief has emphasized God's power. We believe in God, "the Father Almighty, Creator of Heaven and Earth." Liturgical language in particular is filled with the language of God's power, one might say particularly God's patriarchal power, since the language of Almighty Father is so well established in liturgy and prayer and so strongly defended. One need only to read the names of God in the order of the Mass to see how often our prayers are addressed to God almighty, Lord God of all, Lord God of hosts. This language of God's almighty power is not accidental and its effects on the imagination are not insignificant. I am sure that many of us here can vouch for shocked and dismayed student reactions when we propose alternative language for God not just in theology but also, perhaps especially, in liturgical prayer. So much seems to depend on God's almighty power, a point to which I will return later.

Yet as a number of theologians and philosophers have argued, especially in these later postmodern times, the God of Jesus Christ hardly fills the role of a powerful potentate. John Caputo, for example, discusses this extensively in his book *The Weakness of God: A Theology of the Event.*[2] God, Caputo argues, is a "weak force," who "provides a provocation to the world that is otherwise than power."[3] We should speak of God, Caputo argues, not as a name, but as an event—not "an essence unfolding, but a promise to be kept, a call or a solicitation to be responded to, a prayer to be answered, a hope to be fulfilled."[4] Caputo's book is filled with challenges to the various images of God's power as well as challenges to theological power, which he frequently and pejoratively describes as "rouged and powdered."[5] I would note that the gendered implications of this phrase are worth a paper on its own, obviously a play on theology as the "queen of the sciences."

Throughout *The Weakness of God*, Caputo uses the language of weakness to provoke and disrupt but also to invite and cajole, to attract and move the hearer. His challenge to traditional conceptions of creation *ex nihilo*, drawing on the work of Catherine Keller, argues that what God does in creation is to bring goodness to what is already there, coaxing it out of matter, rather than powerfully willing it to be. He juxtaposes St. Paul and Jacques Derrida (whom he calls "Saints Paul and Jacques"[6]) to underscore his point that the ontotheological focus on God's powerful being utterly misses the point of the Christian Gospel, misrepresenting who God is in the New Testament and in the world today. God's real power lies precisely in God's "weakness," a "power" that works not by force but by attraction and persuasion. Throughout the book, he also relies on narratives of Jesus's "weak power" as expressed in the parables and on Paul's language of scandal to make his case that omnipotence has little place in the biblical understanding of God. There are also connections here with theological aesthetics, a point I will return to later in this paper.

Caputo is not the only contemporary thinker to challenge the language of divine power: Richard Kearney, Gianni Vattimo, and Sarah Coakley, among others, also eschew the traditional language of divine omnipotence, might, and strength and argue that the God of the Christian tradition is a reality best spoken of and related to as humble, a "still, small voice," the stranger who knocks at our door. Kearney, for example, ". . . notes that the concept of God as absolute Monarch of the universe stems from a literalist reading of the Bible along with unfortunate misapplications of a metaphysics of causal omnipotence and self-sufficiency."[7] Coakley writes that, in contemplation, one " 'practices' the 'presence of God'—the subtle but enabling presence of a God who neither shouts nor forces, let alone 'obliterates.'"[8] In writing of Jesus's kenosis, for example, Coakley argues against some feminist interpretations that see Jesus as "giving up" a divine power that is assumed that he had and could just as easily have used—and thus he serves as a kind of role model especially for men who need to learn to give up their power. She suggests that there is in fact no plethora of "divine power" that is already there, that Jesus is willingly and deliberately giving up. This is not the God of Jesus Christ—this kind of power isn't even there to begin with and then given up; rather, who God is, is not the almighty and omniscient Lord of All, smiting his enemies and able to effect anything he wills.

When it comes to considering power in the world today, we are in a very interesting time, at least politically, if not in other areas. When policies of diplomacy, strategy, and negotiation are pilloried as those of "weak losers," when brute annihilating force is named as the one and only realistic response to terrorism, when one must demonstrate one's willingness, indeed, one's commitment and desire to use force in order to demonstrate one's patriotism, it is more than clear that any understanding of "weak power" is going to be highly countercultural, to say the least. And I am not so sure that our world today is really so very different from the world of the past, or even the world of a thousand or two thousand years ago. Yes, we have made enormous strides in recognizing the humanity of many people heretofore considered subhuman; yes, there is less poverty, greater access to education; yes, fewer of us starve to death or die of treatable infections. Ideas of equality foreign to biblical and churchly circles have challenged the prevailing narratives of power, perhaps especially the powers of sex, race, and gender. In terms of how military and political power are used, however, we may be more sophisticated, but I am not sure at all whether we human beings are actually less prone to violence and abuses of power than we were in the past. To what extent the human condition and the will-to-power have changed or evolved over the centuries is yet another question I will leave open; I simply acknowledge here its reality and its challenges, especially to a conception of sacramental and liturgical life that relies, to some extent, on weakness.

If we are to take seriously the weak God of these thinkers, how does this speak to liturgy and how can this understanding of a weak God address these issues of power, both in the church and in the world around us? One of the main tasks of liturgy, as I understand it, is to provide us with an alternate narrative, another way of being in the world, than the excesses of worldly and ecclesiastical power and that the least powerful among us are the ones who can best tell this story. The Christian story is not one of good overcoming evil by force, but rather of the one dying in humiliation and defeat, and in that defeat finding new life; indeed, it is a narrative of reversals where the last are first, the prodigal son is rewarded with a feast, and the most cowardly disciple is given the highest authority. I also find it helpful to remember, as any number of liberation theologians have observed, that Jesus himself lacked clerical power; he was a layman in a movement that challenged the powers of the institutions of his day. His own "weak power" proved threatening enough to cause his death.

The question of the purpose of liturgy has a number of possible answers. We can call it "the joining of heaven and earth," as the Orthodox tradition holds; the reception of the Word and our expression of praise and thanks to God; the place where we receive grace through the Sacrament. One simple definition might be: food for the journey, sacred food for the sacred journey, a journey that proposes a different way of navigating in the world. Liturgy is the work of the people, the means by which we enact and signify God's work for the world.[9] We need to be nourished in mind and body, head and heart, with and for each other, and to do this work we cannot do this alone nor can we do this without material reality. So liturgy's role is to call us to life with God in this world so that we can transform it; how liturgy uses material reality will say a great deal about its understanding of power. Since we are not angels, we are incarnate human beings, we come to learn and know through our senses, our imaginations, our feelings, and our ideas. I have always been fond of Thomas Aquinas's discussion of the need for sacraments, and thus, for liturgy. I quote him here, making his own language inclusive:

> It follows, therefore, that through the institution of the sacraments [human beings], consistently with [our] nature, [are] instructed through sensible things; [we are] humbled, through confessing that [we are] subject to corporeal things, seeing that [we] receive assistance through them: and [we are] even preserved from bodily hurt, by the healthy exercise of the sacraments.[10]

While Thomas is assuming a hierarchical universe in which the body's weakness is in some ways an obstacle to be overcome, he is also arguing that this precise weakness is a means—in fact, our only means—of expressing our relationships with ourselves, others, the world, and God. There is a wonderful passage in the *Summa* where he reflects on the relationship between soul and body and, somewhat wistfully (I think), observes that after death, the soul, separated from the body before the final resurrection, "would wish the body to attain to its share."[11] And we should especially remember that God's own self-expression to us comes in bodily form.

Richard Kearney's discussion of Merleau-Ponty's ideas is also helpful here: Merleau-Ponty, Kearney notes, "offers an intriguing phenomenological interpretation of Eucharistic embodiment as recovery of the divine within the flesh, a kenotic emptying out of transcendence into the heart of the world's body, becoming a God beneath us rather than a God beyond us."[12]

The weakness that is our dependence on corporeal things is in fact also our strength and power but not in any traditional sense of "power over." The kind of "attractive power" described by Caputo, Kearney, and Coakley is a power that works by persuasion rather than coercion, and that is also, I would argue, an important avenue to justice. How we use these powers is the key question. Justice is not something that can simply be imposed on someone or a group; the idea of a genuine justice has to come from within. This is, I would argue, where beauty and justice intersect. Like weak power, beauty works by attraction and persuasion, by offering a vision, an alternate reality to which the person is drawn.[13]

To return to the act of submission of my friend David: his action was to submit to the powers of his institutional church which, in effect, had used this power to force him out of office. But at the same time, he demonstrated, through a dramatic and symbolic act of submission, the very power of making even more visible the institution's priorities. Can we see the face of Christ in a gay man? To borrow an idea from Edward Schillebeeckx, this "negative contrast experience" provided a way to make even more visible the injustices of church polity which, as we now know, were eventually changed.[14] It was the "weak power" of this action, and many others like it, that eventually changed the way the ELCA understood the place of sexuality in ministry.

The Ambiguity and Ambivalence of Liturgy as Weak Power

Let me turn now to some of the problems of such a conception of weak power. For all the positive talk of "weak power," there are undoubtedly serious issues with placing weakness at the center of our considerations of liturgical power. Weakness also connotes ineffectiveness, an inability to influence or change others, a ceding of authority to the one with greater power. Especially as a feminist, I am very nervous about celebrating the kind of weakness that suggests an unwillingness to confront injustice, a passive endurance, and one that encourages a simple and humble acceptance of one's lack of power as a kind of pseudo-virtue. Even worse, it can lead to an embrace of something like the "power behind the throne" that supposedly wives or parish housekeepers really exert. While there may be some truth to this, in the sense that it is the oppressed who are the ones who truly understand the dynamics of power, I think one would seriously need also to turn to Hegel and/or Foucault to try to sort out the dynamics of those relationships.[15]

In terms of the role of power and weakness in liturgy and their potential role in speaking to the world, I would identify at least the following. One example is the shift in liturgical emphasis since Vatican II that has had some unintended consequences. With the major liturgical focus on the Eucharist and the consequent loss of emphasis on lay-led devotional practices of the pre-Vatican II church, the presider has in many cases taken on a power that does not always serve him or the liturgy well. I am sure that we have all had experiences of what I sometimes call the "opera singer" presider: "Me, me, me, me, me, me, me." In an effort to make the liturgy more "relevant," presiders of this ilk end up taking "center stage," making themselves the stars of the show, turning the Eucharistic liturgy into a personal performance. This kind of presider will sometimes change the words of the prayers so that, at least in his mind, the congregation can see how much better, how much more powerful, his rendition is than simply speaking the words that are given. One effect of this tendency is that it relegates the congregation to the status of spectators, further weakening their role in participation. When the priest is the most important actor in the liturgy, the congregation is weakened, and not in a positive way. In many ways, I think, our entertainment-based popular culture only seems to support this kind of dynamic.

Unfortunately, a number of the liturgical guidelines from Rome have only made this problem worse. Consider how the rubrics discourage the presider from leaving the altar at the exchange of peace.[16] At my own church, until about ten years ago, the presider sat in the front row of the congregation during the Liturgy of the Word, after which he then took his place at the altar, symbolically signaling his identity first as a member of the congregation, hearing the word of God. The archbishop had made his displeasure about this known, but the location remained unchanged. When our pastor was reassigned and the new pastor came in, he relented to the pressure of the archbishop to move the presider's chair to the platform where the altar was. There was a subtle, but genuine, shift in the dynamics of the liturgy, since the spatial location did in fact make a difference. Another change was the new/old practice of kneeling during the Eucharistic prayer and the prayer before Communion, where the congregation had formerly stood. One of the members of the parish wrote a letter requesting that we return to the old practice, but this did not receive the support of the pastor. And we only need to consider how the Eucharist itself has been used as a gesture of both political and ecclesiastical power, both in terms of how one's public stance on political issues or one's canonical status can determine one's worthiness to receive the Eucharist. These practices are, I suggest, deliberate practices of power as force, which serve to further weaken and disempower the faithful, and thus the people's real power, not only in church but in the world as well. The way that power is exercised in these examples is not an attractive power of invitation but rather a negative power of coercion. I have discussed elsewhere the ways that the power exercised by pastoral staff, especially religious educators, can come to be seen as a threat to the priestly power over the sacraments.[17]

Liturgical language, as I have already suggested, also serves to emphasize where the power is. I am not trying to suggest that we jettison entirely any language of God as "Almighty Father"—for one thing, this language is too firmly embedded in the liturgy—but that we consider how our language exerts a subtle power over our imaginations and consider alternate ways of naming God and ourselves.

Such material uses of power can lead to a kind of passivity on the part of the congregation that works against the very understanding of divine power that Caputo and others encourage and that the work of the people, the *leitourgia*, is meant to foster. But there is still a paradox here that we cannot ignore and, indeed, that I think we have to embrace. That is to say, we need to hold, on the one hand, to God's power as attractive, inviting, noncoercive and "weak," as challenging conceptions of power that we deal with in our daily lives, both secular and religious, on a regular basis, and on the other hand, to recognize that there *is* a need for a power that works against the "overpowering" narratives of so much of the political and even ecclesiastical discourse in the world. Dealing with harassment and abuse, for example, requires a response that is much more than weakness and that also deals with imbalances of power. There need to be strategies of resistance that expose and challenge injustice and that reveal the misuse of power. A more thorough consideration of this topic would touch on the role of law in relationship to injustice and power.

About ten or so years ago, there was a confluence of events at my university that seemed to raise issues of liturgy and power on a number of levels. A group of women students became increasingly angry and frustrated with the situation of women in the church. A number of them felt a call to ordained ministry and decided to express their anger by standing, silently, in the back of the chapel throughout the entire liturgy. They wore stoles that they had made themselves and prepared flyers and passed them out to puzzled visitors that described their silent standing as a visible protest against their being silenced in the church. If they were not to be heard, they would be seen.

At the same time, there were changes in liturgical space and practice at the university. The university's chapel, built in the 1930s, had been renovated in the 1970s so that the interior space formed a large oval. Instead of long rows of pews facing the high altar, the ambo and altar were placed at the two ends of the oval, and chairs were arranged around them. It was, I thought, a successful blending of the pre-Vatican II space with a post-Vatican II sensibility: an intimate and inclusive space within a larger formal space. Masses were usually filled; I recall one Easter Vigil in the late 1980s or early 1990s when I arrived about thirty minutes early and could not find a seat. Then a new president came to the university and raised the funds to restore the chapel to its 1930s glory; there were also a number of changes in liturgical leadership. During the two-year process of chapel renovation, services were held in a nearby auditorium where, incidentally, the silent protests continued, and there were other changes that included giving the Jesuit seminarians more prominent liturgical roles, using more traditional hymns and, in many ways, making a decided shift in liturgical style.

When the renovated chapel reopened, the space was completely transformed. The altar was returned to its elevated place in the front of the chapel, the long rows of pews (with kneelers, of course) were back, and the walls were painted in brilliant whites and golds. The chapel was now "restored" to what it had been intended to be in the 1930s. While I find the renovated space to be aesthetically stunning, I did not then (nor do I now) find it to be liturgically welcoming. The chapel has become a place of ecclesiastical power. And by the time of the rededication of the chapel, most of the women students had graduated, found other places to worship, or simply stopped going to Mass. The silent standing protest as an example of weak power and the renovation of the chapel into a space that highlighted clerical power are two examples of how our material reality embodies a way of being church, how power is expressed and, I think, conveys some powerful messages to the congregation as to its role.

In these examples, action, language, and space all function. And if we were to ask how the liturgy strengthens us and leads us out into the world to be agents of justice, my point would be that one message it conveys through its use of these particular material realities is that the power to do anything significant is left to God and to the clergy. Yet as Pope Francis frequently reminds us, we are called to offer a different story than that of the world, one that does not force its vision, but is rather one that invites: the weak power that does not coerce but welcomes. The church, he has emphasized, is a "field hospital," that opens its doors to the weak, frail, sick, and homeless, and whose ministers are themselves broken. Its purpose is to envision and inspire us to live out the church's mission and for us to become the body of Christ. Expressions of power and its absence work through the actions, language, and spaces in which we dwell. We would do well to consider their power more closely.

Liturgy as Weak Power to Transform

I think it would be fair to say that many of us, perhaps especially women, find ourselves often feeling very powerless in relation to the liturgy and the sacraments, at least according to the official rules that continue to exert strong juridical power. Pope Francis's recent comments to women religious on possibly reviving the diaconate may offer some hope, but I am not holding my breath for any change, at least in my own lifetime.[18] I think there is a longstanding fear of women's power that is disguised by references to complementarity, the "feminine genius," or feeble attempts at humor—all of which have the effect of marginalizing and diminishing women. Looked at from the side of "the world," the magisterial church's claim that it is powerless to go against the mind of Christ, with relation to the question of women's ordination, is disingenuous. We have all heard these arguments too many times, and I am not going to go into them further here. Yet despite the frustration of many, including myself, the liturgy continues to have the potential to nourish, sustain, and inspire, often despite the forceful, powerful actions of the institutional church, presiders, language, and spaces. This is an ambivalent and ambiguous power that can both nourish and starve, elevate and demean.

Here I would like to offer three avenues of thought for "weak power," the liturgy, and the promotion of justice. In all of these considerations, I want to emphasize the significance of context— the environment that shapes our ability to be affected by or exercise power. In some situations, some of these points may be helpful and some may be unhelpful. None of them is intended as any complete "solution," but rather as a suggestion for how we might see ourselves responding when power is at issue. The first is a strategic and critical use of the concept of self-gift. The second is an examination of liturgy as "weak" transformative power. The third is a consideration of what I will call "liturgies of strategic interruption and disruption."

I frequently hear from my students, and I am sure the parents reading this are very familiar with the complaint, that the "Mass doesn't do anything for me." Especially for young people whose quite natural and youthful narcissism leads them to see things from a somewhat narrow perspective, the repetitive nature of the Eucharistic liturgy, combined, perhaps all too frequently, with poorly prepared (if at all prepared!) preaching and anemic music in parish contexts does not make for an attractive combination. Often, parishes and Newman centers go to great lengths to make their liturgies relevant for young people with dynamic presiders and popular liturgical music. By no means do I mean to criticize these valiant efforts, or the work of youth ministers (where parishes can afford them) to make young people feel welcome.

Yet I wonder if there is something important missing in this. If the Eucharistic liturgy is about anything, it is about Jesus's gift of himself to the world, the celebration of this gift of self, and the congregation's becoming the Body of Christ through Word and Sacrament—in a very real sense, losing who we are as a group of discrete individual people to come together with our gifts to be transformed. I want to be very careful here about the language of self-gift, since it is such loaded language. It is used extensively in the Theology of the Body, where every sexual act is to be a complete self-gift of body and soul to the other, an understanding of relationship and sexuality that I find more utopian than realistic or helpful.[19] It can also be used to encourage an unhealthy sense of selflessness which has, as we all know, different effects depending on one's sexual and/or social context, as is true of any language of self-sacrifice.[20] I am not advocating here that kind of selflessness. We need to be very careful when using such language. But the need for care in using this language does not mean that we ought to drop it altogether. It has taken me the better part of a lifetime to learn more and more deeply that the liturgy is not all about me and that my aesthetic or liturgical tastes really don't matter if the liturgy is effective. (Don't take this to mean that music or good preaching is not important; not at all!) My point is that there is an essential dimension of *giving oneself over to the liturgy*, becoming a part of the gathered community, that is, at the same time, very countercultural. The liturgy is the collective act of the people of God, not the act of the individual, and giving oneself over to the community as one part of the Body of Christ is who we are when we worship. This is true for both presider and congregation.

I am trying to walk a very fine line here. On the one hand, I am not arguing that one's particular liturgical community does not matter at all; in fact I do not attend my geographical parish in part because of some experiences of really offensive preaching. But on the other hand, there is no perfect parish, no perfect liturgy (although I keep trying to find one!); the liturgy is not my personal weekly aesthetic experience. There is a giving up of my own needs here in order to become part of a larger reality that is not focused on me and that, in fact, draws me out of myself to others. Only if we recognize this can we link liturgy and justice.

Self-gift needs to be a consideration on the part of everyone involved in the liturgy, and the liturgy itself needs to be seen as nourishment for the gift of self and community to the world. While in a sense the liturgy is an end in itself—it is not utilitarian, to be used only as a means for doing something else—nevertheless the liturgy is one critical part of the life of the Christian community, not the whole thing. There needs to be a connection with the local community and the world as a whole. It is a positive step that the institutional church no longer seems to hold to the requirement of "Sunday or Holy Day of Obligation," as if that were all that was needed to be a "good Catholic."

This means that self-gift as a "weak power" needs to be exercised by both presider and congregation. The Eucharistic presider's role is to be transparent, so that his own distinctive personality is the means of communicating God's presence among us but in such a way that we recall the message rather than the personality. And the entire congregation's role is to become the presence of Christ in the world. As Nicholas Wolterstorff puts it so well, "Liturgy is for giving voice to life oriented towards God."[21] And the God to whom we orient ourselves works through invitation and hospitality, as we should too. Much more can be said here.

Second, the liturgy prepares us to transform ourselves and the world. Drawing on Sallie McFague's helpful characterization of Jesus's ministry as "inclusive, destabilizing and nonhierarchical,"[22] I suggest that we need to pay more attention to the ways that liturgy challenges us to change and how it can incorporate these qualities. Homilies of course need to be well prepared and scripturally based; inclusiveness needs to be the aim of every liturgy and, if we are to consider Jesus's practices with his community, they are, if anything, nonhierarchical. Women's inclusion in the diaconate, if not the priesthood, would in fact confirm the "weak power" that ministry is intended to be, which may well be an unspoken dimension of clerical resistance. Recall Sandra Schneiders' insights about the unexpected gifts of women's spirituality or Christine Gudorf's point that what the sacraments do is what women ordinarily do, but raised up to a clerical level.[23] Schneiders notes that since so much of women's ministry has been unritualized until recently, it is a much more personalized ministry of service than exercise of power. Gudorf makes the point that what the sacraments do is what women ordinarily do, considered to be unremarkable, mere mundane or human actions, but once raised up to a clerical level, they become significant.

The destabilizing force of the liturgy should serve to resist the temptation to set liturgy apart from its lived context. The nostalgia for transcendence in liturgy is too often a desire to have the liturgy be completely "other" than the world, in a place set apart, where one thinks of God, not the world. This is not to say that there is not a transcendent dimension to life that needs to be recognized and expressed in the liturgy, but the tendency, to quote Wolterstorff again, is that "the inclination of most of us religious people is first to do our singing and then, if time, energy, and persistence are left, to tend to justice."[24] Inclusiveness also means paying attention to context, becoming aware of temptations of insularity, making efforts to open a parish's life to challenges in its social and economic situation. The current debate on the worth of Black lives and the apparent lack of discussion in many parishes is a genuine challenge to Catholics.

Third, I suggest that we consider participating in what I am calling "liturgies of strategic interruption." The feminist liturgical movement that arose in the 1970s and 1980s provides one model, but also some cautions. What this movement did was to empower women as liturgical subjects, and that is no small accomplishment! Freed from the idea that the altar was accessible to women only when it needed cleaning, women developed new liturgical practices that celebrated moments otherwise considered unremarkable, not a significant part of human experience, or even a dimension of women's experience that was considered unspeakable, such as menopause.[25]

It is interesting to consider the life of these alternative liturgies. For many, including myself, these liturgies were almost thrilling moments when women could see ourselves as liturgical leaders. They served as a way to give voice to what had been silenced for so long and to inspire action. Yet there is also a life cycle to these liturgies. I was part of some women's liturgical groups for a time in the 1980s and 1990s, and while I found these celebrations inspiring and creative, giving me a community that I did not find in the institutional church, the need to develop something "new" for each liturgy eventually became something of a burden. How many new ways can one celebrate women's creative power, the beauty of nature, the cycles of the moon, without repeating what was done before? In addition, issues of inclusion raised questions, at least for me, of the public character of liturgy and the invited character of the groups. It seemed to me then and now, that the relatively closed nature of these groups posed a challenge to what ought to be the open nature of the liturgy. The Eucharistic liturgy in particular is one place where one should *not* get to decide with whom one sits. So I suggest that "strategic liturgies" have an important place that can remind us what our Christian life and liturgy are all about. My point is to consider how they can be used to energize and perhaps even on occasion disrupt our liturgical "business-as-usual," pointing our attention to the need for action for justice in the world.

The liturgies I have in mind include the Chicago Good Friday Stations of the Cross as practiced in Pilsen each year, stopping at the places where daily crucifixions—shootings, murders, crushing poverty, helplessness in the face of addiction, gross injustices practiced by official government agencies—take place. Such liturgical practices help to more directly connect life as it is lived "on the streets" to what we pray for in church. They are forms of "weak power" that function symbolically to raise awareness and galvanize people to action. They could also include ways in which the racism bred into the American way of life is recognized, lamented, and confronted. In the spring of 2016, Father Michael Pfleger spoke at a colloquium at Loyola on religion and violence and reminded us that the daily death count of lives shattered ought to disrupt our liturgical lives. The frequent marches and protests that he organizes are other examples of these "strategic liturgies of disruption." The power of movements such as Occupy and Black Lives Matter to engage in symbolic actions that help to shake the complacency of the lives of the privileged and comfortable are an important and necessary resource. And it is important to note here their destabilizing role in the community. Encouraging and reclaiming such liturgical actions would also serve to empower the people as a whole to be agents of liturgy rather than simply passive recipients. My point is that some of the "loss" of lay-led liturgical power that followed the almost complete focus on the Eucharist after Vatican II can be reclaimed. There is a need for a variety of liturgical actions, not just regular feasts during the year. I am reminded of what Walter Wink has said about Jesus's actions in confronting power: rather than seeing "turn the other cheek" as an expression of passivity and weakness, he shows how in its context it actually "disarmed" the enemy by forcing the use of weak power.[26]

Eucharistic gatherings themselves are by definition places of weak force where we submit to the power of the liturgy to gather together, to be inclusive, to hear God's word, where the counter-story of Jésus is the meaning of the liturgy: "The liturgy is the place where this process becomes conscious and intentional. It is the place of assent, of openness and meeting."[27]

The liturgical theologian Richard McCall writes: "If human beings are made in the image of God, it is our ability to act in time and space and not some state of being which defines that likeness."[28] McCall's point here is that the *imago dei* is not a static quality but rather something dynamic. He goes on to say, "Because it only 'happens' when there is a sacrifice on the part of each actor, a letting-go of the intention to define the plot, it is not what is happening in most of life. The sacramental plot which is enacted in liturgical events is the very sacrificial act by which Trinity enacts creation in continual letting-go. Because the sacraments involve us (if we will be involved) in the plot which is the 'inner life of the Trinity,' they 'effect what they signify.'"[29]

To conclude: I have tried to offer some ideas that might help us to think and act liturgically in ways that demonstrate the weak power of the Gospel and its transformative power. In some ways, we are all a bit like my friend David: confronted with ecclesiastical, social, and political institutions that wield powers that can exclude and dehumanize. We cannot change all of these powers magically, and resisting by force is most often not even possible. Yet this does not mean we cannot resist at all. Our liturgies and our lives have the power to resist in ways that can transform our imaginations and, perhaps, to move us a little closer to establishing and living in the realm of God's power where death is transformed into life and our fragile bodiliness is where we truly encounter God.

Notes

[1] See http://www.reconcilingworks.org for a description of the movement.

[2] John Caputo, *The Weakness of God: A Theology of the Event* (Bloomington: Indiana University Press, 2006).

[3] Ibid., 13.

[4] Ibid., 5.

[5]Ibid., 8, 12, 33, 42, 59, 153; there are numerous allusions to theology as "rouged and powdered."

[6]Ibid., *Weakness*, 12.

[7]Richard Kearney, *Anatheism: Returning to God After God* (New York: Columbia University Press, 2010), 53.

[8]Sarah Coakley, *Powers and Submissions: Spirituality, Philosophy, and Gender* (Oxford, UK, and Malden, MA: Blackwell, 2002), 35.

[9]Ruth Meyers, in "Unleashing the Power of *Worship*," *Anglican Theological Review* 92, no.1 (January 2010): 55-70, does a helpful job of spelling this out.

[10]Thomas Aquinas, *Summa Theologiae*, ST III, 61, a. 1.

[11]Thomas Aquinas, *Summa Theologiae*, ST I-II, q. 4, a. 5, ad 4.

[12]Kearney, *Anatheism*, 91.

[13]A fuller treatment of this issue of attractive power would need to deal with the role of law. In some important instances, injustice cannot be overcome by persuasion, as in the case of US civil rights.

[14]Edward Schillebeeckx developed this idea over the course of his career. See especially *Church: The Human Story of God*, trans. John Bowden (New York: Crossroad, 1996), 5ff., "The experience of radical contrast in our human history."

[15]For Hegel, see G. W. F. Hegel, *The Phenomenology of Spirit*, trans. A. V. Miller and J. N. Findlay (Oxford: Oxford University Press, 1977), Chapter IV; for Foucault, see Michel Foucault, *Power/Knowledge: Selected Interviews and Other Writings 1972-1977* (New York: Pantheon, 1980).

[16]The USCCB Instructions say: "So as not to disturb the celebration, the priest celebrant normally remains in the sanctuary," with allowances for weddings and funerals. See http://www.usccb.org.

[17]See Susan A. Ross, *Extravagant Affections: A Feminist Sacramental Theology* (New York: Continuum, 1998).

[18]See Jamie Manson's comments in *The National Catholic Reporter* (May 19, 2016) which articulate what many are thinking: https://www.ncronline.org.

[19]See, for example, Christopher West, *The Theology of the Body Explained: A Commentary on John Paul II's "Theology of the Body"* (Boston: Pauline Books and Media, 2003).

[20]The literature on selflessness goes back to Valerie Saiving's pioneering article in 1960 "The Human Situation: A Feminine View," *Journal of Religion* 40, no. 2 (April 1960): 100-112.

[21]Nicholas Wolterstorff, "Justice as a Condition of Authentic Liturgy," *Theology Today* 48, no. 1 (April 1991): 17.

[22]Sallie McFague, *Models of God: Theology for an Ecological, Nuclear Age* (Minneapolis: Fortress Press, 1987), 48.

[23]For Schneiders, see "The Effects of Women's Experience on Their Spirituality," *Spirituality Today* 35 (Summer 1983), 100-116; for Gudorf, see "Sacraments and Men's Need to Birth," *Horizons* 14, no. 2 (Fall 1987): 296-309.

[24]Wolterstorff, "Justice as a Condition," 17.

[25]The literature on this topic is voluminous. Some of the more significant authors to consult would be Teresa Berger, Lesley Northup, Janet Walton.

[26]See Walter Wink, *Jesus and Nonviolence: The Third Way* (Minneapolis:

Fortress, 2003); I am grateful to Anne Patrick who first directed my attention to Wink in her book *Conscience and the Creative Process* (Mahwah, NJ: Paulist, 2011).

[27]Richard McCall, "Liturgical Theopoetic: The Acts of God in the Act of Liturgy," *Worship* 71, no, 5 (September 1997).

[28]Ibid., 410.

[29]Ibid., 413.

The Power of Liturgical Lament to Evoke Ecological Virtues

Anne M. Clifford

Orientation

Pope Francis implores people of our beleaguered planet to respond to the "immensity and urgency of the challenge we face" in *Laudato Si'* (no. 15)[1] and calls for cultivating the "sound virtues" needed "to make a selfless ecological commitment" (no. 211) to end human induced climate change. As a catalyst for the requisite ecological commitment, Pope Francis poses this poignant question, "What kind of world do we want to leave to those who come after us, to children who are now growing up?" (no. 160). Responding to this heart-rending question requires us to heed earth's cries as we acknowledge our role in today's ecological crisis (no. 101). Prayerful lament before our Creator is a step toward choosing to end the *"excessive anthropocentrism"* that blocks us from accepting our rightful place in the world (no. 116). Prayerful lament, as a communal expression of remorse, is not an end in itself. It is an urgent summons to embrace the practice of ecological virtue in the service of life (see no. 189).

To encourage Christians to conserve, restore, and honor God's creation, in the pages to follow a communal para-liturgical day of prayer, inspired by *Laudato Si'*, is proposed. The day's design includes an introduction, reflection on relevant biblical passages and attention to saints featured in *Laudato Si'*, with accompanying reflections on corresponding cardinal virtues conceived as "ecological virtues." Additional biblical passages, hymns, and prayers, including those featured in the encyclical, could complement the proposed schema.[2]

Introduction to the Communal Day of Prayer

The day is envisioned as an opportunity to draw on "the treasure of Christian spiritual experience" (LS, no. 15), including sacred scripture and the witness of saints, to discern communally a virtuous response to Pope Francis' question about the "kind of world" we want to leave to future generations (no. 160). For Pope Francis this question is a priority because "God has joined us so closely to the world that we can feel the desertification of the soil almost as a physical ailment, and the extinction of a species as a painful disfigurement" (no. 89).[3]

Proclamation of Sacred Scripture—The Book of Jeremiah

The powerful sentiments cited from no. 89 of *Laudato Si'* are not new. Similar ones are expressed in this proclamation by the prophet Jeremiah made six centuries before the birth of Jesus:

> Over the mountains, break out in cries of
>   lamentation,
> over the pasture lands, intone a dirge.
> They are scorched, and no one crosses them,
> unheard is the bleat of the flock;
> birds of the air as well as beasts—
> all have fled, and are now gone (Jer. 9:10).[4]

Jeremiah's powerful lament rises from the depths of the human spirit at a time of great distress and draws attention to the negative effects of human choices on the land, resulting in suffering for human and non-human creatures—sheep, birds, and other animals. The call for solidarity with non-human creatures sets this passage apart from most biblical laments. Jeremiah points to the effect of the people's choices: *it is a scorched desert.* Nature is deadly silent; human sinfulness is the cause of a momentous imbalance in creation that God made good (cf. Jer. 27:5). Chapter 9 of Jeremiah continues with this request directed to the women of the community:

Thus says the LORD of hosts: Attention!
Tell the wailing women—come, summon the best
  of them;
Let them come quickly and intone a dirge for us,
That our eyes may be wet with weeping, our cheeks
  run with tears.
The dirge is heard from Zion: Ruined we are, and
  greatly ashamed. . . .
Teach your daughters this dirge, and each other this
  lament.
Death has come . . . (Jeremiah 9:17-20).

This call to the wailing women to sound the dirge of ecological lament is significant. Although women historically have been rarely in a position to make decisions resulting in ecological disaster, it is women (and their young children) who most often bear the brunt of the burden.

The lament of Jeremiah is limited to a relatively small territory and population.[5] Although the majority of the world's current 7.4 billion people[6] do not live in rural areas that resemble the Judah of Jeremiah's era, his words illustrate the power of biblical lament to reach beyond limits of time and place. Humans brought devastation upon themselves and other creatures in the sixth century B.C.E. and continue to do so today. Pope Francis critiques profit-driven economic decisions that negatively impact society and nature as merely "collateral damage" (no. 123).

Silent Prayerful Reflection, Followed by "Faith Sharing"

After the guided reflection on the first biblical selection, participants are provided time for personal prayer and are directed to note areas of their lives in which they recognize an invitation to "ecological conversion" (LS, no. 219) in response to a pattern of treating God's creation in utilitarian ways for one's individual benefit (no. 159).

After the prayer period participants are encouraged to share personal choices harmful to creation, which they lament. It is possible that for some participants this may require ceasing to look upon "doomsday predictions" about our planetary future with disdain or despair. No matter what form the sharing of perceived shortcomings regarding "earth-care" may take, it is important to encourage the participants to regard what surfaced as invitations for lament that open their hearts and minds to deepening their relationship with our Creator-God.

Selected Saints Treated in *Laudato Si'* and Corresponding Ecological Virtues

The biblical passage proposed to set the context for this segment is 2 Peter 1:3-7, chosen not only because the passage features virtue, but also because it is directed to God's "chosen sojourners" (1 Pt 1:1) who, in seeking to live as followers of Christ, feel alienated from the corrupt values of their society.

> His [meaning Jesus's] divine power has bestowed on us everything that makes for life and devotion, through the knowledge of him who called us by his own glory and power.
>
> Through these, he has bestowed on us precious and very great promises, so that through them you may come to share in the divine nature, after escaping from the corruption that is in the world because of evil desire.
>
> For this very reason, make every effort to supplement your faith with virtue, virtue with knowledge, knowledge with self-control, self-control with endurance, endurance with devotion, devotion with mutual affection, mutual affection with love.

The order, supplement your faith with virtue and only then with knowledge, is thought-provoking.

Ecological spirituality has—as any truly Christian spirituality must—authenticating value-based moral practice. The development of an ecological spirituality responsive to today's global climate change problems requires ownership of guilt through heartfelt lament. Ecological lament opens one to cultivating virtues that provide value-based direction for pursuing the knowledge needed to inform one's moral commitment to "earth-healing" (see no. 211).

With regard to the witness of the saints, the focus is on four saints treated in *Laudato Si'* with a proposed connection of each to a cardinal virtue to cultivate in service of "a selfless ecological commitment" (no. 211), expressed in self-giving love for the benefit of "the common home which God has entrusted to us" (no. 232). Focus on virtues exemplified by saints whom Pope Francis "lifts up" as models responds not only to the weak-willed rejoinders of international political agreements and multi-national corporations (neither of which offer effective remedies for climate change), but also (and more importantly) to Pope Francis's call to discover the presence of the Spirit of life who dwells in every living creature (no. 88). This discovery is central to a spiritual conversion that leads one to cultivate the "ecological virtues" (no. 88) needed for effective responses to today's climate-change-induced problems.

It is important to provide the participants in the day of prayer with clarity about the meaning of "ecological virtue." Virtue is more than simple moral goodness; it is practical wisdom with a *telos*—a directedness to God. In the case of ecological virtue, the focus is specifically on following God's will for the sake of life. Such "God-directedness" requires cultivating virtues to achieve the earth-healing needed today (no. 211). In *Laudato Si'* Pope Francis draws attention specifically to the virtue of humility, which he proposes rejects considering ourselves autonomous—replacing God with our own ego, and thinking that our subjective feelings alone can determine the needed moral response. He stresses:

> Once we lose our humility, and become enthralled with the possibility of limitless mastery over everything, we inevitably end up harming society and the environment. It is difficult to promote healthy humility or happy sobriety when we consider ourselves autonomous, when we exclude God from our lives or replace God with our own ego, and think that our subjective feelings can define what is right and what is wrong. (No. 224)

Emphasis on humility in an encyclical from a Jesuit pope is not surprising. Ignatius of Loyola stressed three degrees of humility in the *Spiritual Exercises*,[7] with the third and "most perfect expression of humility" calling for following Jesus, who modeled self-emptying love by assuming the condition of a slave to God's will (Philippians 2:7-8).

Although Pope Francis does not speak directly of Ignatius's

conception of the three degrees of humility in his encyclical, he does draw attention to saints whose exemplary following of Jesus make them guides for virtuous living. Among the saints featured are Thomas Aquinas (no. 86), Francis of Assisi (no. 10-12, *passim*), Benedict of Norcia (no. 126), and Therese of Lisieux (no. 230).

The inclusion of the four above saints in *Laudato Si'* prompts a third biblical text, the book of the Wisdom of Solomon 8:7, which states: "She [Wisdom] teaches *temperance*, and *prudence*, and *justice*, and *fortitude*, which are such things as men [presumably also women] can have nothing more profitable in life." The four are traditionally called the "*cardinal virtues*" and are treated by Thomas Aquinas in his *Summa Theologiae*[8] as foundational for a truly good moral life. But do the cardinal virtues apply to a creation-oriented spirituality in ways that encourage, motivate and "give meaning to our individual and communal activity"? (LS, no. 216).

With this question in mind, I propose that the para-liturgical day of reflection focus two prayer periods on the cardinal virtues as "ecological virtues." To set the context, Aquinas's affirmation of the sacramentality of creation in the *Summa Theologiae* is given attention:

> [God] brought things into existence so that his goodness might be communicated to creatures, and be re-enacted through them. And because one single creature was not enough, he produced many and diverse [creatures], so that what was wanting to one expression of the divine goodness might be supplied by another, for goodness, which in God is single and uniform, in creatures is manifold and divided and hence the whole universe together participates in the divine goodness more perfectly, and represents it better than any single creature whatever.[9]

Expressed in contemporary terms, the bio-diversity of the planet is an inherently good creation with a God-given purpose.

This purpose is integral to the sacramental character of creation. Aquinas affirms that each creature, possessing integrity of its own and in its own distinctive way, is revelatory of God. Further, in his theological reflections on the days of creation, Aquinas calls God's creative processes on days four, five, and six "works of adornment."[10] He professes that birds and fish are called into being by God to embellish creation with beauty. Further, in the richly diverse creation with its multiple "traces" of the Trinity, God provides humans with a window into the divine.

Thomas Aquinas's theology of the sacramentality of creation provides an appropriate context for addressing Pope Francis's concern that "the external deserts in the world are growing, because the internal deserts have become so vast" (no. 217, quoting Pope Benedict XVI). For these deserts to bloom an "ecological conversion," which at its core is an interior conversion, is needed. Such a conversion is a whole-hearted embrace of the vocation to be a protector of God's handiwork through the practice of virtue, especially the cardinal virtues, which are not only character-forming, but also facilitate becoming "one with God."

Prudence and Justice as Ecological Virtues

Following the above introduction, the third prayer period focuses on the cardinal virtues in the order in which Thomas Aquinas addressed them in the *Summa Theologiae*.[11] *Prudence* is first with good reason, for prudence is the principle, in the sense of the "wellspring," of the other cardinal virtues: justice, temperance and fortitude. How is prudence expressed when directed to ecological decisions? Prudence calls for discerning a balance between competing needs and desires in the use of the world's goods. When applied to ecological concerns, it is prudence that prompts one to be attuned to decisions driven by greed that result in ecological harm and to determine the choices required for a life-sustaining world. Prudence also encompasses precautionary action to be taken *now* to ensure the long-term health of an ecosystem and by extension the well-being of our planet.

Thomas Aquinas's works provide no indication about how prudence, as the virtue of practical wisdom, should be applied to water and land issues of his era.[12] Pope Francis also does not address medieval problems, but he does herald the thirteenth-century saint Francis of Assisi as the exemplar of an integral ecology marked by care for the vulnerable, expressed authentically and joyfully (no. 10). Both qualities point to the second cardinal virtue: *justice.*

We have no treatises on justice from the pen of Francis of Assisi, but Thomas Aquinas's description of justice clearly applies to Saint Francis's life choices. For Aquinas justice is giving to each person and, by extension, each form of life, its due—meaning what each needs to sustain life. Saint Francis's life choices model this conception and also transcend it. Pope Francis notes that Saint Francis's actions reveal that he felt called to care for all living beings. His responses to his fellow creatures "take us to the heart of what it is to be human," for "whenever he would gaze at the sun, the moon or the smallest of animals, he burst into song, drawing all other creatures into his praise" (no. 11). Saint Francis's responses to the world around him was much more than intellectual appreciation or economic calculation; for him each and every creature was a sister united to him by bonds of affection. He directly communed with creatures, inviting them "to praise the Lord, just as if they were endowed with reason."[13]

Pope Francis proposes that in Saint Francis's life one finds an invitation to approach nature and the environment with awe and wonder, turning from attitudes of masters and exploiters by justly setting limits based on actual immediate needs guided by a commitment to poverty that refuses to acquire things in order to control them (no. 11). Clearly, justice—guided by prudence—is essential for restoring ecological balance.

Following prayer focused on the virtues of prudence and justice, a musical interlude and/or time for a silent walk may be appropriate.

Temperance and Fortitude as Ecological Virtues

The final prayer period of the day, begins with the third cardinal virtue, *temperance*. According to Aquinas, temperance is the virtue of self-restraint; it disposes one to avoid excess, while seeking balance.[14] Of the saints to whom Pope Francis gives attention, Saint Benedict of Norcia, the sixth-century founder of Western monasticism, undoubtedly is a model of temperance. Benedict proposed a way of life that sought balance—especially of work and prayer. He also encouraged the monks to practice self-control regarding consumption of meat and wine.

Additionally, commitment to temperance is evident in monastic farming practices that emphasized planning and innovation, including three-field crop-rotation and the development of efficient plows for planting and windmills for grinding grain. Temperance is also evident in Benedict's affirmation of the dignity of farm labor and his attention to the importance of agricultural planning to ensure both optimum results and sustainability.

Today the Benedictine form of temperance contrasts sharply with American culture's materialistic values. At present the United States has the world's highest per person level of consumption; in virtually all parts of the world, forests, fisheries, water sources, and whole ecosystems are being jeopardized to support our way of life.[15] Temperance remains a relevant virtue today, because moderating consumption accompanied by voluntary simplicity is imperative for sustaining life on our planet.

The fourth virtue, *fortitude*, Aquinas describes as curbing fear and moderating daring,[16] both qualities evident in the life of Saint Therese of Lisieux. In *Laudato Si'* Pope Francis encourages the practice of Therese's "little way of love," by enacting a commitment to integral ecology in daily choices that break with the logic of violence, exploitation, and selfishness (no. 230). Therese of Lisieux, popularly known as the "Little Flower," may seem like an illogical choice for guidance in the practice of fortitude directed to climate change. But she does exemplify a strong loving concern for nature traceable to her childhood memories of finding in wildflowers, including daisies, buttercups, and roses, reminders of God's love.[17]

As a young adult Therese of Lisieux demonstrated persistent courage, including when she requested to be permitted to join the Carmelite order at age fifteen at a public papal audience in Rome with Leo XIII,[18] and when she struggled with multiple illnesses including the tuberculosis that afflicted her when she was twenty-three that took her life eighteen months later.[19] For Therese fortitude means resisting the temptation to become discouraged by trusting in God's mercy while choosing to live and love until her life's end. It is with good reason that Robert Ellsberg describes Therese of Lisieux as "a woman possessed of a will of steel."[20]

Pope Francis broadens the scope of Saint Therese's exemplary love enacted in her Carmelite convent over a century ago by applying it to today's social and political realm. Calling for mutual care that makes itself felt in every action that seeks to build a better world, Pope Francis stresses, "Love for society and commitment to the common good are outstanding expressions of a charity that affects not only relationships between individuals but also 'macro-relationships, social, economic and political ones.'"[21] When we feel that God is calling us to intervene with others in these social dynamics, such a call is part of a spirituality that encompasses charity, which both matures and sanctifies us (no. 231).

The Closing for the Day of Prayer

After a period of prayerful and optional faith-sharing on the cardinal virtues, as a closing for this para-liturgical day of prayerful reflection on *Laudato Si'*, it seems fitting to draw attention to the hymn of praise of Christ—Creator and Redeemer—in Colossians 1:15-20:

> He [Jesus Christ] is the image of the invisible God,
> the firstborn of all creation.
> For in him were created all things in heaven and
>   on earth,
> the visible and the invisible,
> whether thrones or dominions or principalities
>   or powers;
> all things were created through him and for him.
> He is before all things,
> and in him all things hold together.
> He is the head of the body, the church.
> He is the beginning, the firstborn from the dead,
> that in all things he himself might be preeminent.
> For in him all fullness is pleased to dwell,
> and through him to reconcile all things for him,
> making peace by the blood of his cross,
> whether those on earth or those in heaven.

This Pauline hymn of praise is both the antithesis of Jeremiah's lament and a hopeful reminder that all things are created in Christ and for Christ. The twofold role of Christ as Creator and Redeemer serves as an apt "grounding" for a commitment to an ecologically directed practice of the cardinal virtues in the care of creation and the restoration of our damaged planet. Through such a commitment we can grow closer to Jesus Christ, who not only shared our humanity but also serves as the model of reconciliation that is creation-encompassing (Col. 1:20).

In contemporary American culture with its strong "ego-centered" anthropocentric outlook, the application of prudence, justice, temperance, and fortitude in choices to sustain life on our planet is greatly needed. Mindfulness that creation does not exist for humanity, but rather creation is from Christ and for Christ, and therefore has God-given intrinsic value in and of itself is fundamental to our journeys to redemption via the route of virtuous care for creation.

Hopefully this proposed para-liturgical day of prayer, with its attention to relevant biblical passages and focus on saints who model the cardinal virtues, aptly complements Pope Francis's emphasis on the virtue of "healthy humility" (LS, no. 224), which is "the mark" of those who embrace the commitment to love all of creation in Christ. By actively embracing this commitment in the practice of the cardinal virtues as ecological virtues, not only will we be instrumental in helping our planet flourish, but also we together will become more alive by caring for our fellow creatures with prudence, justice, temperance and fortitude.

Notes

[1] Pope Francis, *Laudato Si'*, "On Care for Our Common Home" (2015), http://w2.vatican.va.

[2] Although a communal day of prayer is proposed, the proposal could be adapted for a weekend retreat or for evenings of reflection.

[3] Here Pope Francis cites his Apostolic Exhortation *Evangelii Gaudium* (2013), no. 215.

[4] The selected verses are excerpted from Jeremiah 8:4-10:25, in which the dominant theme is coping with disaster and the need for repentance. Lamentation is also the central theme of Jer. 14:1-15:9, where drought and war, famine and sword are interwoven. (Recommended: Hosea 4:3, "Therefore the land mourns and all that dwell in it languish and also the beasts of the field and the birds of the air and even the fish of the sea are taken away"; Isaiah 24: 4-5, "The earth mourns and fades, the world languishes and fades; both heaven and earth languish. The earth is polluted because of its inhabitants, who have transgressed laws, violated statutes, broken the ancient covenant.")

[5] The occasion is likely Nebuchadnezzar's campaign against Judah in c. 627-626 B.C.E., Guy P. Couturier, C.S.C., "Jeremiah," in *The New Jerome Biblical Commentary*, ed. Raymond E. Brown, S.S., Joseph A. Fitzmyer, S.J. and Roland E. Murphy, O. Carm. (Englewood Cliffs, NJ: Prentice Hall, 1990), 266, 276.

[6] United Nations, "World Population Prospects" (2015), https://esa.un.org.

[7] Louis J. Puhl, S.J., *The Spiritual Exercises of St. Ignatius* (Chicago: Loyola University Press, 1951), 69.

[8] Thomas Aquinas, treats the cardinal virtues in the *Summa Theologiae* I-II and in II-II (New York: Benziger Brothers, 1946). The cardinal virtues encompass "powers" of intellect, will, emotion and desire.

[9]*Summa Theologiae* I, q. 47, a. 1.

[10]*Summa Theologiae* I, qq.70–72.

[11]*Summa Theologiae* I-II, q. 61, a. 2 (*passim*).

[12]Historians have treated medieval water issues: see Richard Hoffmann, "Economic Development and Aquatic Ecosystems in Medieval Europe," *American Historical Review* 101 (1996): 631–69, and Ellen Arnold, "Engineering Miracles: Water Control, Conversion, and the Creation of a Religious Landscape in the Medieval Ardennes," *Environment and History* 13 (2007): 477–502; for agricultural and land use issues, see Lisa J. Kiser, "The Garden of St. Francis: Plants, Landscape, and Economy in Thirteenth-Century Italy," *Environmental History* 8 (2003): 229–45.

[13]*Laudato Si'*, no. 11, Pope Francis cites Thomas of Celano, *The Life of Saint Francis*, in *Francis of Assisi: Early Documents*, vol. 1, ed. Regis J. Armstrong (New York: New City, 1999), 251.

[14]*Summa Theologiae* II-II, q. 141.

[15]"Use It and Lose It: The Outsize Effect of U.S. Consumption on the Environment," *Scientific American* (September 14, 2015), http://www.scientificamerican.com.

[16]*Summa Theologiae* II-II, q. 123, a. 3.

[17]*Story of a Soul: The Autobiography of St. Therese of Lisieux,* trans. John Clarke (Washington, DC: Institute of Carmelite Studies, 1972), 14.

[18]Ibid., 132-133.

[19]Ibid., 270-271.

[20]Robert Ellsberg, "St. Therese of Lisieux, Doctor of the Church," in *All Saints: Daily Reflections on Saints, Prophets, and Witnesses for Our Time* (New York: Crossroad, 1997), 427.

[21]Pope Francis quotes Pope Benedict XVI, *Caritas in Veritate* (2009), no. 2.

Recovering Liturgy

African American Catholic Liturgical Revivalism

Krista Stevens

The racial turmoil of the twentieth century, coupled with the ecclesiastical renewal of the Second Vatican Council, created what M. Shawn Copeland called a *kairos* for black Catholics in America—a change in both social and ecclesial mood that had significant implications for Black Catholic liturgical life.[1] Out of these social and ecclesial shifts emerged a distinctly black way of worshipping within the Catholic Church. At the heart of these emerging patterns of worship was an insistence that liturgy, while fundamentally about the worship of God, also can be transformative of people and of society. These liturgical movements demonstrate ways in which liturgical practice has been used as a platform for creating black Catholic identity that both advocates for racial justice and helps transform traditional Catholic symbols of faith into symbols that are inclusive, freeing, and liberating for the whole Catholic community.

To draw out the importance of these liturgical practices, this essay begins by examining the intrinsic connection between liturgy and ethics that can inform a worshipping community's understanding of its relationship with Christ and with others. Building on this connection between liturgy and ethics, this essay moves on to describe the emergence of American Black Catholic liturgical revival movements that emphasized social justice as a crucial component of liturgical life. Finally, focus is given to two examples of these liturgical revival movements—Interracial Sundays led by black and white college students in the Jim Crow

South of the 1950s and the work of Fr. Clarence Rivers to create a distinct black liturgical aesthetic.

Liturgy and Ethics: A Practice for Right Living

At the heart of Don E. Saliers's article "Liturgy and Ethics: Some New Beginnings" is his claim that how people pray and worship is intimately linked to how they live their lives. The prayers, practices, songs, sacraments, and stories shared in liturgy create the foundation for living a life of goodness and virtue. Saliers says, "Christian worship, through a complex symbolic pattern of words and gestures in its ritual actions, both forms and expresses dispositions belonging to the life of faith in God."[2] God is both the foundation of worship and orients worshippers to the world around them. Good liturgy, then, should help a person learn both how to address God—to pray—and how to relate to others in God's creation.

Saliers is clear that participating in liturgy and leading a moral life are not simply matters of reciting rote prayers. To live a moral life, "actual orientation of sensibility and intentional acts is involved, as well as a new self-understanding and a 'world-picture.' How we understand ourselves in the world and how we ought to live in relation to society, the neighbor and the self—all these are ingredients in our conception of the Christian moral life."[3] Liturgy helps reorient worshippers to this way of living. Through the practice of liturgy, worshippers can come to an understanding of "who God is and what his intentions for human beings are as revealed in Jesus Christ."[4]

Building on Saliers's work, in his article "Liturgy and Ethics: Something Old, Something New," Stephen Wilson draws out more explicitly how Saliers's emphasis on the connection between liturgy and ethics helps develop Christian identity by identifying how liturgical practice can help cultivate virtue.[5] Wilson begins by unpacking Alasdair MacIntyre's understanding of moral practice discussed in MacIntyre's *After Virtue*. Practices have four defining characteristics: "They are coherent yet complex, social and cooperative, possess internal goods, and have standards of excellence."[6] These characteristics shape liturgical practice. While different liturgical rites might seem to be made up of seemingly dissimilar parts, these rites are still unified by common goals (e.g., a goal of the celebration of the Eucharist is communion with God and with others).[7] Next, liturgy is social and cooperative. The liturgy is a communal celebration, a social gathering in which every person has a role. Wilson goes on to identify three internal goods of liturgy: "the glorification of God, the sanctification of humanity, and communion."[8] These three goods point the participant to communion with God and with each other. Finally, in regard to standards of excellence, the question is not who worships better but "who provides the standard for rendering God glory, holiness, and communion with God?"[9] The answer to this question is Jesus Christ, who

> lived and died in a manner that was focused on self-emptying love or kenosis, allowing the lives of Christians to be depicted in these terms as well. Christ's kenotic love was manifest in his incarnation and ministry, but most fully in his passion. Christ's self-giving, in turn, is presented as source and standard for Christians through the liturgy, especially the Eucharist. In summary, one could say that Christ's kenosis is the basis for the church's offering of itself in thanksgiving in the Eucharist, which in turn becomes a basis from which Christians glorify God, become holy, and live in communion with God and neighbor through the whole of their lives.[10]

These four characteristics of liturgical practice play out in the prayers and stories of Christian liturgy that are intimately tied to the Christian narrative that shapes Christian life. Wilson says, "One of the most significant ways communities form their members through narratives is through the telling and retelling of those stories that express the core beliefs and values that are partially definitive of the community's identity."[11] This telling and retelling of the Christian narrative gives Christians access "to the sacred story of the triune God's relationship with the world. These stories, then, provide a stock of dramatic resources that can help form how Christians see themselves in relation to God, the entire Christian community, and the whole of creation."[12] In this way, Christians are imbued with an understanding of the crucial importance of the Christian narrative—Christ's birth, life, death, resurrection, and ascension—in shaping their own lives.

Saliers and Wilson insist that participation in good liturgy can help shift a person's worldview outward to one that glorifies God and, through this glorification, embraces Christ's own self-giving to the world. Saliers says, "Worship ascribes glory to God alone; but unless the glorification is shown in works of justice, mercy and love faithful to God's commands, Christ's liturgy is not fully enacted."[13] Saliers is making a bold claim. And he realizes that some may ask, "To what extent ought the church as liturgical community make moral and ethical transformation of persons and society the purpose of worship? Is the ultimate thing to be said about the liturgy of Jesus Christ that it is service and love toward mankind?"[14]

Black Liturgical Revival and Social Change

In regard to racial justice and social change, Saliers's questions are important.

Socially, the 1950s and 1960s saw a dramatic push for civil rights. Liturgically, the Second Vatican Council opened the door for liturgical reform and renewal that would have far-reaching effects on the Catholic Church. As the civil rights movement grew, attention was placed on how liturgy could push back against unjust and racist social structures and best reflect and incorporate African American culture. A renewed emphasis among African American communities on black identity and dignity, coupled with the Vatican II document *Sacrosanctum Concilium's* recognition of the place of multi-cultural expressions in Catholic liturgy, opened the door for a variety of different liturgical expressions. African American ministers and religious leaders pointed to a specific passage in *Sacrosanctum Concilium*:

Even in the liturgy, the Church has no wish to impose a rigid uniformity in matters which do not implicate the faith or the good of the whole community; rather does she respect and foster the genius and talents of various races and peoples. Anything in these peoples' ways of life which is not indissolubly bound up with superstition and error she studies with sympathy and, if possible, preserves intact. Sometimes in fact she admits such things into the liturgy itself, so long as they harmonize with its true and authentic spirit.[15]

Many African American Catholic leaders interpreted this passage as validating the use of traditionally African and African American styles of worship and liturgy.

In adapting liturgy to better fit traditional African American cultural identity, the importance of liturgy as a platform for social justice was not lost. Toinette Eugene, a founding member of the National Office of Black Catholics, stresses that "social justice is always a constitutive element of evangelization and liturgical expression."[16] She notes that while traditional forms of liturgy might, at times, butt heads with cultural adaptation, black liturgical reform must focus on both "maintaining 'tradition' in ritual worship" and "sustaining movement for change."[17] This balance of tradition and transition is key. The questions that Eugene is raising are similar to those raised by Saliers and Wilson—how does ritual worship function in sustaining social groups, and how do groups change in and through worship? Eugene responds to these questions by asserting that liturgical worship can foster social change "by focusing a community's 'general conceptions of the order of existence' with the actual circumstances of daily life."[18] The connection between liturgy and life occurs when liturgy is able to lead the worshipping community to a deeper understanding of its own responsibility in shaping the broader society. By shifting the focus of liturgy, Eugene creates space for liturgy to "invite the social group to confront the present, disallow it from living in an ideal and non-confrontational world, challenge the reconciliation with which we are comfortably living, and bring us to a new tradition in a future that is realistic yet full of hope."[19]

Eugene is suggesting that incorporating African American traditions into the liturgy is a profound way of urging liturgy to do what it has always been meant to do—remember, share, and celebrate the Good News of Christ in order to cultivate union with God and with others. In the realm of racial justice and the transformative power of liturgy, Eugene's presentation cannot be overstated. She says, "In the midst of a dominant societal culture of disbelief, epitomized by ennui and apathy, indigenized liturgical renewal within African American Catholic assemblies holds the potential power to transform life in liberating and justice-oriented ways through the process of contextualization."[20] Many of the black liturgical revival movements that emerged in the 1950s through the present sought to use the liturgy not just as a means to transform black Catholic life but of transforming American society into a society that was more just, equal, and inclusive.

"Jim Crow or Jesus": The Southeastern Regional Interracial Commission and Interracial Liturgies

In the late 1940s, the archdiocese of New Orleans became the seat of an emerging Southern Catholic interracial movement. Under the leadership of sociology professor Joseph Fichter, SJ, Loyola University became the center of the regional National Federation of Catholic Colleges commission. The founding Loyola members applied to the university for approval as an official student organization with the purpose of working "for the removal of forced racial segregation." The group argued that their organization was necessary "because forced racial segregation was a social problem that could be overcome by group actions." For these students, racial justice was not just a religious issue but a social one as well.[21] Significantly, these students would use religion in a group action to confront the issues of racial justice.

As the charter members of the NFCC were in New Orleans, the local chapter was originally called the New Orleans Regional Interracial Commission and then the Louisiana Regional Interracial Commission. The name was finally changed to the Southeastern Regional Interracial Commission (SERINCO) in 1950 after other Southern Catholic colleges and universities had joined the NFCC—Xavier University (New Orleans), Ursuline College (New Orleans), and College of the Sacred Heart (Grand Coteau, LA).

In the spring of 1949 the NFCC (which became SERINCO the next year), sponsored its first "Interracial Sunday" to be held at Ursuline College. The schedule for the day included liturgy, breakfast, speakers, and then discussion. In his book *Black, White, and Catholic: New Orleans Interracialism, 1947-1956*, R. Bentley Anderson asserts that the "walls of separation within the Catholic Church in New Orleans began to crumble" when these students sat down together to pray, to talk, and to share a meal.[22]

A year later SERINCO sponsored the second annual interracial Sunday, this time held at the College of the Sacred Heart. Like the previous year, the schedule again called for Mass, breakfast, guest speakers, and discussion. Close to 300 people attended this gathering. Over the next several years, SERINCO would sponsor six more Interracial Sundays centered around liturgy, table fellowship, and discussion. Various themes of the annual gatherings included "Christian Youth at the Crossroads: Jim Crowism or Jesus Christ" and "All the Same in Christ."[23]

At first glance, yearly gatherings of college students may not seem like a significant event, but for the time period in which they occurred, these Interracial Sundays were remarkable and transformative. At the third Interracial Sunday, Norman Francis, a student from Xavier University (the only black Catholic college in the United States) who would go on to be the first black student admitted to Loyola's School of Law, gave a keynote address. Francis declared that the Interracial Sunday was the most crucial component of SERINCO's efforts "because it afforded Catholics the opportunity 'to put into practice the theories and philosophy of our Catholic education. As Catholic college students, we of the Interracial Commission, are striving to foster better race relations in building a Christian atmosphere which is truly part of the Mystical Body of Christ.'"[24]

Francis's word choice is interesting and important given the overall discussion on the place of liturgy in cultivating social change. Francis's recognition of the Mystical Body of Christ likely reflects what John McGreevy identifies as a neo-Thomism that swept through colleges and universities in the early to mid-twentieth century that "fostered a distinctive Catholic worldview" that addressed problems through a "rationality dependent on divine law," sought a "more ordered community," and called for a "renewed focus on the Mystical Body of Christ."[25] This emphasis on the Mystical Body of Christ is found in Pope Pius XII's *Mystici Corporis* in which the pontiff distinguishes between the moral body and the Mystical Body. The goal of the moral body—society—is directed toward a common good through cooperation and collaboration of all members of the society. The Mystical Body brings a different dimension to the moral body with the ultimate common goal of union with Christ.[26] This transcendence of the Mystical Body broke down racial, ethnic, and geographical boundaries. Racial ideologies, therefore, "destroyed hopes for a genuinely corporate community, one united through faith."[27]

In an April 17, 1960, interview on *Meet the Press*, Martin Luther King Jr. lamented, "I think it is one of the tragedies of our nation, one of the shameful tragedies, that eleven o'clock on Sunday morning is one of the most segregated hours, if not the most segregated hour in Christian America.... Any church that stands against integration, that has a segregated body, is standing against the spirit and teachings of Jesus Christ."[28] In southern parishes marked by both *de jure* and *de facto* segregation, the Southeastern Regional Interracial Commission embodied the Mystical Body of Christ. They recognized that the moral body in which they were living—a society marked by racism—was broken. Often, Catholic worshipping communities, which should be reflections of the Mystical Body of Christ, were also broken with racism. These students recognized the goals of liturgy as union with God and with others. In their liturgical practice, these students embraced the narrative of Christ's self-giving actions. By coming together as one body in Christ, these students embraced a way of living that more truly reflected Christ's desire for Christians. Participants in these liturgies were trying to reorient how people understood themselves in relation to others.

Fr. Clarence R. J. Rivers and the African American Liturgical Aesthetic

The work of groups like SERINCO was a small, but important, piece of larger movements for racial justice and civil rights in the United States. While SERINCO's goal was to use liturgy as a platform for interracial communion and fellowship in response to God's call of the Mystical Body of Christ, little effort was made to revise or reshape the liturgy itself. Though black priests presided over some of these liturgies, the liturgical practice and rites reflected traditional pre-Vatican II liturgy. Picking up on the movement started by SERINCO and furthered by Vatican II, Fr. Clarence R. J. Rivers led the movement for an indigenized and contextualized liturgy in the mid to late twentieth century. Rivers, described as a "musician, dramatist, author, scholar, liturgist, and composer . . . [who] was convinced that the treasure of African American art, culture, and religious expression could revitalize Catholic worship," developed an African American liturgical aesthetic that brought a more spontaneous and improvised approach to the liturgy, incorporating drums, music, and poetic preaching.[29] Introduction of these modes of worship would serve to "free" the church from what Rivers and other Black Catholics saw as a rather inert and non-participatory form of traditional Catholic worship. A quote from an unpublished sermon by Rivers is telling. Worship, he says, should be "a dramatic dance of life." Instead "it is all too often like the dry bones in the vision of Ezekiel, a static, stagnant, sprawl of lifeless limbs."[30] Rivers attributed this "static, stagnant sprawl of lifeless limbs" to a Western culture trapped by "puritanicalism" and an emphasis on the ocular over the oral. What he means here is that Western religion has embraced reason over emotion, what can be seen over what can be felt. Emotion is a threat to intellect and reason, and things that "feel good" cannot actually be good for us. This worldview results in a disconnect between the belief that religion is incarnational and sensual and actual religious practice that tends to be dull and lifeless. Liturgy in this worldview is often characterized by detachment and suspicion of emotion. Here liturgy is not meant to be enjoyed but an obligation to be endured.[31]

Instead, Rivers emphasized the aural tradition, or what he calls "the sound of the soul." The aural tradition, deeply embedded in black life, embraces oral tradition and tends to be more poetic than literal. Worshippers in this tradition will be more attuned to the poetic meaning of the sermon, the pastor's word play, syntax, and metaphor.[32] Rivers is not suggesting that people immersed in the ocular culture cannot or do not use their senses. He is suggesting that these types of worshippers are less likely to be moved by worship. Rivers insists, however, that "the members of a Christian assembly are there not merely as sponges to absorb; they are also there as witnesses of their faith and must therefore be active in the entertainment. And if anything is to be done away with, it is not entertainment, it is merely objective passivity and detached noninvolvement."[33] Here Rivers creatively is flipping traditional understandings of entertainment. He is not suggesting that liturgy should be entertaining in the same way that a movie or TV show might be—something to be consumed passively as a diversion from daily life. Liturgy as entertainment is something that is meant to be actively enjoyed and shared with others.

Effective worship is, of course, dependent on God, but liturgy must also be "facilitated by two dynamics—discerning the *dramatic structure* of a whole worship event, and ensuring the *artistic performance* of each of its elements."[34] Like Saliers, Wilson, and Eugene, Rivers recognizes the crucial importance of the Christian narrative—the *dramatic structure*—in shaping liturgical practice and worshippers. At the same time, he insists that the Christian narrative is a living tradition that should be continuously and creatively reinterpreted in ways that best affect worshippers. Worship that moves its practitioners helps the Christian narrative come alive. Thus, worshippers are better able to understand and live out the values that Christ himself lived.

In light of these emphases, what Rivers calls *effective worship* must reflect several key characteristics. Mary McGann pares these characteristics down to four main themes: (1) Effective worship draws people to the transcendent God. (2) Though worship draws people to the transcendent, it also must be grounded in the reality of human life and the needs of others. (3) Effective worship must be joyful, bringing delight to the heart and soul. (4) Effective worship must lead to continual conversion of the heart as people become disciples of Jesus Christ, committed to his mission to the marginalized.[35]

These four themes underscore the transformative power of liturgy and offer a profound and active "yes" to Saliers's question posed above: "Is the ultimate thing to be said about the liturgy of Jesus Christ that it is service and love toward mankind?" Both SERINCO and Rivers rightly insist that liturgy should open up the worshipper's worldview to see beyond himself or herself. Participation in the symbols and practices of faith that are themselves remembrances and retellings of Christ's life, death, and resurrection, draws people to God and recognizes God's ongoing work in the here and now. Liturgy and ethics are best connected in and where a connection is created between "praying and being."[36] Praying that shapes being has the potential to shape how people understand and relate to each other, an essential component of transforming society.

Notes

[1]M. Shawn Copeland, "African American Catholics and Black Theology: An Interpretation," in *Black Theology: A Documentary History, Vol. 2: 1980-1992*, ed. James H. Cone and Gayraud S. Wilmore (Maryknoll, NY: Orbis Books, 1993), 99-115.

[2]Don E. Saliers, "Liturgy and Ethics: Some New Beginnings," *Journal of Religious Ethics* 7, no. 2 (1979): 178.

[3]Ibid., 179.

[4]Ibid., 180.

[5]Stephen B. Wilson, "Liturgy and Ethics: Something Old, Something New," *Worship* 81, no. 1 (January 2007): 24-45.

[6]Ibid., 27. Wilson is drawing upon Alasdair MacIntyre, *After Virtue*, 2nd ed. (Notre Dame, IN: University of Notre Dame Press, 1984), 187.

[7]Wilson, "Liturgy and Ethics: Something Old, Something New," 31-32.

[8]Ibid., 32.

[9]Ibid., 32-33.

[10]Ibid., 33.

[11]Ibid., 37.

[12]Ibid., 42.

[13]Saliers, "Liturgy and Ethics: Some New Beginings," 181.

[14]Ibid., 183.

[15]*Sacrosanctum Concilium*, in *Vatican Council II: The Conciliar and Post-conciliar Documents*, ed. Austin Flannery, OP (Collegeville, MN: Liturgical Press, 1996), no. 37.

[16]Toinette Eugene, "Between 'Lord Have Mercy!' and 'Thank You, Jesus!'" in *Taking Down Our Harps: Black Catholics in the United States*, ed. Diana L. Hayes and Cyprian B. Davis, OSB (Maryknoll, NY: Orbis Books, 1998), 164.

[17]Ibid.

[18]Ibid.

[19]Ibid.

[20]Ibid., 170.

[21]R. Bentley Anderson, *Black, White, and Catholic: New Orleans Interracialism, 1947-1956* (Nashville: Vanderbilt University Press, 2005), 24-25.

[22]Ibid., 41.

[23]Ibid., 40-43, 69, 87-89, 96-97, 113, 121-122, 133-134, 153-157.

[24]Ibid., 88.

[25]John T. McGreevy, *Parish Boundaries: The Catholic Encounter with Race in the Twentieth-Century Urban North* (Chicago: University of Chicago Press, 1996), 41-43.

[26]Pope Pius XII, *Mystici Corporis Christi* (Whitefish, MT: Kessinger, 2007), no. 22. Also see John LaFarge, *Interracial Justice* (New York: America Press, 1937).

[27]McGreevy, *Parish Boundaries*, 43-44.

[28]*Meet the Press* Archives: MLK on Non-Violent Resistance, http://www.nbcnews.com/video/meet-the-press/52856624#58523601.

[29]Mary E. McGann, RSCJ, and Eva Marie Lumas, SSS, "The Emergence of African American Catholic Worship" in McGann, *Let It Shine!: The Emergence of African American Catholic Worship* (New York: Fordham University Press), 7.

[30]Clarence Rufus J. Rivers, "The Oral African Tradition versus the Ocular Western Tradition," in *Taking Down Our Harps*, ed. Hayes and Davis, 232.

[31]Ibid., 234.

[32]Ibid., 240.

[33]Ibid., 235.

[34]Mary E. McGann, RSCJ, "Clarence R. J. Rivers' Vision of Effective African American Worship," in *Let It Shine*, 71.

[35]Ibid., 56-58.

[36]Saliers, "Liturgy and Ethics: Some New Beginnings," 180.

Traditional Devotion, Radical Witness

Insights from Fieldwork in Conflict Northern Uganda

Todd Whitmore

In the United States, interpreters of Catholicism often divide the faith into "liberal" and "conservative" camps. For instance, the College Theology Society's description of its 2017 meeting on "American Catholicism in the 21st Century" cites "news and op-ed pieces" that themselves draw "from multiple sources, including sociological data concerning the devotional practices of American Catholics" to depict "fracture among U.S. Catholics over political and economic issues ('Social Justice' Catholics vs. 'Right to Life' Catholics)."[1] However, the setting of Northern Uganda during the conflict between the Ugandan government and the rebel Lord's Resistance Army (LRA) suggests that, in some contexts, it is precisely what are considered to be conservative devotional practices in the United States that fund a dramatic witness on behalf of justice. Such witness is evidenced in the testimony, as one among many, of Sister Perpetua of the Little Sisters of Mary Immaculate of Gulu:

> Every day we experience war, war, horrible war . . . such that people came and then we had to take care of them in the mission. . . . We have to struggle to take care of them. That was in 1985. Even before the LRA, yes. . . . This is when [current Ugandan President] Museveni had thrown out Okello and the NRA [Museveni's army] is chasing [Okello's troops]. The life was difficult because those who run and took refuge in the mission, we up to now accommodate them. And then this accommodation—we could not put them in our rooms

[any longer]. We are sleeping in the what?—in the church. All of us. The Sisters and the priests. We were sleeping in the church. . . . It was not for weeks; it was for some months.[2]

Then the LRA, and the prospect of abduction, came, as described by Sister Esther Arach of the Little Sisters:

And then I also came across the rebels in 1998. Mm. When we met them, I was saying the Rosary. Then one of them jumped in the middle of the road. Then I told the driver, I said, "Driver, they are the ones. Stop." Then the driver just went with the car on the side of the road, and stopped. When he stopped, the students collected all their things and go. They all ran away. My interest was to see that nobody was there left in the vehicle. So I was just seeing that everybody should jump. After all of them had gone, what I wanted was also now to see what I could do.

By then, the rebels had already surrounded me. One came, said, "Get the watch." I give. Another one came, "Give the lady bag," and I give the lady my bag. Their leader was ordering those who were in the bush to come out and collect the things from the vehicle. I was the first to get out of the vehicle. Of course I was in front, but I didn't run. And then, their commander was standing just near me there. He said, "Give the rosary here if you cannot come with us." I said, "I can help you with the rosary." Then I give the rosary to him. When I gave the rosary, he bowed down with it. When he got up, he said with a very sweet voice, "You can go." Then I started going. So I believe that it was Our Lady who released me, the rosary.

And whenever I was troubling, I would hold the crucifix. If I entered a vehicle I would hold a crucifix like this, in front of me, I said, "Jesus you clear for me the way, you clear the way, go ahead and clear the way." And in fact I was protected many times. . . .

Jesus would tell me through the cross, "I have gone through it. And the first have already made it. Follow me." So when I see the cross I would say, what kind of suffering has Jesus not gone through? And as I am his follower I am also to do the little I can, too. Mine is not much if I compare my suffering to Jesus. There is nothing to be done except, this is the way." Mm. So I cannot long for any other things which do not follow the way he has shown me. That is why I am devoted to the cross. It helps me a lot. It gives me encouragement. Mm. Jesus has gone through it, so. And he also said it: "If you want to follow me, take up your cross. Then you come after me."[3]

What sustained the Little Sisters? Over the course of six years, during and immediately after the conflict there with the Lord's Resistance Army, I did eighteen months of field research in Northern Uganda, spending over half of that time living in Internally Displaced Persons (IDP) camps. When in Uganda, I had frequent, almost daily, interaction with the Little Sisters. It became clear during the course of my fieldwork that what sustained them was a mix of devotional practices handed on to them by Comboni missionaries, practices that constituted (and continue to constitute) an embodied and thus lived cosmology wherein God has love and a providential design for each and every human being, particularly the marginalized. As is evidenced from the testimony from Sister Perpetua above, here the "conservative" or "traditional" devotions—the imitation of Christ and the saints, the Rosary, Eucharistic Adoration, mortification on behalf of those in purgatory, novenas, the Stations of the Cross—all work to empower radical—that is, life-risking—witness on behalf of justice. And this linkage between devotional life and lived witness—though pressed into particular poignancy by the exigencies of being in a conflict zone—is deliberate on the part of the practitioners. Many of the services they offered—the works of mercy to the displaced that flooded the schools and parishes—might have been *ad hoc* during the war, but the spiritual infrastructure that made them possible was not.

In what follows, I draw on extensive interviews with members of the Little Sisters to provide first of all an *emic*—that is, in their own terms—account of how their devotional practices serve as conduits for the Holy Spirit to, in the local parlance, "animate" the Sisters with the charism of their order's founder and, ultimately, Christ.[4] In the second section of this article, I draw from the work of an early anthropologist, James George Frazer, to provide an *etic* interpretation of the Sisters' practices in terms of "magic." In the end, we will see that the Sisters do not reject Frazer's interpretation, only his denigration of magical portrayals of the world. In their case, what Frazer would call magical practices provided the wherewithal for them to carry out their radical witness in the midst of war.

The Emic Interpretation: Imitating Negri, Imitating Christ

Set on a floor-stand in a corner of the sitting room of the Mother House of the Little Sisters is a six-foot painting of their founder, the Comboni Bishop of Gulu, Angelo Negri (1889-1949)—hair combed straight back, black eyebrows, precisely trimmed goatee of mostly silver-white. He is holding a streamer at waist-level that bears his motto: "Light in Darkness." The lower half of the painting features not Bishop Negri from the waist down, however, but a painted reproduction of an aerial photograph of the Little Sisters's main compound, including the Mother House, schools, dorms, and meeting rooms. It is a God's-eye view. Negri is looking out at the viewer of the painting, but he is clearly also watching over everything that might go on in the compound below. An archway painted over his head reads, "LSMIG Golden Jubilee in the Year 2000." The painting commemorates the fiftieth year since Negri's death.

"Our founder has a special charism," Sister Miriam Kozoa tells me in the present tense, as if he is still alive. She is in tinted glasses, Marian blue everyday habit, white veil. She has just stepped down as Mother General, and is part of an effort by the order to reclaim and revivify in themselves the kind of life led by Bishop Negri, now after a generation of war. "His charism is what we are living on. He imparts that charism to us, and that is why the Little Sisters of Mary Immaculate, we are who we are—because of the burning love of Christ that we have to attend to the most vulnerable people. . . . In fact, as a Congregation we are trying our best to follow the footsteps of our founder, Bishop Negri."[5]

* * *

Our founder has a special charism. His charism is what we are living on. He imparts that charism to us. How does this happen? Negri died in 1949. The Combonis and the Little Sisters have only fairly recently—the mid-1990s—attempted to write brief, article-length biographies of him.[6] For the most part, knowledge of him is still passed on orally: "Our older sisters, they used to teach us, those who have seen him."[7] Otherwise, the Sisters have only photos and paintings based on photos of the bishop. But the photos have, the Sisters claim, a real capacity to transmit an authoritative *power*—a charism—to them, a power that enables them to, in their words, live lives of "burning love" for "the most vulnerable people." One Sister, after having told me of her various trials—government soldiers killed her mother, Ebola took two of her Sisters—went on to elaborate on what supported her during such times: "I love our founder so much, Bishop Angelo Negri. I have not seen him, but looking at his picture, hearing about some of his stories. This kept me in this place."[8]

The Sisters do not hesitate to describe Negri's character traits: "a good shepherd," "loved all categories of people without discrimination," "clever," "open-minded," "prayerful."[9] Specific stories give life and context to the traits. Perhaps the story that most displays his love for the people of northern Uganda, such that he was willing to lay down his life for them, regards his decision to return after a trip abroad:

> He went to America to look for someone who could build the convent, because there was no money. When he was coming back, he felt very sick. Then he went to the doctors. The doctors said, "Bishop, you are very sick. Don't go back to Africa. You need to go back to Italy, so that you can live longer." And then the Bishop said, "Better to shorten my life among my sheep than to stay longer in a comfortable place in Italy."[10]

Such character traits, given life by the stories, make Negri a role model for the Sisters.[11]

But it is clear that for them he is more than simply an exceptionally good person. He carries the burning love of Christ for the most vulnerable in a way that shares in the traits of Christ, such that he merits veneration. "Now I've developed also a deep devotion to our founder, Bishop Negri," says one Sister. And the stories become miracle stories. One Sister tells of his intervention—years after his death—in a four-year court case over disputed land claims, and the dramatic events afterwards.

For four years, I was alone with the rosary and the relics of our founder, Bishop Angelo Negri. And the lawyers wanted to eat the money of the rich man who was taking me to court. People said, "Sister, you are a religious, God assisted a miracle [in your winning the case]." I did not know that it was a miracle. When I finished the court, I continued to pray to our founder, Bishop Negri. Then the surveyor came and marked the land. Eight acres. The land was released. I marked the land title on the fifth of November, 2003.

I went to pray. Immediately, I could see a cloud, a brilliant white, a different white. What is this? What is this? What is this? I was looking as the thing went oooooh, at the distant border with Sudan. And a sea of snow. What is this? What is this? What is this? And I saw a big . . . it seemed to be a mountain, very black, up there, falling at the edge of the white ocean of cloud. Very white. Immediately it came here. It came. It came on the water.

What is this, then? I started to see the what?—the cloud of the bishop, and the mitre. On that cloud, I suddenly realized, is Bishop Negri. Bishop Negri was transparent. Brilliant. Beautiful. He put on the *pianeta* for Mass. And glittering—chit!-chit!-chit!—with something. The *pianeta*. Pulsing spots-spots. Pt!-pt!-pt! Heavenly color.

It was Negri. He was still. He was tall. Beautiful. Then I said, "Bishop Negri is so beautiful in heaven, it burns."

I began to see the room as it was. And I seated there. Till the cock crowed, I was sitting there. Until morning. I could not sleep.[12]

While waking visions as dramatic as this one are not everyday among the Sisters, Bishop Negri and other heavenly figures do come to them regularly in dreams that have portent. Through such dreams, Bishop Negri exercises a capacity—a power—to com-

municate with the Sisters, and even call them to take up specific
actions or a way of life, a capacity that in other of the Sisters's
dreams is carried out by Jesus:

> It was in 1960 when I had the experience which led me
> to become a Sister. I had dreamt that I was in the chapel,
> praying. Then, the Divine Mercy appeared at the corner of
> the chapel in our place near Pabbo. He was standing on the
> world—globe—with rays of light; red, bluest, whitest. Shin-
> ing. He did not say anything to me, but I just outstretched
> my hands, just like this, eh? I went to him, and he put a ring
> on my finger. And disappeared. So it was at this time that
> I confirmed that God was calling me. I was in P4 [fourth
> grade].[13]

For the Little Sisters, then, Bishop Negri is both a person to
be imitated and a venerable spirit who invites and enables that
imitation. It is important for our understanding to keep these
two aspects of their personas together. The figure visiting in the
dreams is no less a person, and the embodied person of Negri bears
his charism. This double characteristic carries over to the various representational objects like the photographs and paintings.
These, in important respects, *are* Negri in that, as representations
of him, they participate in and serve as conduits of his charism,
even to the point where the objects "speak" to the Sisters, as we
saw earlier in Sister Esther's testimony with regard to the rosary,
the crucifix, and Jesus: "And whenever I was troubling, I would
hold the crucifix like this, in front of me, I said, 'Jesus you clear
for me the way.' Jesus would tell me through the cross, 'I have
gone through it. And the first have already made it. Follow me.'"

The role of the representational objects in the lives of the Sisters—their capacity to communicate God's charism to them—is
perhaps most evident in the practice of Eucharistic Adoration.
Here, Jesus of Nazareth, born two thousand years ago, *is* the Host
now, in front of them, and the Host *is* Jesus the Nazarene the
Christ. This co-presence allows the Sisters to carry on colloquies
with the Host as if Jesus is right there before them, because, according to the Sisters, He is. As one Sister described, "As girls, we
were taught what to tell Jesus when you're in front of the Blessed
Sacrament. But then in the novitiate, we went deeper, because we

had times for quiet whereby you allow Jesus to speak to you."[14]
Sometimes, Jesus speaks quite specifically:

> When the Blessed Sacrament is exposed, we were told to
> wait on two knees. Then I also do that practice. But one day
> when I entered the chapel in the Motherhouse, the Blessed
> Sacrament was exposed, so I genuflected on both knees.
> Then the voice told me, "When I am on the altar exposed,
> you genuflect on both knees, but when I'm in the tabernacle,
> you genuflect with only one knee. Am I different when I'm
> on the altar [than] when I'm in the tabernacle?" So then I
> ask Him, I say, "What message do you have for me? What
> do you want me to do?" [He replied,] "Worship me the way
> you do when I'm exposed on the altar." And from that day,
> I never genuflect with one leg when I'm in the church. And
> when I genuflect on one knee, I am haunted. I feel I'm not
> giving enough devotion, enough respect, to Jesus.[15]

So critical is Jesus's presence in the Eucharist, that the Sisters,
together with others of the faithful, would walk miles on roads
they knew to be dangerous just to bring it back with them to
locations where priests either would not or could not go to con-
secrate the Host.

The emic answer to the question of what sustains the Sisters,
then, is that their founders are bearers and transmitters of a
charism that is ultimately the charism of Jesus the Nazarene,
the Christ, that is, the charism to, in the Sisters words, exhibit a
"burning love" to "attend to the most vulnerable people." The
Little Sisters draw the same animation, therefore, from photos of
Negri as they do from the consecrated Host and material representations of Christ.

An Etic Interpretation: Contact and Similarity

If the fact of charism is the emic answer to what enables such
faithful witness, the question remains as to more precisely *how* that
charism is passed, and here an initially etic or externally sourced
response is helpful. Much of anthropology since James George
Frazer has answered the question of charism transmission under
the rubric of "magic." (Frazer, like other early anthropologists,

understands "magic" to be a low form of relating to the world.) In *The Golden Bough*, he distinguishes two ways through which practitioners of magic understand their acts to work: the "law of similarity" and the "law of contact or contagion." The law of similarity works such that, in Frazer's words, "the magician infers that he can produce any effect he desires merely by imitating it." In contrast, the law of contact, according to Frazer, "proceeds upon the notion that things which have once been conjoined must remain ever afterwards, even when quite dissevered from each other, in such a sympathetic relation that whatever is done to the one must similarly affect the other." Both kinds of magic, according to Frazer, "assume that things act on each other at a distance through secret sympathy, the impulse being transmitted from one to the other by means of what we may conceive as a kind of invisible ether." [16] Though *The Golden Bough* was first published in 1890, the distinction between the two "laws of magic" remains in prominent use in academic disciplines, even while Frazer's hierarchy of cultures is rejected.[17]

The role of the paintings, photos, and rosary crucifixes in transmitting Jesus's charism displays aspects of both "similarity" and "contact," with the movement being from similarity to contact. There is an initial act—whether through paintbrush, camera, or chisel—that produces an artifact that is *similar* to the original; thereafter, *contact* with the artifact transmits the charism through what Frazer calls the "invisible ether." Sister Margaret Aceng puts it this way in her essay for the Sisters' golden jubilee:

> [W]ithin the Sisters' environments, there are holy pictures on the walls. These include the cross and the crucified Christ, pictures of Our Lady the Virgin Mary, the Pope, the Bishops, the authorities of the Congregation and other holy pictures. These purify the Sisters' environment so much that on entering the Sisters' house one feels that he/she has entered a holy place, a place where God dwells.
>
> Pictures of Superior Generals and their councilors hung on the walls have a special significance to the Sisters. God the Father and His Son Jesus Christ, whose footsteps the Sisters follow in the vows of Obedience, Chastity and Poverty, do not speak and deal with the Sisters directly but through his

chosen instruments—the Superiors whose presence in the pic-
tures on our walls reflects the presence of God in our midst.[18]

In the case of the Blessed Sacrament, Jesus's words at the last supper, "This is my body," are sufficient to secure the similarity. The
bread need not look like the person Jesus for Jesus to be present in
it and to speak quite specifically to persons who come into contact
with it. The claim of the Sisters is that the transmission of Jesus's
charism gives them the wherewithal to witness to the most vulnerable in a war where, in the words of Sister Esther, "Peace and joy
disappeared."[19] And again in Sister Esther's words, "When I see
the cross I would say, what kind of suffering has Jesus not gone
through? . . . There is nothing to be done except, this is the way."
   Although the photos, paintings, crucifixes, and Host move
from similarity to contact to transmit the charism, the flow is in
the reverse direction—that is, from contact to similarity—in the
overall formation process with the Little Sisters. Formation in this
case places candidates for the order in carefully guided extended
contact with the Sisters (who already participate in the charism)
until the candidate becomes "like"—that is, similar to—the Sisters.
In the words of one Sister, "You have to be guided by the Sisters
if you want to be a Sister."[20] The period from first vows—taken
after the candidate has already spent three and a half years as an
aspirant, postulant, and novice—and final vows can be as long
as nine years. The formation process becomes highly structured
and deliberate in postulancy and the first year of the novitiate,
where the women receive instruction about the order, its founder
and co-founder, and communal life in Christ. In the second year
of novitiate, the women go out to live in one of the order's communities in an apostolate serving the people. One Sister comments,
"This is, I would say, a pre-test of community life."[21] If the novice
passes the pre-test, she takes first vows. Though she now becomes
a professed Sister, the vocational discernment continues. "So we
groom them. Then eventually when they become Sisters, they know
their part. And then after becoming a Sister, there's still spiritual
growth. So retreats, spiritual courses, like that."[22] All of this extended contact and subsequent similarity with the Little Sisters
aims at one primary goal: similarity with Jesus Christ: "We were
formed to understand our religious core, Christian core, based on

the life of Christ. So the knowledge and the love of Christ are made the foundation during our formation. That is how I understood it. Knowing and living the life of Christ."[23]

Traditional Devotion, Radical Witness

The Little Sisters say that they are simply imitating their founder in following Christ. An array of devotional practices that Westerners in the developed world type as being "traditional" enables a radical witness that refuses to abandon a suffering people even when the Sisters' own lives are at stake. Such an example suggests that the traditional-radical division sometimes found in contemporary discourse is inadequate to interpret the religious and social practices of communities like the Little Sisters. These practices can be described in etic terms using the work of James George Frazer. The Sisters do not disagree with Frazer's contact and similarity account of the workings of what he denigratingly calls magic; they simply say that it is the work of the Holy Spirit. And that Spirit has enabled them to remain in zones of the armed conflict long after the members of the Ugandan military and the representatives of NGOs have run away.

Notes

[1] See http://www.collegetheology.org/Annual-Convention.
[2] Interview with Sr. Perpetua (pseudonym), 8-9.
[3] Interview with Sr. Esther Arach, 38-39.
[4] I interviewed twenty of the Sisters, gathering about thirty hours of material.
[5] Interview with Sr. Miriam Kozoa, 1.
[6] Fr. Lorenzo Gaiga, *Short Life of Bishop Angelo Negri*, trans. the Comboni Missionaries (Gulu: Catholic Press, 1994).
[7] Interview with Sr. Josephine, 21.
[8] Interview with Sr. Beatrice Lalam, 1, 9, and 17.
[9] Interview with Sr. Delfina Aywelo, 11; Sr. Esther, 10-11; Sr. Josephine Oyella, 20; Sr. Susan Clare, 10.
[10] Interview with Sr. Delfina, 13.
[11] Interview with Sr. Delfina, 12.
[12] Interview with Sr. Veronica Achola, 12-13.
[13] Interview with Sr. Esther, 3-4.
[14] Interview with Sr. Beatrice, 5.
[15] Interview with Sr. Mary Clementina, 15.
[16] James George Frazer, *The Golden Bough* (Oxford: Oxford University Press, 1998), 26, 37, and 27.

[17]See Paul Rozin and Carol Nemeroff, "Sympathetic Magical Thinking: The Contagion and Similarity 'Heuristics,'" in *Heuristics and Biases: The Psychology of Intuitive Judgment*, ed. Thomas Gilovich, Dale Griffin, and Daniel Kahneman (Cambridge: Cambridge University Press, 2002), 201-216.

[18]Sr. Margaret Aceng, "The Little Sisters of Mary Immaculate and Environment," in Little Sisters of Mary Immaculate of Gulu, *Golden Jubilee Celebrations*, 47.

[19]Interview with Sr. Esther Arach, 12-14.

[20]Interview with Sr. Dosoline Lakworo, 2.

[21]Interview with Sr. Josephine, 22.

[22]Interview with Sr. Miriam, 2.

[23]Interview with Sr. Martha, 2.

Women's Silent Suffering

Constructive Theological and Liturgical Responses

Cynthia L. Cameron and Susan Bigelow Reynolds

The following two contributions by Cynthia L. Cameron and Susan Bigelow Reynolds and the response from Susan Ross employ feminist theological methodologies to engage non-suicidal self-injury and prenatal loss, two forms of suffering that uniquely and disproportionately affect women. They foreground gendered experiences of suffering that are otherwise shrouded in shame and secrecy to ask: Does attention to these realities illuminate inadequate or even harmful dimensions of Catholic liturgical practice? Can resources from our theological and liturgical tradition contribute to healing and the transformation of those social structures that contribute to women's suffering? Both essays engage the work of Susan Ross, who provides the language to understand the ambiguity of these forms of women's suffering and lays the groundwork for constructive liturgical response.

Hidden Self-Injury and Public Liturgy
Cynthia L. Cameron

Young women are growing to adulthood in a culture that can seem confusing and fragmented. They are hearing messages about who they are supposed to be from a wide variety of sources, and these messages are often conflicting. Some young women respond to this cacophony and their resulting sense of being out of control by resorting to self-injurious behaviors.[1] Since these young women may attend church and participate in its sacramental life, ministers cannot ignore this phenomenon. Because young women who self-injure likely do not hear any public recognition of their pain from the church, they may not know that they can turn to the church's ministers for pastoral care. And even though the sacramental life of the church is not able to address all the issues that lead some young women to self-injure, it does provide ministers with resources to draw upon in helping these young women. Therefore, in this essay, I argue that, while the Sacrament of Anointing of the Sick is an appropriate sacramental response for young women who self-injure, they and the whole church also need the more public sacramental response that can be found in the Sacrament of the Eucharist.[2]

Self-Injury in Young Women

Non-suicidal self-injury—the deliberate harming of the body with the intention to cause injury but not to cause death—has been a part of the psychological literature since the nineteenth century and has become a more intensely researched behavior in the past few decades.[3] Beth Hartman McGilley, psychologist and professor at the University of Kansas medical school, defines self-injury this way:

> [Self-injurious behavior] includes cutting; burning; hitting; biting; head banging; excessive scratching; hair pulling; interfering with wound care; breaking bones; chewing lips, cheeks, tongue or fingers; ingesting or inserting toxic or sharp objects; excessive sun burning; and unnecessary surgeries. Most that engage in self-harm are female, use multiple methods . . . and begin this behavior in early adolescence. Considered a pervasive problem in the United States, [self-injury] cuts across geographic, cultural, age, class, and psychiatric boundaries.[4]

Some studies suggest that 1.5 percent of all Americans have or currently are hurting themselves and that as many as 15-25 percent of young women have self-injured at least once in the past year. Of those who self-injure, 60-70 percent are female; 90 percent of self-injurers begin hurting themselves as teenagers, often beginning around the age of fourteen.[5] While men and boys do engage in self-harming behaviors (including those behaviors most often associated with women who self-injure, such as cutting and burning), the majority of self-injurers are young women, and this essay will focus on their experience. However, men and boys who self-injure cannot be ignored simply because there are fewer of them, and further psychological and theological research is warranted.

While the causes of self-injury are debated among mental health professionals, there is significant consensus that it is a maladaptive behavior rooted in trauma and/or mental illness, particularly depression and anxiety.[6] McGilley argues that self-injury is best understood as the attempt to self-medicate—an attempt by a young woman to manage her own pain when she lacks appropriate or healthy ways to self-soothe or self-regulate.[7] Self-injury remains a hidden phenomenon; young women who self-injure tend to do so in ways that are hidden from view, such as by cutting themselves on parts of the body covered by clothing and by refraining from seeking medical attention for their self-inflicted wounds.[8]

Given that self-harming behaviors are more common among women and girls, feminist psychologists have described the behavior not as simply a self-destructive one, but as an attempt to save oneself. Feminist theorists who engage the issue of self-injury contend that women, regardless of class, race, age, appearance, sexual orientation, or religious affiliation, are subject to the oppressive forces of patriarchy. They "argue that women's bodies are subjugated to relentless constrictions, overtly and insidiously designed to circumvent [women's] social, economic, and political status."[9] McGilley contends that this patriarchal culture perpetuates an oppressive disregard for women's bodies and that patriarchy is the context in which women and girls "operate 'as if' under constant scrutiny, embattled within and between themselves, their bodies host and hostage to self-harming dynamics."[10] In a culture that silences them and forces them to turn their emotions inward so as to never show a negative feeling,[11] self-mutilation is an attempt to give voice to these overwhelming emotions. For McGilley, self-harming behaviors in young women are a misdirected but not illogical attempt to assert control and to communicate in a patriarchal culture that silences the voices of young women and dictates how they should act and look. Self-injury is, at least in part, a reaction to the devaluation of the body in general, and of women's bodies in particular, that is characteristic of patriarchy. It reflects individualized expressions of the ways that young women are socialized to think about their bodies and themselves.

The phenomenon of self-injury among young women presents particular challenges to Roman Catholic churches. Under consideration here are the responses of local instantiations of the church—parishes, schools, and colleges, for example. Such communities are the likely spiritual homes of Catholic women who self-injure and, as such, have the potential to play a critical role in addressing and responding to this phenomenon. However, because they are also institutions that exist in the larger culture, these communities are not immune to the patriarchal forces that shape the lives of young women. This means that, despite a desire to serve everyone including young women who self-injure, Catholic communities often participate in this patriarchal culture.[12] For the young woman who self-injures, this participation in the patriarchal culture might be seen in an exclusively male hierarchy, an absence of women and women's voices in the church's teachings and practices, or an inadequate theology of embodiment that leads to the devaluing of women's bodies.[13] While feminist theologians continue to challenge this patriarchal culture, it is also important for ministers in local communities to create a culture that enables young women who self-injure, and all those with mental illness and trauma, to move out of the margins and come out of hiding. The pastoral counseling offered by individual ministers is an important starting place, but the public liturgical celebrations of the church can also serve as a powerful tool in reaching out to young women who self-injure.

Liturgical Responses to Young Women Who Self-Injure

How are Catholic communities, then, called to respond to the phenomenon of young women who self-injure in light of the sacramental resources available to them? These communities can be in a unique position to help young women grow into healthy adulthood and manage the stresses they face along the way. Communities can begin to do this by raising awareness of self-injury, by striving to break down taboos, by inviting the community to a greater consideration of the brokenness of the Body of Christ, by inviting women to work towards healing in ways that name their struggle instead of perpetuating their sense of voicelessness, and by working to become a community that cares for all of its members. Gathered around Jesus and the ministry of the church, these communities can become places where young women can find healthier options for dealing with emotional turmoil than self-injury. And those young women who do hurt themselves can find a community of care that will hear them and help them heal.

Young women who self-injure and who come to the attention of ministers are usually referred for mental health services. And this is, of course, good; providing care must begin with good mental health care. But young women who come to the church for help may be seeking not only clinical responses but also pastoral, spiritual, and liturgical care. In these situations, ministers often focus their responses on individual pastoral care and private sacramental responses. The impulse to keep this care private is, in part, due to the private nature of mental health care and the need to protect the privacy of individuals. In such instances, a private or semi-private celebration of the Sacrament of Anointing of the Sick may, for some or even most young women, be the most appropriate response. While not taking the place of appropriate medical care, the Sacrament of Anointing can play a role in the healing process. The Sacrament of Anointing provides an opportunity for young women who self-injure to experience care—the care of God and, through the minister, of the church. The sacrament can serve as a way to initiate or confirm a commitment to healing, as a recognition of healing that has been accomplished, and as a bolster for the hard work that is required when young women struggle with maladaptive behaviors like self-harm.

Liturgist Kristyn Russell argues well that mental illness in general and self-injury in particular are serious, debilitating, and destructive of relationships and that the Sacrament of Anointing can validly be used with young women in these situations.[14] Although most commonly associated with those who are near death or in danger of dying, this sacrament has evolved such that believers with less obviously life-threatening but still serious illness are encouraged to avail themselves of it.[15] In the particular case of a young woman who self-injures, according to Russell, this sacrament can help her begin to reorient her understanding of her own body, heal relationships with herself, others, and God, and "rediscover herself as loved."[16]

In the Sacrament of Anointing, young women who self-injure can encounter God's grace and have the opportunity to view their lives and their bodies in healthier ways.[17] In addition, these young women challenge ministers to think more clearly about how bodies can be sites where we experience profound pain caused by accident, illness, or self-injury, and how bodies can both reveal and hide that pain. They also expose how the patriarchal culture encourages young women to, as psychologist Mary Pipher puts it, "carve themselves into culturally acceptable pieces."[18] For women who self-injure, their experience of their bodiliness can be conflicted; when cutting becomes a useful self-soothing strategy, bodies become both a source of a longed-for healing and a source of shame and pain. Bodies for these women are also where they act out their pain, blurring the lines between mental and physical illness. As theologian Susan Ross contends, there is need for ritual attention to these more conflicted experiences of embodiment.[19] The Sacrament of Anointing has the potential to help young women who self-injure embrace a healthier sense of their own embodiment. They are affirmed as embodied persons as their bodies are anointed with oil and they can experience confirmation of their worth to God and the community as they experience God's care and grace.

However, in confining responses to self-injury to private celebrations of the Sacrament of Anointing, there is a danger of reinforcing the private and hidden nature of self-injury, perpetuating the silencing of these women, and failing to publicly challenge the patriarchal messages that make self-injury seem a useful coping strategy. Ross suggests that the practice of "'making public' the kinds of activities that have been formerly seen as private" can be valuable in the process of naming a need and raising awareness in the community.[20] While an individual woman might prefer not to have the story of her self-injury as public knowledge, Catholic communities have the liturgical resources to address self-injurious behavior in ways that are public by locating this pastoral response within the heart of the church's sacramental life.

Given the centrality of the Eucharist in the lives of Catholic communities, it is a sacrament that can aid in the task of providing a more public voice for young women who self-injure. Ross suggests that sacraments are inherently ambiguous, something that is particularly true of the Sacrament of the Eucharist: "Sacraments are a dimension of finite human existence and thus sacramentality is, by definition, fluid in that the concrete reality at issue points *both* to itself *and* beyond itself. There is both an opacity and a transparency to the sacraments, as there is to human life."[21] Because sacraments are expressions of human life and are grounded in history and culture, they are not static events; they point beyond themselves. This ambiguity, which is a part of the power of sacraments, means that they always point to the deeper mystery of God and call Christians into relationship with that mystery.[22] Beyond this inherent ambiguity, which helps expand our vision of the sacrament, the Eucharist can also be ambiguous in less constructive ways, particularly for young women who self-injure. The absence of women at the table, the remembering of saints who self-injured,[23] and the tendency to downplay the physicality of the Eucharist while emphasizing its spiritual meanings all contribute to this ambiguity.[24]

However, the Eucharist also has the potential to speak in powerful ways to women who self-injure. It is a sacrament that celebrates the body: the bread and wine become the body and blood of Christ. We ingest Christ's body; we become the Body of Christ. The Eucharist is also a public sacrament: the table is, at least theoretically, open to all the baptized. It initiates believers into a community that cares for all members; it is a public statement of the community's quest for unity and wholeness; it insists that weakness and death are not the final word. The Eucharist has the potential to break down dualisms: both body and spirit are celebrated; it both is public and has moments of private reflection; it brings together the natural and the supernatural; it speaks to the senses and the mind. The Eucharist and the Mass as a whole have the power to bring public voice to the need for healing in the community. The homily, the prayers of the people, the acclamation that "our souls shall be healed," the sign of peace—all of these can be moments for the church to speak to women who self-injure and to all those with mental illnesses. The celebration of the Eucharist provides ministers with a place to say out loud, and to put into practice, the conviction that those who self-injure are welcome, have a voice, can find healing and wholeness.

The Eucharist is not the only public sacrament of the church, and ministers can consider ways that other public sacraments can become opportunities to reach out to those who self injure. Can Confirmation be a chance to say something to adolescent girls about their value and their voices in the community? Can Marriage be a chance to preach about the value of women's bodies? Can Baptism be a reminder to the whole community of its responsibilities to be attentive to those most likely to be marginalized in our faith communities? In addition, other public celebrations of what Ross calls "sacramental moments" are ripe for providing recognition of the presence of young women who self-injure.[25] Some of these sacramental moments might take place in more traditional contexts: the Stations of the Cross, practices of fasting, devotions to Mary and the saints, Eucharistic adoration.[26] Others might be more experimental: celebrations of milestones in women's lives like menarche or menopause, or prayer groups that explore embodied prayer styles.[27]

One of the reasons that the Sacrament of Eucharist and other public sacraments have such potential to speak to young women who self-injure is that sacraments form Christians into communities in which they care for one another. Ross suggests that "the sacraments do involve a responsibility to care. . . . Thus they grow out of an understanding of Christian community as the place where we have obligations to others as we do to our own families."[28] Since the Eucharist is the preeminent sacrament in the life of the church, and the one most often celebrated, it plays a prominent role in building up these communities of care where all people find that they can "care about," "take care of," give care, and receive care.[29] For young women who self-injure, the presence of this community of care means that they can find ministers who have named their presence to the whole community and who are prepared to provide pastoral care for them.

There remains a great deal of work to be done to increase awareness of mental illnesses in our faith communities and, while individual communities may not be immediately able to break down the patriarchal culture that makes self-injury seem like a useful coping strategy, they can make it possible for the young women in these communities to resist that culture. The public liturgies of the church are an opportunity to say out loud, with words and actions, that young women who self-injure are not unnoticed, uncared-for, unwanted; these liturgies are an opportunity to publicly claim, in word and action, that they are not hidden or silenced, and to call all in the community to care for young women who self-injure. Public recognition in the Eucharist of the presence of young women who self-injure, coupled with the more private nature of pastoral counseling and the Sacrament of Anointing and, of course, in cooperation with mental health professionals, means that faith communities can be the kinds of caring communities that Ross calls for: "Our recognizing the needs of the other and our taking responsibility because of our interdependence also means that we see these needs in concrete ways and meet them, as best we can."[30]

Catholic Liturgy and Prenatal Loss:
Ritual, Ambiguity, and the Miscarrying Body
Susan Bigelow Reynolds

A colleague of mine once shared with me a powerful memory from her childhood, growing up in the pre-Vatican II Catholic world of mid-1950s south side Chicago. One night a week, her mother would gather with other women from the parish to pray a devotional to Our Lady of Sorrows. As she recalled, "Mothers suffering from various afflictions and sorrows were out in force, often encouraged by other women from the parish—relatives, neighbors, friends." There were mothers grieving the loss of their sons in World War II and the Korean War. Others, including her own mother, were caring for children with disabilities. Some, she suspected in retrospect, were suffering from domestic violence and husbands with alcoholism and undiagnosed PTSD. Many were mourning miscarriages and stillbirths. The group was ever evolving—some women would join in the devotion for the length of a novena, others for years. As she understood it, the women never explicitly defined the purpose or mission of the group. And yet, in her words, "they all knew why they were there."

Not long before our conversation, I had suffered a miscarriage of my own. As my colleague spoke, I found myself yearning for something like the group she described at my own parish: A space where I could share my sorrow with other women who would take seriously the magnitude of what I felt I had lost, and where I could be drawn beyond my grief in empathy for their sufferings. A space able to bear the weight of such a complex, untidy form of loss characterized by confusion and deep ambiguity. A space constructed out of the walls and symbols and stories of my own tradition, indicating that my particular grief had a home in, not apart from, the Christian story.

This paper will draw on the work of Serene Jones and Susan Ross to make two mutually interrelated claims about prenatal loss[31] in the Catholic Church today. First, it will demonstrate that communal liturgical and sacramental embrace of women and families who have suffered the loss of a child in the womb is an area of ministerial concern in the church that has been critically neglected and is desperately needed. At the same time, bringing to light the socially and pastorally silenced reality of prenatal loss has the power to deepen and transform the church's liturgical theology and practice.

Sacramental Imagination and the Miscarrying Body

Miscarriage is an experience in which social taboos converge with medical and biological ambiguities.[32] These function to silence the multiple and varying forms of grief women experience in the wake of such losses. This silencing cultivates around miscarriage a myth of anomaly, isolating women within the seeming unshare-ability of their grief and obliterating the possibility of communal support. This imposition of silence is reflected in advice commonly given to newly pregnant women that they wait until their second trimester, when the risk of miscarriage decreases, to share the news that they are expecting. While such advice is perhaps sound on some level, it also communicates to women that a miscarriage, should one occur, is something that is supposed to remain a secret, even to friends and loved ones. When a miscarriage does occur, then, women can encounter a painful dissonance: their deeply felt desire to grieve, to ritually mark and give meaning to their loss, is met with a stifling socially and culturally mediated sense that their grief is not to be shared. In contrast with, for example, the Japanese Buddhist practice of *Mizuko Kuyo*, which marks the death of an unborn child (called a *mizuko*, or "water child"),[33] the absence of language and rituals (both religious and non-religious) that follow a miscarriage in a U.S. context ultimately communicates to women that their loss is both unimportant and fundamentally without meaning. The veil of public silence that surrounds prenatal loss heightens the internal sense of alienation from their own bodies that many women experience in the wake of such loss. The body once trusted to nurture and defend the new life within can suddenly seem like a traitor, a failure, perhaps even a murderer.[34]

In order to begin to speak about prenatal loss with an eye of hope and expectation toward the cultivation of communal, liturgical responses, we must begin by attending to the deep theological significance of the miscarrying body. Speaking of the miscarrying body is not intended to abstract or isolate the bodily experience of prenatal loss from its many other dimensions (the social, familial, and psychological, for example), as if to reduce the multifaceted experience of losing a child in the womb to a stark medical descriptor. Rather, I would suggest, the incarnational impulse of the Catholic sacramental tradition invites and demands particular attention to the created and embodied, to flesh and blood in all its forms. The miscarrying body, in this respect, is long neglected and has much to reveal theologically: it has carried within its organs and bones the body of another. It has become a living grave. For some, it may yet become in some unknowable future a conduit of new life.

In her powerful, personal theological reflection on miscarriage, theologian Serene Jones illustrates how an honest, unsanitized understanding of the miscarrying body points to ambiguous dimensions of bodiliness and selfhood. When her child dies in her womb, a woman suffers multiple "undoings" that at once upend and render ambiguous her own self-understanding, and at the same time reveal the deeply relational character of such loss and the startlingly porous boundaries of the self.[35] When a miscarriage occurs, a woman experiences a loss of bodily integrity expressed in what Jones calls the "rupturing of the self."[36] She feels "fragmented, dispersed, like she [is] leaking into the world."[37] She leaves "pieces of herself and another in rags, in toilets, in medical waste cans; she tries to hold all this together but can't."[38] When loss occurs early in a pregnancy, it is nearly impossible to distinguish embryonic or fetal remains from the mother's own blood. In a surprising way, death does not sever her bodily relationship to her child but renders it, for a time, even more inextricable.

Indeed, Jones observes, when a woman loses a child in the womb, "her body becomes to her 'the space of death.'"[39] Jones contends that "[t]here is no other experience, in the mix of our many human griefs, that comes close to mirroring this. She carries death within her body . . . but she does not die. Death becomes her."[40] "What does it mean," she asks, "to know one's self as a walking site of death itself? To have death quite literally inside you?"[41] When the boundary between life and death is severed in a woman's own body, what is experienced is the sense that one has, quite literally, lived through hell.

What could this image of the self—this "non-agentic, hopeless, fragmenting, death carrying self"[42]—possibly reveal? I would suggest that it forces us to grapple with the deep ambiguity of bodily reality in ways that are consequential for liturgical and sacramental theology and practice. Holding the image of the fragmented, death-carrying body—this self-as-grave—alongside the more common maternal image of the life-bearing body has the surprising capacity, Jones suggests, to propel us deep into the Trinity, into God's very being. On the cross, Jones suggests, "the whole of the Trinity . . . takes death into itself." Like the enwombed child,

> this is a death that happens deep within God, not outside of God but in the very heart—perhaps the womb—of God. It is a death that consumes God, that God holds, making a grave of the Trinity. And yet . . . this death-bearing grave of a God paradoxically does not die but lives. And She lives to love yet again and to offer to the world the gift of the future.[43]

As several feminist scholars have noted in reflections on the maternal body, the pregnant woman can be understood as a communion of persons.[44] When the child dies within her, however, the communion of her body does not cease. Her body, like the multipersoned body of the Trinity, becomes the site of rupture and undoing. Among her organs and bones, she contains death. Her womb becomes a tomb, and yet she lives. Any resurrection that will occur in the wake of her loss, any hope or consolation, cannot be imposed from without but must necessarily emerge from deep within—an embodied resurrection, an embodied hope.

When Bodies Talk Back:
Ritual, Ambiguity, and Complex Grief

For Catholic women, the silencing that surrounds experiences of prenatal loss is reinforced and reinscribed by pastoral neglect.

Catholic pastoral responses to miscarriage, where they exist at all, typically disclose an improvisational, *ad hoc* character. Historian Agnes Howard captures the painful absence of ritual and pastoral resources in the days following her miscarriage. She writes,

> We were visited by our priest. With warmth and prayer, he gave care there in the hospital and later at the gravesite, but there was a provisional sense about his gestures, as though he were improvising out of his own kindness rather than acting on long liturgical practice that the church had devised in meeting these crises from time immemorial.[45]

Both within and beyond the Catholic Church, women's accounts of their miscarriages suggest that many feel very palpably the lack of prescribed ritual in the aftermath of what many experience as a traumatic loss.[46] Jones recalls that, after both she and a friend suffered miscarriages almost concurrently, they "did not first and foremost yearn for a conceptual argument about such things as Divine providence or feminist notions of freedom. . . . What we yearned for," she recalled, "was more basic. We wanted images, a drama, a story, a vivid language that . . . could give meaningful shape to this particular event."[47]

Catholic liturgical practice acknowledges prenatal loss in the Roman Catholic Book of Blessings, which contains among its many occasion-specific prayers a "Blessing of Parents After a Miscarriage or Stillbirth." The short rite contains a reading from the Book of Lamentations, followed by intercessions and by a prayer of blessing for the parents of the child lost.[48] The existence of the blessing is, unfortunately, little publicized by clergy and thus little known or utilized by women or families. Yet the blessing itself also falls short of capturing the reality of the grief for which it seeks to offer healing. The beginning of the selection from Lamentations (3:17-18) echoes well the feeling of "time undone" and "future lost" that Jones suggests marks the aftermath of a miscarriage:

> My soul is deprived of peace,
> I have forgotten what happiness is;
> I tell myself my future is lost,
> All that I hope for from the LORD. (Lam 3:17-18)

At that point, however, the selection prescribed in the rite skips several verses and jumps abruptly from mourning to hope (Lam 21-24). So too do the prescribed intercessions cascade smoothly over pain to comfort. This is not, in itself, a critique. Consolation is an important part of what Christian rituals of mourning do. They hold together the cross with the resurrection, lament over a future lost with communal memories of God's healing and renewing action. Yet the distinct bodily reality and form of knowing that emerges when we take prenatal loss seriously calls forth from the Christian tradition memories, stories, and symbols with the capacity to dwell perhaps more patiently in complex grief and deep ambiguity.

We find few images in Scripture or in the aesthetic tradition of the Church that resonate with this particular experience of motherhood jarringly interrupted. The concluding prayer of the Catholic blessing recalls the image of Mary at the foot of the cross, grieving the death of her crucified son. While the image is an evocative and important one, and like any potent symbol transcends the particularity of its circumstances, there nevertheless remains a dissonance in its use in a ritual meant specifically for women who have suffered a miscarriage or stillbirth. Mary's tears at the foot of the cross point to a quite different genre of grief—one in which "maternal barrenness and bodily disintegration are not at issue."[49] Perhaps it can be construed as validation of the miscarrying mother's tears to unite her hidden story of loss with Christianity's archetypal story of maternal sorrow. But not to differentiate between the death of a (born) child and a miscarriage is to fail to recognize the complexity and ambiguity of having experienced *oneself* as the site of death.

The disconnect exemplified in the Book of Blessings can be understood as suggestive of the ongoing ecclesial neglect of women's embodied reality more broadly. Despite Catholic theology's incarnational impulse, the tradition has typically regarded bodies, particularly women's bodies, with varying degrees of suspicion. It is not surprising, then, that in a patriarchal context, sacramental theology and practice have evolved in ways that have neglected, subordinated, or spiritualized the embodied experiences of women. As a consequence, notes Susan Ross, the neglect of women's embodied realities in the church's liturgical life and sacramental imagination has propelled women to cultivate and claim "spaces apart from the church's institutional structure"[50] for worship and community. In her now-classic work *Extravagant Affections,* Ross explains, "Since the church's official liturgical celebrations have been so exclusive of women, women have turned to 'unofficial' religious practices, to ways of celebrating, mourning, and remembering significant events in their lives that are on no liturgical calendar."[51] Such alternative practices transgress the fabricated boundary between public and private that has long served to exclude women's experiences of suffering from the church's public consciousness and liturgical practice.

As the story with which this paper began suggests, this is not a new phenomenon—Catholic women have been claiming "unofficial" communal spaces of worship for a long time. Yet in some ways, the cultivation of such alternative spaces and practices is more constrained and viewed with greater clerical suspicion than sixty years ago when my colleague's mother would gather with other women to offer their prayers to Our Lady of Sorrows. As post-Vatican II liturgical reforms consolidated Catholic devotional practice around the Eucharist and "full, conscious, and active participation"[52] in the sacred liturgy became the primary aim of this renewed liturgical life, non-Eucharistic forms of devotion—the majority of which were organized, practiced, and led by women—increasingly came to be regarded as superfluous and superstitious.[53] Devotions that were not done away with were "recast . . . in what [reformers] considered a new, more spiritually mature idiom"; the popular was tidied up with authoritatively sanctioned set texts and clerical oversight.[54] As a consequence, women seeking to ritually mark their griefs and joys through non-Eucharistic forms of prayer are in some ways forced even farther outside the institutional bounds of the church today than they once were.

Ross argues that what is revealed in women's alternative practices of worship is the shape of a renewed sacramental theology. This renewed vision is characterized by four features: an openness to ambiguity; an honoring of women's embodiment; a sensitivity to the multivalence of symbols; and an impulse to do justice.[55] Embodied experiences of loss and women's constructive practices of commemorating such losses open us up to precisely this sort of porous and capacious sacramental imagination. An understanding of sacrament conditioned by a recognition of the ambiguity inherent in lived reality, particularly the lived realities of women, takes a critical approach to the interpretation of bodies and gender roles and recognizes the multivalent and socially mediated nature of Christian symbols. As we have observed, this "lived ambiguity"[56] is central to understanding both the bodily reality and liturgical-sacramental implications of miscarriage. Unsilencing the complex and ambiguous grief of miscarriage complicates in consequential ways our understandings of birth and death, maternity and sacrifice, bodiliness and agency. I would thus argue that a feminist theological recovery of the miscarrying body has the potential, as Ross contends, to both "affirm in creative ways, but also to correct, clarify, subvert, and transform this [sacramental] tradition."[57]

The experience of prenatal loss reveals in the language of human bodies the deeply, divinely relational nature of Jesus's death. This is a dimension of the crucifixion that is often overlooked, particularly when we compartmentalize all of women's embodied experience into a narrowly understood Marian framework and fail to let these bodies and experiences speak back to doctrine and symbol. Indeed, the miscarrying body reveals to us the deep inadequacy of the dualistic manner of thinking that has long served to constrict the Christian sacramental tradition and, within this tradition, to naturalize the subordination of the lives and bodies of women. The forced division of reality into spirit and flesh, sacred and profane, public and private, self and other, even life and death, has conditioned "our ways of thinking about the sacred [in ways that] rule out its potential to be revealed in new or seemingly inappropriate places."[58] Yet, as we have seen, the miscarrying body renders these seemingly rigid distinctions that form the brick and mortar of our sacramental imaginations ambiguous, even invalid.

In the context of prenatal loss, women's ritual "spaces apart" serve as important sites of solidarity, community, and healing. Yet as much as such alternative spaces serve as a remedy for institutional pastoral neglect, we should not view them as its solution. By relegating the experience of miscarriage to the margins and shadows of the institutional church's practice, the church not only deprives women of needed support by communicating to them that their grief has no home in their tradition. It also deprives itself of a profound and sacramentally revelatory way of understanding embodied reality, human relationality, and the porous boundary between life and death. Relocating this experience of prenatal loss—a phenomenon as basic to and inseparable from human experience as birth and death—from the periphery of our social and theological consciousness to its center has the capacity to deepen the prevailing understandings of bodiliness that inform our sacramental imagination at a fundamental level. The miscarrying body must be allowed to "talk back" to the tradition so as to enrich and transform it.

Response to Cynthia Cameron and Susan Reynolds
Susan A. Ross

First of all, let me thank both Cynthia Cameron and Susan Reynolds for these thought-provoking and sensitive essays touching on issues seldom, if at all, dealt with in the Catholic sacramental tradition. Both the issues of self-harm and of pregnancy loss are experiences that many women find have no place in the sacramental tradition, but both authors make a compelling case for greater (ritual) attention to them. Both discuss the role of ambiguity, as it is developed in *Extravagant Affections*, both emphasize the importance of naming, and both also discuss how women carry these experiences with them in a way hidden to those around them.

First, a brief comment on ambiguity. I want to note that I cannot take credit for the concept of ambiguity itself. In researching my book, I came upon the work of Donald Levine[59] and Ruth Page,[60] in addition to the work of David Tracy,[61] who was my graduate school mentor. All three of them emphasized the place of ambiguity in cultural, linguistic, theological, and philosophical discussions. I found these discussions helpful as a way to understand the place of many women like myself who felt both in and out of the church and its sacramental contexts. Ambiguity is, as Tracy describes, a feature of the postmodern context, but in the sense I use it, it is a way to talk about how many Catholic women find ourselves both included and excluded in the church. It is the one concept from the book that is most often raised in discussions, and I am happy to see that it continues to have relevance.

Second, the naming of self-harm and of pregnancy loss is crucial to dealing with these experiences both personally and communally.

My understanding of self-harm is that it offers both control and release: another kind of pain replaces psychic pain. The suggestions that Cynthia Cameron raises—of bringing these experiences to the larger worshiping community—have both positive and negative potential. It might be difficult to find the proper "sacramental" context for ritual recognition, but Cameron makes a significant point that communal prayers need to name all of the community's pain publicly. Such a public recognition acknowledges the broken and wounded Body of Christ and in naming these wounds, opens the door for women to realize that they are not alone. In addition, the larger context of Catholic theology of the body fails to empower women as agents in its stress on feminine qualities of maternity and receptivity. These emphases can perpetuate the sense of helplessness that can accompany self-harm, and indeed, the fact that feminism is often seen by the hierarchy as a form of evil makes such agency itself appear to be sinful.

In the case of pregnancy loss, I was reminded of a number of losses experienced by women in my own family: my sister, whose pregnancy losses included premature twins who both died shortly after birth, a miscarriage, and a stillbirth, all within four years between her second and third children; my mother, who miscarried her seventh pregnancy, and about which she was deeply conflicted, since her youngest had just begun school and she had begun to experience a measure of freedom for the first time in fifteen years; women I know who had abortions and had expected to have children later on but did not. Both the deep grief that Reynolds describes as well as the ambivalence experienced by some with pregnancy loss fail to be acknowledged sacramentally. I found Reynolds' description of the "womb as tomb" to be a very powerful expression of the ambiguity of the female body, and that this understanding opens up ways of thinking about not only women's bodies but of the deep suspicion in which our imperfect bodies are seen by the tradition.

Both of these papers speak to the church's inability to respond to women's pain—indeed, even to acknowledge it—and both raise yet again the gaping chasm left by women's exclusion from any formal ritual role. Women are always recipients, never agents, of the church's "official" sacramental grace, but both papers nevertheless show the immense possibilities for women's sacramental agency. The fact that women have, in a number of ways, reclaimed these ritual spaces despite the church's position, speaks to the power of women themselves.

Notes

[1]Until relatively recently, it was assumed that self-injurious behaviors were more prevalent in white and middle- or upper-class populations. Because of this, one of the research priorities had been to explain why self-injury was more of a problem with these young women. Subsequent research has shown that self-injury is a problematic behavior in a wide range of communities, including poor communities and communities of color. However, because white middle- and upper-class girls and women come to the attention of medical professionals at a higher rate, it is their experiences that are reflected in the medical and psychological literature.

[2]Beyond the scope of this paper is the question of whether the existing seven sacraments are sufficient for ministering adequately to young women who self-injure. In addition, the broader question of sacramental responses to mental illness is likewise beyond my scope here; self-injury is one behavior that is rooted in mental illness and trauma and it points to some of the ways in which churches fail this group of people. So, taking self-injury as one instantiation of the hidden side of mental illness and trauma in the life of the Christian community, I argue that our sacramental theologies need to take this into consideration and that our sacramental responses need to be more robust.

[3]Beth Hartman McGilley, "Feminist Perspectives on Self-Harm Behavior and Eating Disorders," in *Self-Harm Behavior and Eating Disorders: Dynamics, Assessment, and Treatment*, ed. John L. Levitt, Randy A. Sansone, and Leigh Cohn (New York: Brunner-Routledge, 2004), 76. Non-suicidal self-injury is often called "delicate self-cutting" in order to distinguish it from a more dramatic or "coarse" self-injury like eye enucleation or genital amputation, behaviors more common among men and in psychotic illness. Self-injury is also distinguished from high-risk behavior (like dangerous driving), more common in adolescent boys.

[4]McGilley, "Feminist Perspectives," 77.

[5]Shana Ross and Nancy Heath, "A Study of the Frequency of Self-Mutilation in a Community Sample of Adolescents," *Journal of Youth and Adolescence* 31, no.1 (February 2002): 69; Martha B. Straus, *Adolescent Girls in Crisis: Intervention and Hope* (New York: W. W. Norton, 2007), 59.

[6]For further information on the causes or potential causes of self-injury, see Lori M. Hilt, Christine B. Cha, and Susan Nolen-Hoeksema, "Nonsuicidal Self-Injury in Young Adolescent Girls: Moderators of the Distress-Function Relationship," *Journal of Consulting and Clinical Psychology* 76, no.1 (2008): 63-71; John L. Levitt, Randy A. Sansone, and Leigh Cohn, eds., *Self-Harm Behavior and Eating Disorders: Dynamics, Assessment, and Treatment* (New York: Brunner-Routledge, 2004).

[7]McGilley, "Feminist Perspectives," 78. "Psychic relief from feelings of

depersonalization, emptiness, shame, rage, tension, and emotional pain is mitigated through the physical pain that inevitably registers. Though often exquisitely unbearable in its own right, physical pain is preferred over the mental anguish it was otherwise intended to assuage."

[8]Straus, *Adolescent Girls in Crisis*, 59. "We do know that the problem is significantly greater than published reports generally suggest. . . . Many miserable girls appear to be 'writing' messages to us on their bodies, even if there is only a very small chance we will notice and 'read' them, and respond. In the absence of more adaptive self-soothing strategies, millions of girls have discovered that self harm provides a reliable short-term solution for them."

[9]McGilley, "Feminist Perspectives," 79.

[10]Ibid., 83.

[11]For a discussion of how a patriarchal culture forces women and girls to silence themselves and to meet unrealistic expectations of what being a woman means, see Stephen Hinshaw with Rachel Kranz, *The Triple Bind: Saving Our Teenage Girls from Today's Pressures and Conflicting Expectations* (New York: Ballantine Books, 2009).

[12]Elizabeth A. Johnson, *She Who Is: The Mystery of God in Feminist Theological Discourse*, 10th anniversary ed. (New York: Herder & Herder, 2002), 26-27; Anne E. Carr, *Transforming Grace: Christian Tradition and Women's Experience* (New York: Continuum, 1988), 14-17.

[13]Susan A. Ross, *Extravagant Affections: A Feminist Sacramental Theology* (New York: Continuum, 2001), 25-28, 57-59.

[14]Kristyn Russell, "Sacrament of Anointing: A Step in the Healing of Young, Self-Harming Women," *Worship* 86, no. 6 (November 2012): 531; *Pastoral Care of the Sick* (Collegeville, MN: Liturgical Press, 1983), no. 53.

[15]Russell, "Sacrament of Anointing," 531-532.

[16]Ibid., 539.

[17]An understanding of the sacrament of anointing as affirming of embodiment assumes that Roman Catholic theology has an adequate theology of embodiment. While theologians such as Susan Ross have taken up this task, there remains much to be done. See Ross, *Extravagant Affections*, 102-136; Susan A. Ross, "'Then Honor God in Your Body' (1 Cor. 6:20): Feminist and Sacramental Theology on the Body," *Horizons* 18, no. 1 (1989): 7-27.

[18]Mary Pipher, *Reviving Ophelia: Saving the Selves of Adolescent Girls* (New York: Putnam, 1994), 157.

[19]Ross, *Extravagant Affections*, 227.

[20]Ibid., 225.

[21]Ibid., 39.

[22]Ibid., 40.

[23]Ariel Glucklich, *Sacred Pain: Hurting the Body for the Sake of the Soul* (New York: Oxford University Press, 2001). Consider the following: "Blessed Clare of Rimini had herself bound to a pillar and whipped on Good Friday. Hedwig of Silesia scourged herself, and Blessed Charles of Blois wrapped knotted cords around his chest.... Christina of Spoleto perforated her own foot with a nail" (79). It is important to note that we cannot assume that self-injurious behavior by the saints was meant to be a form of self-soothing

or a manifestation of mental illness. Women and men who self-mutilated for spiritual reasons were often seeking self-control, self-mastery, and self-transcendence, but this behavior was not always rooted in a mental illness.

[24]Ross, *Extravagant Affections*, 55.

[25]Ibid., 211-213.

[26]Colleen M. Griffith and Thomas H. Groome, eds., *Catholic Spiritual Practices: A Treasury of Old and New* (Brewster, MA: Paraclete Press, 2012).

[27]See, for example, the liturgies suggested in Rosemary Radford Ruether, *Women-Church: Theology and Practice of Feminist Liturgical Communities* (San Francisco: Harper &Row, 1985), 107-121; Janet R. Walton, *Feminist Liturgy: A Matter of Justice* (Collegeville, MN: Liturgical Press, 2000), 48-80.

[28]Ross, *Extravagant Affections*, 198.

[29]Ibid., 199-200. Ross is drawing on the work of ethicist Joan C. Tronto, *Moral Boundaries: A Political Argument for an Ethic of Care* (New York: Routledge, 1993).

[30]Ross, *Extravagant Affections*, 200.

[31]In this essay, I use the term "prenatal loss" to refer to experiences of miscarriage and stillbirth. According to the Centers for Disease Control and Prevention, in the United States, a miscarriage refers to involuntary fetal loss before 20 weeks gestation. Stillbirth refers to a loss after 20 weeks gestation. (Some other countries utilize different cut-offs to differentiate between a miscarriage and stillbirth.) Estimates indicate that at least 15 to 20 percent of clinically recognized pregnancies end in miscarriage. In the U.S., stillbirth occurs at a rate of roughly 6 in 1,000 live births (CDC/HCHS National Vital Statistics System, *National Vital Statistics Reports* 64, No. 8 [July 23, 2015]). By referring to both categories of loss concurrently in this paper, I do not seek to conflate them. Medically, and in many other ways, they can be quite distinct. The goal of this paper is to bring recognition to the necessity of taking seriously both miscarriage and stillbirth as sites of needed liturgical, pastoral, and theological engagement. Such responses can and must look different depending on the particularities of the loss. The jarring, inexplicable loss of a new pregnancy at seven weeks and a third-trimester umbilical cord accident both call forth pastoral care and theological reflection with equal urgency, though what each loss demands pastorally and evokes theologically will be in many ways distinct.

[32]I engage in a deepened and expanded exploration of the causes and consequences of these taboos, ambiguities, and contestations, in Susan Reynolds, "From the Site of the Empty Tomb: Approaching the Hidden Grief of Prenatal Loss," *New Theology Review* 28, no. 2 (2016): 47-59. The present paper represents the more constructive side of the largely deconstructive argument presented in that article.

[33]The Japanese Buddhist ritual of *Mizuko Kuyo* is a memorial ritual for a miscarried, stillborn, or aborted baby. In contrast to English, which lacks a word for a deceased unborn baby, in Japanese a deceased fetus is called a *mizuko*, meaning "water child." See, for example, Jeff Wilson, *Mourning the Unborn Dead: A Buddhist Ritual Comes to America* (New York: Oxford University Press, 2009). For a brief and personal account that highlights the distinction between U.S. and Japanese societies in ritually commemorating

a miscarriage, see Peggy Orenstein, "Mourning My Miscarriage," *New York Times Magazine* (April 21, 2002).

[34]From a theological standpoint, Serene Jones explores the complex dynamic of powerlessness, guilt, and self-blame in the wake of a miscarriage in S. Jones, "Rupture," in *Hope Deferred: Heart-Healing Reflections on Reproductive Loss*, edited by Nadine Pence Frantz and Mary T. Stimming (Eugene, OR: Resource Publications, 2005), 51-53.

[35]L. Serene Jones, "Hope Deferred: Theological Reflections on Reproductive Loss (Infertility, Miscarriage, Stillbirth)," *Modern Theology* 12, no. 2 (2001): 238.

[36]Ibid., 234.

[37]Ibid.

[38]Ibid., 234-235.

[39]Ibid., 235.

[40]Ibid.

[41]Ibid., 236.

[42]Ibid., 238.

[43]Ibid., 242.

[44]See, for example, Bonnie Miller-McLemore, *Also a Mother: Work and Family as Theological Dilemma* (Nashville: Abingdon Press, 1994); Miller-McLemore, "Epistemology or Bust: A Maternal Feminist Knowledge of Knowing," *The Journal of Religion* 72, no. 2 (1992).

[45]Agnes R. Howard, "Comforting Rachel: How Christians Should Respond to Prenatal Death," *Commonweal* (November 4, 2013), 11, https://www.commonwealmagazine.org/comforting-rachel.

[46]See Deborah J. Brin, "The Use of Rituals in Grieving for a Miscarriage or Stillbirth," *Women & Therapy* 27, no. 3/4 (2004), 123-132. On the relationship between miscarriage and trauma, see T. M. Walker and K. M. Davidson, "A Preliminary Investigation of Psychological Distress following Surgical Management of Early Pregnancy Loss Detected at Initial Ultrasound Scanning: A Trauma Perspective," *Journal of Reproductive and Infant Psychology* 19, no. 1 (2001): 7–16; L. Born, C. N. Soares, S. Philips, M. Jung, M. Steiner, "Women and Reproductive-Related Trauma," *Annals of the New York Academy of Sciences* 1071 (2006): 491–94; and I. M. Engelhard, M. A. van den Hout, A. Arntz, "Posttraumatic Stress Disorder after Pregnancy Loss," *General Hospital Psychiatry* 23, no. 2 (2001): 62–66.

[47]Jones, "Hope Deferred," 228.

[48]The blessing can also be accessed on the USCCB website at: http://wwwmigrate.usccb.org.

[49]Jones, "Hope Deferred," 239.

[50]Ross, *Extravagant Affections*, 222.

[51]Ibid., 27.

[52]*Sacrosanctum Concilium* 14.

[53]Robert A. Orsi, *Thank You, St. Jude: Women's Devotion to the Patron Saint of Hopeless Causes* (New Haven, CT: Yale University Press, 1998), 33. The Notre Dame Study of Catholic Parish life, conducted throughout the U.S. from 1981-1989, concluded that a quarter century after Vatican II, "The liturgy as reformed by Vatican II is now central to parish spirituality

and community experience; public devotions such as novenas and the rosary have greatly declined" (Joseph Gremillion and David C. Leege, "Post-Vatican II Parish Life in the United States: Preview and Review," Report No. 15, Notre Dame Study of Catholic Parish Life [1989], 8). Ross affirms and nuances these conclusions, noting that while this devotional decline is particularly true in the context of Anglo-American women, it tends to be less the case in, for example, U.S. Hispanic communities, where non-Eucharistic forms of devotion and popular religiosity continue to thrive (*Extravagant Affections*, 206).

[54]Orsi, *Thank You, St. Jude*, 33.

[55]Ross, *Extravagant Affections*, 209.

[56]Ibid., 211.

[57]Ibid., 28.

[58]Ibid., 40.

[59]Donald Levine, *The Flight from Ambiguity: Essays in Social and Cultural Theory* (Chicago: University of Chicago Press, 1985).

[60]Ruth Page, *Ambiguity and the Presence of God* (London: SCM Press, 1985).

[61]David Tracy, *Plurality and Ambiguity: Hermeneutics, Religion, Hope* (San Francisco: Harper and Row, 1987).

PART III

LITURGY AND POWER
IN LIVED RELIGION

The Liturgy of Life

The Eucharist, Power, and Lived Religion

Ricky Manalo, CSP

Introduction

The liturgical movement that began in Europe during the nineteenth century has had a lasting impact on Christian worship.[1] One of its many goals was to address the interrelationship between liturgy and Christian life. Two types of worship practices were prevalent during this time, one emphasizing the sacramental and mediatory power of the official church, and the other emphasizing "the popular" as it was practiced by the laity in daily life and was often viewed with suspicion by the clergy.[2] As a way to articulate this relationship, the ecclesial leaders and liturgical scholars of the movement sought to renew official liturgy, especially the Eucharist, by promoting diverse images of the Eucharist as source (*fons*) and summit (*culmen*) as a means to renew the active participation of the laity during liturgy and, at the same time, to maintain hierarchical control over all other types of worshipful practices. Variations of this image emerged,[3] culminating in article 10 of the *Constitution on the Sacred Liturgy* (1963) which stated that "the liturgy is the summit toward which the activity of the Church is directed" and "the source from which all her power flows."[4]

As a result of the solidification and promotion of the Eucharist as source and summit, less attention was given to articulating a genuine evaluation of popular religious practices in the everyday lives of Christians, at least within official documents. Popular religious practices were defined in relationship to—*in harmony and in accordance with*—official liturgy, while the Eucharist remained above all other worship practices, including the other sacraments. But throughout this process of reordering and solidification, the fluidity of interactions between official liturgy and nonofficial worship practices remained.

In this essay, largely drawn from my doctoral dissertation and subsequent book, I contend that liturgical scholars need to consider the place of non-official worship practices in their reflections on Sunday Eucharist. My goal is to expand the contextual horizon of liturgical scholarship and to include a broader range of worship practices as appropriate subject matter for our inquiry. First, I will entertain Peter Phan's revision of source and summit as a theological paradigm that includes both Eucharist and other, non-official, worship practices, all of which constitute the one worship that humanity renders to God. With this theological perspective as a basis I will introduce the perspectives and methods of sociologists of religion, as well as my own ethnographic exploration of one community's perception of these relationships. It is my contention throughout that by examining the dynamic interrelationship between Sunday Eucharist and other forms of worshipful practice that occur in everyday life, new theological, ecclesiological, and ritual understandings of "liturgy" emerge that expand and inform the contextual horizon of liturgical scholarship.[5]

Peter Phan: The Liturgy of Life as Source and Summit[6]

That the liturgy is the source and summit of church life is not without critique. Peter Phan challenges this theological trajectory by raising "a genuine *quaestio disputata*" regarding the relationship between worship and life.[7] He offers a theological paradigm that does not limit the contextual horizon of liturgical scholarship to eucharistic liturgies alone but, instead, broadens the scope and spectrum of what constitutes "liturgy" by borrowing Karl Rahner's "liturgy of the world" and renaming it "the liturgy of life." Further, Phan proposes that the liturgy of life is the summit and source of the official liturgy *and* popular religion and that *both* of these worship practices *together* constitute the *one* worship that humanity renders to God.

First, drawing from Josef Jungmann, Phan notes the objections and proposed amendments regarding the wording of Article 10 of *Sacrosanctum Concilium* (SC), the *Constitution on the Sacred Liturgy*:

> The summit and goal of the activity of the church [is not the liturgy, but] . . . [but] the salvation of souls and the glory of God; the highest value is not religion, but love; the liturgy was rather a means than an end, the fountain being Christ and the Holy Ghost; the liturgy [as it was presented in this article] appeared here in a sense only very meagerly explained.[8]

Despite these objections Phan acknowledges that the use of the metaphors *culmen* (summit) and *fons* (fount) in Article 10 may be theologically justified.[9] He also highlights the last sentence of Article 10, which states that the activities of the church are directed toward the sanctification of humanity and the glorification of God "as toward their end." Thus, the liturgy should only be viewed as "indirectly" being the summit of church activities.[10]

Phan then asks if the image of source and summit has led to "one-sided theological interpretations and skewed pastoral practices."[11] First, the image of "summit" suggests "a mountain or a pyramid," a medieval paradigm that "sets up a scale of values and willy-nilly devalues all other activities, ecclesial or otherwise, that do not qualify as liturgical or sacramental."[12] The question here is not to deny the *centrality* of the Eucharist for church life but to search for a metaphor that fosters fundamental equality, mutual relationship, reciprocal dependence, openness, change, and novelty in the way the liturgy and the Eucharist interact with the other activities of the church.[13] Second, the metaphor *fons* suggests a "one-way relation between the original source and the body of water that flows out of it . . . from the top to the bottom." This image systematically excludes "any possibility of fecundation and enrichment of the liturgy and the Eucharist by other forms of worship or sacramental celebration, let alone popular devotions and daily life in general."[14] And third, the two metaphors support a post-Tridentine theology that views Christians as living in two different and separate worlds, the secular and the sacred. The larger world, the world of everyday life, the world of Monday through Saturday and even the greater part of Sunday, is secular

and devoid of grace because it is only "nature" and worse, fallen
and sinful.[15]

The Liturgy of Life as the Everyday Mystical Encounters with God[16]

In response to these interpretations and pastoral practices,
Phan wishes to widen the liturgical horizon beyond Sunday Mass
in order to account for the everyday generative experiences and
worship practices through which Christians encounter God. He
draws inspiration from the theological writings of Karl Rahner,
in which *the entire world* is viewed as being wholly permeated
by God's grace:

> Strictly speaking, therefore, there are no secular and sacred
> zones in human history, no profane marketplace and holy
> temple, but only the saved (where God's self-gift is accepted)
> and the damned (where it is rejected).[17]

Due to the permeation of God's grace *in the world*, Christians
are called to be "mystics" in the world, that is, be *attuned* to the
presence of God during everyday moments that would otherwise
go unnoticed. Experiences of God are not rare, one-time moments,
but are available to everyone at all places and at all times. Where
Rahner calls these mystical encounters with God "the liturgy of the
world"/ "the Mass of the world," Phan, for his part, encapsulates
these terms into his own, "the liturgy of life." This includes the
"universal experiences of God and mystical encounters with God's
grace in the midst of everyday life, made possible by God's self-gift
embracing the whole of human history, always and everywhere."[18]
     Phan proposes that the liturgy of life "is the very source of
fecundity and effectiveness of the liturgy of the church," since
"humanity's ongoing communion with God in grace in daily life
is, according to Rahner, the primary and original liturgy." The
worship of God, then, involves those explicit moments when
Christians celebrate these encounters, made even *more explicit*
during the church's official *public* liturgies. But "one-sided theological interpretations and skewed pastoral practices" may result
if Christians do not acknowledge that official liturgies take place
within the wider horizon of these everyday mystical encounters.[19]

By demonstrating how the liturgy of life is the source and summit of the liturgy of the church, Phan essentially sets up a dialectical paradigm between the liturgy of the church and other forms of worship activities. To this end, he considers the place of popular religion within his schema and proposes that, in addition to the liturgy of the church, popular religion may also be viewed as a real symbol of the liturgy of life. Arguing how popular religion has often been placed in a subservient role in relationship to the liturgy of the church, at least in official documents, Phan places popular religion in a more intentional and mutual dialogue with the liturgy of life. He defends how this new paradigm for interrelating popular religion and the liturgy of the church by placing both of these worship practices in alignment with one another, while maintaining the distinctiveness of each. Collectively, these mystical encounters with God's grace in the world create a dynamic and mutual *interdependency* that point toward the unity of the one worship to God through Christ and in the power of the Holy Spirit.

Tools from the Sociology of Lived Religion[20]

How do the manifold religious/spiritual practices that Christian people cultivate create a continuum with their participation in more official liturgical rites, and what kind of reciprocal interactions and mutual influences are/are not created along this continuum?

To help answer this question, I borrow from the fields of sociology and ethnography in order to stretch the contextual horizon of the study of liturgy.

The discipline of sociology, since its beginnings, has taken seriously the relationship between religion and societal analysis. This includes sociologists who have placed religious studies in more intentional dialogue with everyday life, otherwise known as "lived religion."[21] Sociologists of lived religion seek to rethink traditional binary approaches that pitted "official religion" against "popular religion." Lived religion, instead, is located in the middle of these two oppositional categories; that is, it occupies "the space . . . between official . . . and [non-institutional] . . . culture."[22] The intention of these sociologists is to alleviate past approaches to popular religion that presumed a high-low distinction "in which 'official religion' was authoritative and 'real,' in contrast to popular religion, which was presented as constituted by unofficial and even degraded forms."[23] Sociologist Mary Jo Neitz goes even further and suggests that "popular religion" is often "tainted by associations with racist and colonial writings."[24] Further, within this middle space two aspects of lived religion are brought to bear: (1) that lay people enjoy "a certain measure of autonomy"; and (2) that religion encompasses "a range of possibilities, some with the sanction of official religion and others not, or perhaps ambiguously so."[25]

Catherine Bell: Ritualization, and Power

Many of these non-official worship practices could be viewed as ritualization strategies that include power negotiations between what is official and what is non-official. In *Ritual Theory, Ritual Practice,* Catherine Bell critiques past approaches to ritual theory that saw ritual as a vehicle for social control and change.[26] For example, Emile Durkheim postulated that rituals promote social cohesion through the use of dramatic displays. And Max Gluckman and Victor Turner believed that ritual was a means for the channeling of social conflicts that threatened social unity. However, Bell states that ritual does not, in any useful understanding, control or change individuals.

To this extent, I would contend that official liturgies as a form of ritualization do not control individual worshipers. Rather, ritual practices themselves are the very production (location) of power relations. In other words, where Victor Turner located power as preliminarily existing outside the immediate ritual context (i.e., power from the outside-in), Bell does not see the workings of ritual as existing *external* to ritual activities.

Borrowing from the writings of Michel Foucault, among others, Bell demonstrates how ritual practices become the means through which power relations are produced. First, Foucault viewed power as being contingent, relational, organizational, imprecise, and local. This is a different perspective on power from that which presumes power as coercive. For Foucault, power is exercised upon free subjects only insofar as they remain free. The movement of power is not just from top to bottom, but also involves bottom to top. Furthermore, Foucault postulates that it is the social body that becomes the political field in the exercising of power. The body becomes the link between the individual and larger societal frameworks. For Bell, then, ritualization is a way that this form of power is expressed. It is a "political technology of the body."[27] But there are limits in the exercising of ritualization. Because ritualization involves the distinguishing and privileging of certain actions over other actions, the *boundaries* of ritual activities remain flexible and porous. While those in charge of rituals may objectify their office, create a hierarchy of practices, and utilize tools for the purposes of traditionalization, there are certain limits. While those in charge of controlling ritual events may feel empowered, at the same time, practitioners and participants during ritual practices are capable of negotiating various levels of resistance and appropriation.

Five Principles for Enquiry into Practices of Lived Religion

From the works of sociologists Nancy Ammerman, Meredith McGuire, and Giuseppe Giordan, and William Swatos,[28] I have drawn five principles for enquiry into practices of lived religion:
(1)*That a new measuring stick be used to study religious and spiritual practices that broadens the definitional boundaries of "religious practices" and, by extension, worship practices.*
Given the pervasiveness of worship practices in today's modern life, Ammerman[29] calls for a new "measuring stick" with which to observe and analyze how people come to practice everyday religion. She notes that older models of measuring the relationship between religion and society[30] led to predictions that blind faith would one day be replaced by reasoned investigation, that religious traditions would soon fade away as secularization increased. As a result, by the mid-twentieth century, the measuring stick of religion's impact in society had become a "zero-sum" proposition, postulating that the religious sphere and the secular sphere were "tightly bounded against each other."[31]
What these sociologists suggest is that the boundaries between the sacred and the secular, between what constitutes religious practices and what constitutes individual embodied expressions of religious beliefs, are quite permeable. This is due, in part, to the plurality of religious and spirituality practices, including those practices that may be considered "impure" by religious

institutions. Such practices do not necessarily lead to the demise of religion's presence and significance in society. Thus, contrary to past "zero-sum" propositions, the manifestations of religious practices, rituals, and behaviors today cannot be narrowed down to quantitative surveys that list how many people "attend" worship services that are often presumed to be institutionally bounded.

The permeability and fluidity of religious boundaries lead to overlapping and intersecting religious practices that consequently extend definitional boundaries of what constitutes "religion." These sociologists do not subscribe to earlier theories that compartmentalize social domains which, in turn, presume there is no interaction between domains. "Each domain colors the other," since a variety of domains "often exhibit spiritual influences . . . [while other domains] have failed to become spiritually neutral."[32] As such, worship practices, which include devotional, spiritual, and/or institutionally prescribed rituals, occur "in unpredictable places."[33]

(2) *That the insights of nonexperts and nonclerical people be privileged in the study of lived religious practices more than had been the case in the past.*

As I noted earlier, in order to move beyond past approaches to popular religion that presumed a high-low distinction (i.e., "official religion" vs. "popular religion"), sociologists of lived religion, more often than not, focus on the everyday worship practices of "nonexperts," that is, "the people who do not make a living being religious or thinking and writing about religious ideas."[34]

In addition to the term "nonexperts," I would add the term "nonclerical leaders," since some of the studies in these three volumes consider "theological experts" who may not be in positions of clerical leadership as it applies within the Roman Catholic Church.

(3) *That researchers assume the interchangeability of the terms and understandings of "religious" and "spiritual."*

One of the themes that often comes up in these works is the interchangeability between the terms "religious" and "spiritual" or, as Swatos and Giordan describe, the perceived "religious-spiritual contrast."[35] While acknowledging the complex history of how Western Christian writers and thinkers came to define "spirituality" (often in contrast to "religion"),[36] most of these sociologists promote an approach that is more in line with Wade Clark Roof's call for an integrated analysis of both terms. Roof borrows Robert Wuthnow's observation that practices of religion, over the past half-century, have led to juxtapositions of "dwelling" and "seeking," particularly during practices of lived religion. Roof suggests that "dwelling" and "seeking" are better viewed as "modes of apprehending the spiritual, either through existing rituals and symbolic systems or through more open-ended, exploratory ways."[37] Sociologists of lived religion suggest an ethnographic method that pays closer attention to how subjects often use these terms interchangeably.

(4) *That attention be given to the micro-level and macro-level negotiations of religious and spiritual identities of those studied.*

Cathy Holtmann's study of Catholic women is a prime example of why sociologists of lived religion use the term "negotiation" as a chief metaphor when examining how their subjects interchange religious identities and "spiritual options." The "multiple solidarities" that lead to the "permeability of institutional boundaries" (as noted above) may lead to various negotiations of social action that occur "between predictability and improvisation."[38]

(5) *That narrative analysis be used as an ethnographic tool in the study of everyday worship practices.*

Ammerman writes that, unlike "didactic lessons or moral recipes," which often mark the literature of theological experts and official leaders, narratives allow for the unfolding of plots, characters, relationships, and motivations that often mark the everyday lives of people. These stories may include "ritual interruptions" or other activities that "may be more or less explicit."[39] In a previous study of the linkages between one's religious identity and the religious institutional affiliation, Ammerman proposes that the study of "narrative construction" allows social scientists to "move past the words themselves" and calls for a closer attention "to the *relationships* and *actions* that give words their meaning" (emphasis in original).[40]

While my list of five summary points does not intend to be exhaustive, it does provide other possibilities of how one might frame the wider sociocultural context within which practices of religiosities and spiritualities occur. A church building where such practices may occur is just one among many locations. One should also consider domestic, leisure, and workplace locations, particularly since these "social domains" often intersect with one another. Sociologists of lived religion privilege locations outside of institutional boundaries as starting points of inquiry, but they also remain open to how individuals and collective social groups perform these practices within and around these boundaries. Each social actor and/or social group, in turn, negotiates varying levels of membership, ritual participation, power, and accountability, often doing so simultaneously.

Ethnographic Study

From February 2010 to May 2013, I pursued ethnographic research within one Catholic community in San Francisco, St. Agnes Church, seeking to delve deeper into experiences of lived religion of eight of its members.[41] This includes some of my participant observations of the community's Sunday 10:30 a.m. eucharistic liturgies. Mary McGann writes:

> The purpose of liturgical ethnography is to open to new insight, to receive new paradigms, to make new connections, to welcome fresh deposits of spirit. Its goal is appreciation rather than critique, understanding rather than evaluation. Within the work of liturgical studies, which necessarily seeks to establish normativity, contemplative ethnographic scholarship can bring to light and reflect on the salience of these new paradigms. For this reason it is integral to the work of critical liturgiology, inviting new paradigms to both confirm and critique our existing normative claims. It introduces new hermeneutics into the fabric of interpretive liturgiology, a process essential to a liturgical scholarship that can truly serve a world church.[42]

The interpretations that I gleaned from in-depth interviews explored the community's everyday worship practices and how they interrelate these practices with Sunday Eucharist.[43] How do they perceive the sources and the summits of their lives? What metaphors do *they* use and how do they express this through measurable practices of everyday religion and relate these practices to Sunday Eucharist? Here are eight samples of what I learned from my subjects regarding these interrelationships.[44]

Helen Rosario

- Feelings (as distinct from more abstract theological/doc-trinal statements) expressed through the recalling of past memories fortify different degrees of personal favorites and personal "sources and summits" among a variety of worship practices.

- While favorite prayer forms may emerge and distinctions may be made between various everyday worship practices (including daily Mass), God and not the Eucharist [accord-ing to Helen] is the source and summit of her life and this may be perceived as showing no discrimination among the variety of prayer forms.

Edward Williams

- Positive experiences of community and fellowship can mo-tivate more participation during communal worship rituals, while negative experiences can lead to the abandonment of official worship participation.

Jude Pendland

- Everyday worship practices may utilize different objects and resources as aid during ritual performances, includ-ing prayer booklets and electronic tools such as iPads and iPhones.

- Everyday worship practices may coincide with functional activities, such as drinking coffee and taking medicine, or be integrated with other prayer forms, such as meal blessings.

Rachel Durst

- God as "source and summit" may be expressed in different ways within the same person during individual, ecclesial, and familial worship practices and contexts.

Irene and James Robinson

- One's spiritual life is not contingent upon weekly participa-tion in official liturgies.

Helen Chen Abrams

- Non-theological or non-liturgical terms, such as "my family," may become expressions of what constitutes the source and summit of one's life. While family members may become a source of support "on earth," God may still be perceived as the source of everything else.

The nonexperts of my study demonstrate the complexity of worship practices that continually and inextricably become "woven through the fabric of human life." As a result, they demonstrate that the official worship boundaries of St. Agnes Church remain porous, while, at the same time new paradigms are created for how we may approach the interrelationship of Sunday Eucharist and the everyday worship practices of religiosities and spiritualities.

Ethnographic Study Assessment[45]

From my ethnographic project, I learned that nonexperts interrelate various forms of worship practices in their everyday lives and, at times, develop and sustain their own degrees of reordering their worship practices. Among these interrelationships, four themes emerged in my assessment:

(1) Communal and Emotional Links

There exist communal and emotionally embodied links between worship forms, and these links between persons and communities could be potential starting points in accessing and reflecting upon the interrelationship of worship forms. During my participant observations of the annual *Flores de Mayo* devotion, I noticed how the eyes of several worshipers would well up with tears during the recitation of the rosary; the linkage between their affiliation with the group provided a safe environment for the display of feelings and emotions.

To a large measure, these examples of interrelating worship practices demonstrate one of the reasons why I chose to pursue an ethnographic component to my dissertation: namely, the official documents and the writings of liturgical theologians more often than not focus on prayer *forms*, theological doctrine, and/or ritual prescriptions in their attempts to interrelate worship practices. What remained missing in these past approaches were descriptions of the heartfelt rituals and emotionally embodied sensibilities and negotiations by the worshipers themselves and how these sensibilities and negotiations influenced what for them constituted worship.

(2) Hybrid Prayer Forms with Functional Needs

There is an integration of functional needs (including the use of cultural products) and the creation of hybrid prayer forms during the ritual performances of everyday worship practices. In official documents consideration of legitimizing hybrid worship forms remained mostly non-existent, primarily due to the efforts of the pioneers of the liturgical movement to demarcate popular religious practices from official worship practices. In the interrelationship of everyday worship practices I learned that worshipers often utilize cultural products, such as electronic devices or prayer books, as worship aids during ritual performances: e.g., an iPad for morning and evening prayer or an iPhone. What we learn is that technological "gadgets" that are used during the performance of worship rituals are simultaneously used for other non-worship practices, such as making phone calls and using other apps. This does not assume that concern over the usages of cultural products during the liturgical movement does not exist, nor that worshipers' usages of technological products are only a contemporary phenomenon that has not been investigated by liturgical theologians.[46] My point is that these products may contribute to the dialogue between official and nonofficial worship practices since the products themselves (as well as the worshippers who use them) cross boundaries between designated social domains (a hospital office, the inside of a train, a sidewalk in downtown Chicago) as they also interact with one another.

(3) Expansion of Ecclesial Boundaries and Identities

There is an expansion of ecclesial worship boundaries as a result of interrelating worship practices. For Irene and James, the starting point of their experiences of worship is located *outside* of official worship, as well as beyond official expectations of accountability (for example, the church's teaching on the weekly obligation of Sunday eucharistic worship); there is an interplay between the terms "spirituality" and "religion": while both Irene and James use the term "spirituality" to describe their everyday worship practices.

(4) Expansion of Academic Inquiry

And fourth, as an extension, there is an expansion of academic inquiry of the liturgy of life as the result of interrelating *associative terms* for source and summit by nonexperts and nonclergy. Regarding this last and fourth assessment point, some qualifications remain in order. At one level, it would be unfair to evaluate my subjects' responses to these questions with the same academic criteria of official statements and the writings by liturgical theologians. The official and theological writers used the phrase "source and summit" as an overarching term and metaphor in order to articulate the relationship and interplay between official liturgy and all other activities in Christian life. Having stated this, I wanted to learn and discover how nonexperts came to associate these popularly used terms which were/are often used in theological discourse. My aim was not to pit the written discourse by theological experts up against nonexperts, but rather to use their responses as a means to stretch my own imagination and develop conceptual tools for how their experiences and associations may inform and even expand present academic inquiry on this subject. Further, what we can learn from their answers could influence pastoral implementation of interrelating official and nonofficial worship practices.

The Liturgy of Life and Divine Initiative[47]

I will place the fruits of what I have learned from my ethnographic project and demonstrate how they complement and align with a current concern of the primacy of the divine initiative in liturgical theology, that is, a concern of how liturgical scholars, in their reflection of what liturgical events mean theologically, maintain the primacy of God acting upon the assembly during worship, rather than placing more emphasis on what the assembly does.

In 2003 Kevin Irwin expressed concern that the issue of maintaining reflection on the divine initiative in liturgical scholarship remains one of the more critical issues that liturgical theologians face today. He writes:

> There is a delicate balance in liturgy: divine initiative and human response, the action of God and the sanctification

of humanity. How one "achieves" this is part and parcel of liturgy as an art and a craft. . . . But even then it is not about what *we* achieve but what God works among us and through us.[48]

In 2007 Michael Aune rearticulated Irwin's concern in his own assessment of the state of liturgical theology. Agreeing with Irwin that the field of liturgical theology needs "to recover once again an awareness of God's initiative, the divine action in liturgy—what God does among us and for us," Aune states that "awareness" of divine action in liturgy "has been all but lost or certainly overshadowed in the nearly endless emphasis on church, assembly, and so on."[49]

One of the hallmarks of Phan's proposal, namely, that "the liturgy of life and the liturgy of the church constitute the one worship that humanity renders to God and whose center and supreme fulfillment is Jesus Christ," is that it better articulates and more directly maintains the divine initiative during acts of official and nonofficial worship practices than the phrase "the liturgy/Eucharist is the source and summit of Christian life." In the liturgy of life, God is viewed as *The Source* from whom all Christian life and activity flows and *The Summit* toward which all Christian life and activity returns. Recall the articulation of how God was viewed as source and summit was one of the four points of resistance and debate over Article 10 of SC during Vatican II. Yet a careful reading of the last sentence of Article 10, as Phan demonstrated, reveals that *all* activities of the church are directed toward the sanctification of humanity and the glorification of God . . . "as toward their end."

It is my assertion that the contextual field upon which official and nonofficial worshipful practices transpire will always need to be considered seriously and placed in continuous dialogue with the historical and the theological for two reasons. First, the call to utilize tools from the social sciences (such as sociology and ethnography in my case) and to consider the cultural context of liturgical practice remains faithful to the pastoral vision of the Second Vatican Council. Second, as long as liturgical scholarship exists and liturgical theologians continue to reflect upon the liturgy theologically, there will always be a need to qualify the cultural assumptions and contextual locations of each scholar. Recall that the development of how the liturgy and the Eucharist came to be solidified (as the source and summit of Christian life) has largely been a Western enterprise. Because the demographic backgrounds of my subjects represented a cross-section of race, gender, sexual orientation, age, and ethnicity, the interpretive data that emerged became a richer and deeper reservoir from which to correlate the theological and the historical components that were raised.

What my study has demonstrated is that dialogue with the social sciences, including the call to consider more intentionally the expanding sociocultural context of worship through sociological and ethnographic tools, could not only lead to new paradigms of how we come to understand *what* liturgy is and *how* liturgy is performed, but do so while maintaining the divine initiative. Furthermore, theological reflections and frameworks that take these interrelational dynamics into account could lead to other articulations and variations of the term "source and summit," variations that are capable of maintaining the primacy of God's divine action:

- *God,* as experienced and explicitly expressed in the eucharistic liturgies that take place within communal settings, *is the source and summit of Christian life.*
- *God,* as experienced and expressed during the everyday worship practices of the liturgy of life, *is the source and summit of Christian life.*
- *God,* as experienced and expressed during celebrations of the Eucharist in the immediate presence of friends, loved ones, and family members and through affective ritual expressions and embodiment, *is the source and summit of Christian life.*

The chief metaphor that arises from these worship experiences remains the liturgy of life, a liturgy whose scope and spectrum of interactional worship activities communally and officially centers around the Eucharistic liturgy, and a liturgy whose end goal is the sanctification of humanity and the glorification of God. It consists of our individual and communal grace-filled responses to the spectrum of mystical experiences of everyday life, experiences that are initiated by God who continually invites us to deepen our relationship with the Triune God and with one another.[50]

Finally, we must be attentive to new and developing concerns with regard to the ever-expanding contextual horizon of worship practices. In more recent times, an emerging subfield within the sociology of religion has been focusing on "religion, media and culture" and "religion and digital culture."[51] In my book, I touch upon some of the implications that the use of electronic devices (the iPad and iPhone) may have in the interrelationship dynamics between worship practices. My concern is that liturgical theologians may ignore the very likelihood that such forms of worship practices will increase among Christian worshippers and that the acceleration rate of advancing technologies may, in the end, outpace exclusive foci on historical and theological considerations.

Notes

[1] The following text from my plenary address draws mostly from my book, *The Liturgy of Life: The Interrelationship of Sunday Eucharist and Everyday Worship Practices* (Collegeville, MN: Liturgical Press, 2014).

[2] See Edward Muir, *Ritual in Early Modern Europe*, 2nd ed. (Cambridge: Cambridge University Press, 2005), 224; Mark C. Francis, "Liturgy and Popular Piety in a Historical Perspective," in *Directory on Popular Piety and the Liturgy: Principles and Guidelines: A Commentary*, ed. Peter C. Phan (Collegeville, MN: Liturgical Press, 2005), and his more recent *Local Worship, Global Church: Popular Religion and the Liturgy* (Collegeville, MN: Liturgical Press, 2014).

[3] Chapter 2 of *The Liturgy of Life* presents how the terms "source" (*fons*) and "summit" (*culmen*) and other terms were used throughout the movement, including citations from the writings of Dom Prosper Gueranger, Leo XIII, Pius X, Dom Lambert Beauduin, Virgil Michel, and Pius XII. In my analysis and correlation of these variations, three threads emerged: (1) there were more uses of the term *fons* than the term *culmen* in the interplay between official liturgy and practices of popular religion; (2) while the majority of writings referred to "the liturgy" as *fons*, Pius XII specifically located *fons* in the person of Jesus Christ (*Mystici Corporis Christi*, Articles 9, 51, and 56), while other writings demonstrated an interchange of locations between liturgy and Jesus Christ; and (3) there was more variety of opinions concerning what effects flowed out of the *fons* of liturgy, thus indicating the attempts by these writers to consider all forms of worshipful practices.

[4] The following year, Article 11 of the *Dogmatic Constitution on the Church* (1964) reasserted this relationship, but further specified "the eucharistic sacrifice" as "the source and summit of the whole Christian life." And Article 5 of the *Decree on the Ministry and Life of Priests* (1965) stated that "the Eucharist shows itself as the source and summit of the whole work of preaching the Gospel."

[5] Manalo, *Liturgy of Life*, 11-12.

[6]Ibid., ch. 4.

[7]Peter C. Phan, "Liturgy of Life as Summit and Source of Eucharistic Liturgy: Church Worship as Symbolization of Liturgy of Life?" in *Being Religious Interreligiously: Asian Perspectives on Interfaith Dialogue in Postmodernity,* by Peter C. Phan (Maryknoll, NY: Orbis Books, 2004), 257-78. An earlier version of this article appeared as "Liturgy of Life as the 'Summit and Source' of the Eucharistic Liturgy: Church Worship as Symbolization of the Liturgy of Life?" in *Incongruities: Who We Are and How We Pray,* ed. Timothy Fitzgerald and David A. Lysik (Chicago: Liturgy Training Publications, 2000), 5-33.

[8]Josef Andreas Jungmann, "Constitution on the Sacred Liturgy," in *Commentary on the Documents of Vatican II,* vol. 1, ed. Herbert Vorgrimler (New York: Herder and Herder, 1967), 15. In Manalo, *Liturgy of Life,* 86.

[9]See Phan, "Liturgy of Life as Summit and Source," 260.

[10]In addition to this justification, Phan presents a second theological argument for the inclusion of these metaphors: namely, the liturgy's efficacy since "[n]o other action of the church is said to equal its efficacy 'by the same title and to the same degree' " (Article 7). If the supreme excellence of the Eucharist "lies in the special presence of Christ 'in the Eucharistic species,' " then this needs to be understood in relationship with the other modes of Christ's presence, as stated in SC 7: Christ is present in the minister, in the word of God, and in the assembly (Ibid., 260-61).

[11]Ibid., 261.

[12]Ibid., 261-262.

[13]Ibid., 262.

[14]Ibid., 262.

[15]Ibid., 262-263.

[16]Manalo, *Liturgy of Life,* 90.

[17]Phan, "Liturgy of Life as Summit and Source," 267.

[18]Ibid., 268-269.

[19]Ibid., 271.

[20]Manalo, *Liturgy of Life,* ch. 5.

[21]The American roots of this field of inquiry may be traced back to September 1994, when a group of mostly historians of religion and a few ethnographers were invited to Harvard Divinity School in Cambridge, Massachusetts, for a conference known as "the lived religion project." The project, headed by David D. Hall, focused on perspectives on how Christians practiced their religious beliefs in everyday life during different time periods of American history. See David D. Hall, *Lived Religion in America: Toward a History of Practice,* ed. David D. Hall (Princeton, NJ: Princeton University Press, 1997).

[22]Ibid., viii.

[23]Mary Jo Neitz, "Lived Religion: Signposts of Where We Have Been and Where We Can Go From Here," in *Religion, Spirituality and Everyday Practices,* ed. Giuseppe Giordan and William H. Swatos, Jr. (New York/Heidelberg, Germany: Springer, 2011), 47.

[24]Ibid., 47.

[25]Hall, *Lived Religion,* viii.

[26]Catherine Bell, *Ritual Theory, Ritual Practice* (Oxford: Oxford University Press, 1992). The third section of this monumental work is devoted to ritual

and power. This portion of my essay specifically draws from pp. 197-223.
[27]Ibid., 202.

[28]Nancy T. Ammerman, ed., *Everyday Religion: Observing Modern Religious Lives* (Oxford: Oxford University Press, 2007); Meredith McGuire, *Lived Religion: Faith and Practice in Everyday Life* (Oxford: Oxford University Press, 2008); Giordan and Swatos, eds., *Religion, Spirituality and Everyday Practices*.

[29]In addition to Ammerman and McGuire, the contributors to *Everyday Religion* include Grace Davie, Enzo Pace, Lynn Davidman, Lynn Schofield Clark, Mia Lövheim, Peggy Levitt, Ziad Munson, Paul Lichterman, John P. Bartkowski, Kelly Besecke, and Courtney J. Bender.

[30]Here she quotes Max Weber who "envisioned a trajectory from Calvinist shopkeepers to heartless capitalists." Weber, *The Protestant Ethic and the Spirit of Capitalism* (New York: Scribner, 1958), 181-82, quoted in Ammerman, *Everyday Religion*, 3.

[31]Ammerman, *Everyday Religion*, 9.
[32]Ibid.
[33]Ibid.
[34]Ibid., 5.

[35]In the introduction to their book, Swatos and Giordan write: "These chapters take up the religious-spiritual contrast specifically through investigations into *practice*: In what ways do people who claim to be 'religious' or 'spiritual' define these self-images as manifest in their own lives? How do people who make this contrast believe people who see themselves in these ways implement their convictions in practice (or should implement them)? We also explore whether there are institutions of spiritual practice to which those who term themselves 'spiritual' turn or whether the difference implied by these terms may instead be between institutionalized and de-institutionalized expressions of practice, including but not limited to self-spiritualities" ("The Spiritual 'Turn' in Religion as Process and Outcome," in *Religion, Spirituality and Everyday Practice*, xi.)

[36]Linda Woodhead names five historical aspects: (1) early spirituality as a radicalization and "Easternization" of liberal Christianity; (2) ritual, esotericism and nativism in Christianity and spirituality; (3) New Age and its parallels with charismatic-evangelical Christianity; (4) the holistic turn in spirituality and its links to "lived" religion in the West; and (5) contemporary neo-Paganism and its links with Christian tradition, ritual, and place. See her "Spirituality and Christianity: The Unfolding of a Tangled Relationship," in *Religion, Spirituality and Everyday Practice*, 3-21.

[37]Wade Clark Roof, "Religion and Spirituality: Toward an Integrated Analysis," in *Handbook of the Sociology of Religion*, ed. Michele Dillon (New York: Cambridge University Press, 2003), 139. Roof draws on Robert Wuthnow, *After Heaven: Spirituality in America since the 1950s* (Princeton, NJ: Princeton University Press, 1998), 3.

[38]Cathy Holtmann, "Workers in the Vineyard: Catholic Women and Social Action," in *Religion, Spirituality, and Everyday Practice*, 228.

[39]Ammerman, *Everyday Religion*, 226.

[40]Ammerman writes: "If we are to understand the nature of identity in a

complex world that involves multiple solidarities that both constrain and are continually reconstructed, we need a dynamic mode of analysis that moves beyond categorizing words and analyzing syntax . . . . Narrative . . . renders an event understandable by connecting it to a set of relationships and practices—historically and spatially, particular people doing socially patterned things" (Ammerman, "Religious Identities and Religious Institutions," in *Handbook of the Sociology of Religion*, 213).

[41]My ethnographic methodology primarily draws upon scholars who, each in their own way, consider the porous and fluid boundaries of ethnographic field sites. These include Mary E. McGann, *A Precious Fountain: Music in the Worship of an African American Catholic Community* (Collegeville, MN: Liturgical Press, 2004); and James Clifford, *Routes: Travel and Translation in the Late Twentieth Century* (Cambridge, MA: Harvard University Press, 1997).

[42]McGann, *Precious Fountain*, xx.

[43]A general introduction to the worship life of St. Agnes parish and the backgrounds of the eight participants is presented in ch. 1 and the appendices. Quotes from the eight ethnographic participants that emerged from my interviews are interwoven throughout *The Liturgy of Life*, usually at the beginning of each chapter.

[44]Manalo, *Liturgy of Life*, 147-149.

[45]Ibid., ch. 7.

[46]For an historical survey of Christians' use of worship aids, see Edward Foley, *From Age to Age: How Christians Have Celebrated the Eucharist: Revised and Expanded Edition* (Chicago: Liturgy Training Publications, 2008). For the historic development of the use of modern technological products during worship, see Eileen D. Crowley, *Liturgical Art for a Media Culture* (Collegeville, MN: The Liturgical Press, 2007).

[47]Manalo, *Liturgy of Life*, 162-174.

[48]Kevin W. Irwin, "A Spirited Community Encounters Christ: Liturgical and Sacramental Theology and Practice," in *Catholic Theology Facing the Future: Historical Perspectives*, ed. Dermot A. Lane (Mahwah, NJ: Paulist, 2003), 120.

[49]Michael B. Aune, "Liturgy and Theology: Rethinking the Relationship—Part One," *Worship* 81 (January 2007): 47. Aune sharply critiques the line of liturgical scholarship which he calls "The Schmemann-Kavanaugh-Fagerberg-Lathrop line of liturgical theology." Alexander Schmemann, in seeking to articulate the relationship between worship and theology, placed emphasis on the ecclesial context of liturgy as starting point, to the detriment of the primacy of God's action.

[50]Manalo, *Liturgy of Life*, 171.

[51]See Eric Michael Mazur and Kate McCarthy, eds., *God in the Details: American Religion in Popular Culture*, 2d ed. (New York: Routledge, 2011); Gordon Lynch, Jolyon Mitchell, and Anna Strhan, eds., *Religion, Media and Culture: A Reader* (New York: Routledge, 2012); Daniel A. Stout, *Media and Religion: Foundations of an Emerging Field* (New York: Routledge, 2012); Rachel Wagner, *Godwired: Religion, Ritual, and Virtual Reality* (New York: Routledge, 2012). In the field of liturgical studies, see Teresa Berger et al., in *Liturgy in Migration: From the Upper Room to Cyberspace*, ed. Teresa Berger (Collegeville, MN: Liturgical Press, 2012).

Words Uttered by God

Reformulating "Source and Summit" Language with Karl Rahner

Michael Rubbelke

Working to unite creatures to God's Self, God's power operates in the church through both the liturgy and Christians' actions in the broader world. However, balancing these sites of divine power proves difficult. *Sacrosanctum Concilium* focuses attention on the liturgy as a site where the church preeminently receives power from God: "Nevertheless the liturgy is the summit toward which the activity of the Church is directed; at the same time it is the font [or source] from which all her power flows" (no. 10).[1] Even though the constitution situates the liturgy in the context of non-liturgical worship and everyday life in its surrounding paragraphs, this statement is often cited by itself and out of context.[2]

Peter Phan and Ricky Manalo rightfully argue that "liturgy as summit and source" language seems to disconnect God's power from life outside the sanctuary. According to Phan, referring to ecclesial liturgy as "source and summit" without qualification separates the liturgy from spiritual practices and social action.[3] Phan prefers to say: "[I]t is the liturgy of life that is the summit and source of the church liturgy and not the other way around."[4] Agreeing with Phan's assessment, Manalo prefers to speak of God as the source and summit of the liturgy and everyday life.[5] In their revisions, Phan and Manalo appeal to Karl Rahner's understanding of "the liturgy of the world." Rahner argues that grace does not emerge from restricted sacred spaces to affect an otherwise profane world; rather, liturgies efficaciously manifest God's power welling up in the experiences of everyday life.[6] These reformulations correctly rectify an imbalance, but they risk underemphasizing the church's liturgy as a site of God's power.

Using "source and summit" language, can one balance liturgy and world as sites of encountering God's power in the church? Drawing on Rahner's theologies of prayer and the Word of God, I want to argue for an alternative construction: "becoming *a* word of God to the world is the source and summit of Christian life, and this is revealed and empowered by *the* Word of God, Who is the source and summit of the church's liturgy."[7] For Rahner, prayer is a dialogue in which God's word to human beings is themselves "as those who are spoken by God."[8] He further argues that everyday choices—discerned in light of God's will—concretely express one's identity as a word of God. Becoming a word of God is thus intrinsically tied to life outside the sanctuary. Moreover, Rahner claims that the person's status as a word of God receives definitive illumination from the Word of God, Jesus Christ, and His continuing presence in church and sacraments. Becoming *a* word of God only has meaning in light of *the* Word of God, including the Word's liturgical expression.[9]

My argument will proceed in three parts. After first briefly elaborating Rahner's understanding of prayer, a second part will explore key characteristics of both human words as primordial words and the Word of God seen analogically in Christ, the church, and the sacraments. Finally, the implications of becoming a word of God will be both unfolded in light of Rahner's treatment of the Word of God and related to the formulation above. The argument thus primarily offers a coherent interpretation of Rahner to support this formula. Given the essay's aims, limited attention will be paid to broader critiques of these Rahnerian elements.

Prayer's Response: Becoming a "Word of God"

In his 1973 essay "Dialogue with God?" Rahner applied his definition of human beings as hearers of revelation in the context of prayer.[10] According to Rahner, the divine-human dialogue cannot be univocally compared with a creaturely dialogue.[11] God's utter transcendence ensures that this dialogue is *sui generis*. The one praying "does not hear 'something' additional to himself as to someone presupposed in his inert facticity."[12] Prayer's answer does not come as something added onto an otherwise unaffected human being; it is not an additional quality or external object which would affect the one praying by efficient causality. Rather, the answer to prayer is the person "himself as the word spoken to him, in which God constitutes him a hearer and to whom He promises Himself as answer."[13] God's answer to prayer is the person concretely existing in relationship to God as one open to becoming a word of God.

Becoming a word of God emerges concretely in everyday life insofar as the one praying discerns and does God's will. For Rahner, discernment is the process of testing options for choice in terms of how they restrict or enlarge one's openness to God. Discernment is successful when the person chooses the option which best renders her actions and herself open to God. As such, the human being can understand her choices as enabling her to become a word of God. Even if such discernment can be provisional or even erroneous, it "is here and now the best medium of this indifferent, transcendental openness in which man knows himself as God's spoken word and consequently salvifically God's will."[14] By discerning and choosing to do God's will, a person allows herself to be open to God, that is, to become a word of God spoken into her concrete situation by means of a particular choice.

Prayer thus reveals that a human being can become a word of God in every situation. For Rahner, the dialogue of prayer requires human beings to be open to God and thus to receive themselves as a word of God. Everyday choices and actions which keep the person most open to God's initiative are the concrete expression of God's word in response to prayer.

Human Words and the Word of God

Rahner's philosophical-theological reflections on human primordial words further illustrate what becoming a word entails. In his 1956 essay "Priest and Poet" Rahner describes the poet as the one who speaks the human word in its concentrated essence: as the primordial word (*Urwort*).[15] In dialogue with Heidegger, Rahner describes everyday speech in terms of instrumental-technical words which divide things, distance the hearer from things, clarify things, and master things. In contrast, primordial words unify things, incarnate things, obscure things, and master the hearer.[16]

The poet reveals three characteristics about human words. First, words can show a particular thing in its mysterious and obscure unity with all reality: that is, a primordial word can manifest a being in unity with other beings and against the whole of Being.[17] Second, the human word can incarnate the thought and the thing described within the poetic form. Primordial words serve as the bodily form of thought insofar as they make thought and the object uniquely present to the senses.[18] Third, the human word can reconcile the speaker's being and consciousness, intimately uniting her with the world. Primordial words effect an aesthetic return to a prelapsarian Eden, before concupiscence cleaved the natural and personal as well as the inner and outer of human beings.[19]

Rahner decisively parts ways with Heidegger when he indicates that human primordial words need to be completed by God's Word.[20] Rahner contrasts the poet—the speaker of human primordial words—and the priest—the speaker of God's Word—on two major points. First, the poet speaks the *human* word which, for Rahner, is a question about God which only gestures toward this distant infinite: "it does not bring and contain *the* infinite."[21] The priest, meanwhile, speaks *God's* Word as an answer to this question. God's Word is the divine Self-revelation that communicates God's life to human beings and brings them into ultimate proximity to this divine mystery. Second, the poet's primordial word unites being and consciousness in herself in a purely aesthetic reconciliation. The priest makes present the Incarnate Word of God Who eternally reconciles everything in Himself.

For Rahner, God's power in the world decisively depends upon the Word of God, revealing God's Self-offer to human beings and empowering them to accept God. This divine Word is an analogous reality, descending from Christ to the church to the sacraments and beyond. Throughout these different modes of presence, certain consistent characteristics emerge. These are most visible in the primordial Word of God: Jesus Christ, the revelation and promise of God's victorious Self-offer.

First, God does not wish to speak a purely divine Word apart from human beings. Rather the definitive and final Word of God is spoken in Christ, the God-Human. Jesus is the perfect union of the human question about God—that is, the human primordial word—and the divine answer manifested in this question.[22]

Second, the Word of God is historically and tangibly manifested in Jesus's life, death, and resurrection. Jesus is the definitive and ultimate Self-offer and Self-revelation of God in everything pertaining to Him. His words, His actions, His deeds manifest what God's Word is to human beings; they show what divinized life—life completely liberated into God's power—looks like in historical and concrete terms. Furthermore, for Rahner, Jesus's life "becomes final and definitive through death."[23] In death, all that Jesus was and did is crystallized. His last words on the cross show both the agony of the human question about God—"My God, my God, why have you forsaken me?" (Matthew 27:46; Mark 15:34)—and the total self-surrender of the human into God—"Father, into Your hands I commend my spirit" (Luke 23:46). This death only becomes "complete" and "manifest historically" in the Father's acceptance of it as God's answer to the human question, that is, in the resurrection.[24] The Father accepts and upholds Jesus's life to all eternity, such that the life of this human being can never be seen apart from God's own life.[25]

Finally, the Word of God is efficaciously triumphant. From the Cross and Resurrection forward, God's own Trinitarian life becomes manifest and triumphantly present as the destiny of human beings and all creation.[26] Looking to the crucified and risen Jesus, we need not fear that God will withdraw from us into the infinite Mystery and reject us from God's life. Only our own choice can do this. In Christ, the history of God's Self-offer in grace which pervades the whole history of the world becomes manifest, pledged, and irreversibly triumphant.[27] Christ's cross and resurrection concretely reveals the victorious reach of God's life into all situations, even into the maw of death.

The church is a derivative but analogous Word of God: Christ's continuing presence in history. Like Christ, first, the church is human. It is a community of persons through whose human rituals, words, and actions God's life becomes manifest. Second, while God's Self-offer occurs outside the church and while the church is composed of sinners, the church is God's Word uttered to the world in a uniquely visible and social form "as an ongoing event with historical tangibility and with incarnational corporeality."[28] This historical and incarnate tangibility makes Christ present in many modes, from the words of Scripture and preaching to the eucharistic words of institution.[29] Finally, Rahner views the church as the Word of God's efficaciously triumphant presence in two supreme realizations: the sacraments and the saints.[30] In these, the church is the Word of God's triumphant and efficacious offer of the divine life to the whole world, making it the "basic sacrament of the salvation of the world."[31]

Sacraments are Christ's mode of presence in the church as objective word-events which illuminate the recipient's identity as a word of God and conform the recipient to the Word of God in the most decisive life-situations.[32] First, sacraments are always composed of human words. Second, through these words, God's Word becomes incarnate and historically tangible. This is primordially the case in the eucharistic liturgy where Christ's words at the Last Supper make the Crucified and Risen One present. Sacraments are the visible manifestation of God's victorious Self-offer in Christ *within* the world—not interrupting the world—for its transformation. Finally, as word-events, they effect what they signify precisely *by* signifying (e.g., the baptized is plunged into the death of Christ).

Rahner inseparably links the sacramental and non-liturgical manifestations of God's power. Considered solely in the sacraments' signifying, Christ is present and manifest as God's irreversibly victorious Word. However, the sacraments are not intended only as liturgical significations. They are meant to illuminate human persons and empower them to accept God's Word in the whole of their lives. For Rahner, there are not two ways to God—sacramental/liturgical and individual/mundane—but one. The sacraments allow the person to accept God's life and thus become *a* word of God.[33]

Implications for Liturgy and Everyday Life

Extrapolating from Rahner's account, a person who becomes a word of God shares certain characteristics of primordial words and the Word of God. Reflecting the unifying function of primordial words, the person who opens herself to God is dynamically oriented to opening every level of her being and every circumstance of her life to God. She is meant to incarnate her reality as a word of God in the whole of her life, and this transformation gradually diminishes the disparity between nature and person as well as being and consciousness. Finally, becoming a word of God entails participation in the manifest, irreversible, and efficacious victory of the Word of God in Christ. It is the manifestation of grace's victory over sin in a person's life. This participation occurs socially in the church and extends—like the sacraments—to all important aspects of human life.[34] The believer is meant, in other words, to become a word of God in the liturgy of the world: a word spoken into her worldly situation as an efficacious manifestation of God's victory in Christ.

Rahner's theologies of prayer and the Word of God thus can generate "source and summit" language that gives equal weight to the liturgy and the non-liturgical world as sites of God's power. The sacramental liturgy serves as a continuing manifestation of the efficaciously triumphant Word of God, Jesus Christ, present in His church. This liturgical presence illuminates the deepest reality of personal prayer and openness to God in discernment, and it empowers a person to become a word of God to the world. One can relate liturgical and non-liturgical action vis-à-vis God's power in this way: "becoming *a* word of God to the world is the source and summit of Christian life, and this is revealed and empowered by *the* Word of God, Who is the source and summit of the church's liturgy."

This reformulation explicitly connects the liturgical and non-liturgical operation of divine power in Christological terms. As Rahner insists, becoming *a* word of God depends upon openness to God, and ultimately *the* Word of God simply is this total openness to the Father. At its most intense, Christ's greatest openness to the Father occurs on the cross and in His validation by the Father in the resurrection. The openness which lets one become a word of God can be seen as an entrance into the Paschal Mystery, represented in the Eucharist. Choices stemming from this openness make personal participation in the Paschal Mystery concretely present today.

Moreover, if becoming *a* word of God becomes most visible in the process of discerning God's will, the dichotomy between liturgy and spirituality or socio-political action disappears. Becoming aware of how particular choices allow or restrict one from being open to God depends on a profound level of discernment. A word of God cannot exist only in personal depths; what is most interior must somehow be expressed, and a person's everyday life becomes a site into which God can speak her. This emphasis on discernment also preserves a level of freedom for persons to act in the many different ways that the Spirit of God in Christ can lead. God speaks to new situations with unique words, and becoming a word of God entails a readiness for being surprised. This new formulation runs up against certain limitations as well. Rahner might ask if and how a non-Christian could become a word of God.[35] How consciously available *can* one's openness to God be? One might also ask about the liturgy's communal and transformative significance for individual Christians, which seems underplayed here. Finally, the Christological focus calls for a more robust pneumatological balance. Though these concerns cannot be answered within this essay, they would be well worth addressing from the perspective of this new formulation.

The sanctuary and the world cannot be separated without diminishing the power of God Who acts through them. Karl Rahner concretizes this unity by means of God's word. The dignity of the human being is that she can open herself to God, becoming a word of God in her everyday life. Yet her existence as a word of God must be illuminated and empowered by the Word of God, living and active in the church and the sacraments. In and beyond the liturgy, then, the Word of God continues to act in power through any person who becomes a word of God, drawing all things into union with God, the destiny and happiness of creation.

Notes

[1]Second Vatican Council, *Sacrosanctum Concilium* [Constitution on the Sacred Liturgy], December 4, 1963, no. 10, http://www.vatican.va.

[2]Peter C. Phan, *Being Religious Interreligiously: Asian Perspectives on Interfaith Dialogue* (Maryknoll, NY: Orbis Books, 2004), 257-261.

[3]Ibid., 263-264.

[4]Ibid., 265.

[5]Ricky Manalo, *The Liturgy of Life: The Interrelationship of Sunday Eucharist and Everyday Worship Practices* (Collegeville, MN: Liturgical Press, 2014), 166-171.

[6]Karl Rahner, "Considerations on the Active Role of the Person in the Sacramental Event," in *Theological Investigations, Vol. XIV: Ecclesiology, Questions in the Church, the Church in the World,* trans. David Bourke (New York: Seabury Press, 1976), 161-184; especially 169-176; Karl Rahner, "On

the Theology of Worship," in *Theological Investigations, Vol. XIX: Faith and Ministry,* trans. Edward Quinn, ed. Paul Imhof (New York: Crossroad, 1983), 141-149; here, 146, 149.

[7]Throughout this essay, the term "the Word of God" will refer solely to Jesus Christ and His continuing presence in the church and the sacraments. The term "a word of God" will refer to any human being who is open to God and thus allows God to "speak her." This terminology more closely links the way in which God's power conforms human beings to Christ. Rahner himself sometimes distinguishes Jesus from other words of God by the definite article: for instance, Jesus "is *the* Word of God to us, not simply *a* word" (Karl Rahner, "Christology Today?" in *Theological Investigations, Vol. XVII: Jesus, Man, and the Church,* trans. Margaret Kohl [New York: Crossroad, 1981], 24-38; here, 33 [Rahner's emphasis]).

[8]Karl Rahner, "Dialogue with God?" in *Theological Investigations, Vol. XVIII: God and Revelation,* trans. Edward Quinn (New York: Crossroad, 1983), 122-131; here, 127.

[9]Phan would agree with this Christological emphasis, even if he might not agree with this essay's relation of sanctuary and world: "[T]he true summit, center, and source of both the liturgy of life and the liturgy of the church is Jesus Christ" (Phan, *Being Religious Interreligiously,* 273).

[10]Rahner, "Dialogue with God?" 125, n. 8.

[11]Ibid., 127.

[12]Ibid., 129.

[13]Ibid.

[14]Ibid., 130.

[15]Along with "Priest and Poet," Rahner treats the primordial word in at least three other essays: Karl Rahner, "Poetry and the Christian," in *Theological Investigations, Vol. IV: More Recent Writings,* trans. Kevin Smyth (Baltimore, MD: Helicon Press, 1966), 357-367; Karl Rahner, "'Behold This Heart!': Preliminaries to a Theology of Devotion to the Sacred Heart," in TI IV, 321-330; Karl Rahner, "Some Theses for a Theology of Devotion to the Sacred Heart," in TI IV, 331-352 (especially 331-332). There is an obvious overlap in his understandings of the *Urwort* and the *Realsymbol.*

[16]Karl Rahner, "Priest and Poet," *Theological Investigations, Vol. III: The Theology of the Spiritual Life,* trans. Karl Rahner and Boniface Kruger, O.F.M. (Baltimore: Helicon Press, 1967), 294-317; here, 301-302.

[17]Ibid., 297.

[18]Ibid., 295, 299.

[19]Ibid., 309, 315. Rahner treats concupiscence in "The Theological Concept of Concupiscentia," *Theological Investigations, Vol. I: God, Christ, Mary, and Grace,* trans. Cornelius Ernst (Baltimore: Helicon Press, 1961), 347-382.

[20]As Peter Fritz convincingly argues, "Priest and Poet" draws upon Heidegger's valorization of the poet in order to refute it in relationship to the priest: cf. Peter Joseph Fritz, *Karl Rahner's Theological Aesthetics* (Washington, DC: Catholic University of America Press, 2014), 90-97.

[21]Rahner, "Priest and Poet," 316 (Rahner's emphasis).

[22]Karl Rahner, *Foundations of Christian Faith: An Introduction to the Idea*

of Christianity, trans. William V. Dych (New York: Crossroad, 1994), 225: The human "is the radical question about God which, as created by God, can also have an answer, an answer which in its historical manifestation and radical tangibility is the God-Man, and which is answered in all of us by God Himself. … [Jesus] is the union of a question which as a question about God is the manifestation of the answer. This is the union which is meant in Christology."
    [23]Ibid., 284.

    [24]As Rahner writes, "This death *as* entered into in free obedience and *as* surrendering life completely to God reaches fulfillment and becomes historically tangible for us only in the resurrection" (ibid., Rahner's emphasis).

    [25]Cf. Karl Rahner, "The Eternal Significance of the Humanity of Jesus for Our Relationship with God," *Theological Investigations, Vol. III: The Theology of the Spiritual Life*, 35-46.

    [26]Rahner, *Foundations*, 284.

    [27]As Rahner writes, "Through Jesus Christ the drama and the dialogue between God and His world has entered into a phase which already implies God's irreversible triumph, and which also makes this victory in the crucified and risen Jesus Christ historically tangible" (ibid., 412).

    [28]Ibid., 416.

    [29]Karl Rahner, "The Presence of the Lord in the Christian Community at Worship," *Theological Investigations, Vol. X: Writings of 1965-1967*, trans. David Bourke (New York: Seabury Press, 1977), 71-83; here, 78-81.

    [30]For this understanding of saints as the subjective ecclesial correlate to the sacraments' objective manifestation of Christ's victory, see Karl Rahner, "The Church of the Saints," in *Theological Investigations, Vol. III: The Theology of the Spiritual Life*, 91-104.

    [31]Karl Rahner, "What Is a Sacrament?" in *Theological Investigations, Vol. XIV: Ecclesiology, Questions in the Church, the Church in the World*, 135-148; here, 142.

    [32]Rahner describes a sacrament "as that kind of exhibitive and effective word in which Christ, through the mouth of the Church, utters himself as the eschatological 'sacrament' of salvation to a specific man in a situation which is significant for his life as a whole and in a form in which it can be apprehended at the level of concrete human living. From this standpoint it is clear that every sacrament signifies and effects a presence of Christ" (Rahner, "The Presence of the Lord," 79).

    [33]Cf. Karl Rahner, "Personal and Sacramental Piety," *Theological Investigations, Vol. II: Man in the Church*, trans. Karl-H. Kruger, O.F.M. (Baltimore, MD: Helicon Press, 1963), 109-133.

    [34]This is further reinforced by Rahner's refusal to separate liturgical prayer and other modes and methods of prayer: cf. Karl Rahner, "Some Theses on Prayer 'In the Name of the Church,'" in *Theological Investigations, Vol. V: Later Writings*, trans. Karl-H. Kruger (Baltimore, MD: Helicon Press, 1962), 419-438, *passim*.

    [35]In other words, how does the supernatural existential relate to becoming a word of God? Though this essay cannot answer that question, one would have to explore how non-Christians accept grace in the supernatural existential.

One could argue that the openness required to become a word of God and the openness required for a person—even unthematically—to accept God's grace are essentially the same. The degree to which a person recognizes this openness in terms of the Word of God's efficacious and manifest victory constitutes the major difference. However, this formulation highlights the importance of conscious and explicit participation in the Word of God, insofar as the central question is recognizing and affirming a balance between liturgical and non-liturgical sites of God's power in the Word.

The Power to Bless

The Negotiation of Ecclesial Authority and Christian Identity in Roman Catholic Liturgical Blessings of Parents and Children

Anne McGowan

The Ordinary General Assembly of the Synod of Bishops on the Family in October 2015 gave Catholics many opportunities to reflect anew on how families bless the church,[1] but the church has a longstanding tradition of blessing families through its liturgical rites that deserves renewed attention as well. Christian blessing prayers invoke God's power—through Christ and in the Holy Spirit—to reveal the ordinary and extraordinary situations of human life, including family relationships, as manifestations of God's generosity, love, and mercy. They then petition God for further gifts and protection so that the person(s) or object(s) blessed might serve as tangible signs of God's goodness and motivate the recipient(s) of the blessings—and others—to praise and glorify God.[2]

Building on permission given in *Sacrosanctum Concilium* for laypeople to administer some ecclesial blessings, *The Book of Blessings*—as an official collection of Roman Catholic liturgical rites—acknowledges by its publication that parental blessing of children can be a liturgical act. Considering the Church's collection of familial blessings as a whole, however, reveals significant theological and social ambiguities that threaten the correspondence between the *lex orandi* prayed in the rites and the *lex vivendi* lived in domestic churches. In particular, contemporary Roman Catholic liturgical blessings (a) privilege ordained clergy over parents as ministers on theological grounds without sufficient consideration of the unique dynamics of family life, (b) almost invariably present fathers as active agents of faith development in the family setting and mothers as relatively passive cooperators, thereby minimizing the complexity and flexibility of both parental roles, and (c) neglect distinctive features of childhood that could broaden appreciation of the working of God's power and grace among *all* God's children. The interrelationship among these issues will be explored through analysis of some significant textual aspects of orders of blessing pertaining to parents or children contained in official liturgical books of the Roman Rite.[3]

Parents Blessing Children:
Devotional Practice Becomes Liturgical Act

The traditional dividing line between liturgy and devotions concerns how closely certain practices are aligned with the public, official authority of the church. Rites conducted publicly according to a prescribed form found in a liturgical book of the Roman rite are liturgical; all other rites, even when conducted in a group and presided over by ordained clergy, are devotional.[4] Before Vatican II, therefore, parental blessing of children generally was classified as a laudable private devotion, as stated explicitly in the entry on "Benedizione" in the Italian *Enciclopedia Cattolica*: "[T]he blessing of children by their parents is no more than a private act, not an act of the Church."[5]

Blessings belong to the category of sacramentals, which are instituted by the church, not by Christ.[6] Two significant statements in *Sacrosanctum Concilium* illuminate the current theological understanding and scope of ministerial power pertinent to these rites. SC 60 characterizes sacramentals as "sacred signs by which, somewhat after the manner of the sacraments, effects of a spiritual nature, especially, are symbolised and are obtained through the church's intercession";[7] thus *both* sacraments (SC 59) and sacramentals can now claim the common designation as *signa* and should be understood in relationship to each other as enacted rites.[8] Therefore, the blessings of persons, places, and objects in *De Benedictionibus* (ET: the *Book of Blessings*) are *liturgical* blessings whereby the gathered church, drawing on its ministries and services and celebrating according to an authorized form, mediates the power of God's blessing.[9] The two central components involved in each order of blessing in the *BoB* (see 20–22) are the Word of God (Scripture) and a Prayer of Blessing. Furthermore, each blessing prayer features two parts: praise (blessing God for who God is) and petition (a request for God's further blessing, typically framed in terms of protection and help for living as a person of faith in this life and/or hope for a share in eternal life).

Furthermore, SC 79 directs: "Provision should be made for the administration of some sacramentals, at least in special circumstances and at the discretion of the Ordinary, by qualified lay persons," thereby implying that the power to bless is ultimately grounded in the priestly power of baptism.[10] Taken together, SC 60 and 79 make it possible for parents to bless their children not only in their own name but also in the name of the church when their familial function (i.e., their status as parents) qualifies them to assume a ministerial role in a liturgical rite.[11] The inclusion of an Order for the Blessing of Sons and Daughters in the *BoB*, in which the minister(s) of the rite may be the parent(s) of the child(ren) blessed, therefore affirms the blessing of children by their parents (at least when cast in a ritual, corporate, authorized canonical form) as within the legitimate scope of the church's liturgical activity.[12] The priestly power of the baptized and that of the ordained coexist somewhat uneasily, however, in the current rites of blessing.

Hierarchy and the Ministerial Mediation of the Church's Blessing

The ordained seemingly have a more expansive power to bless family members in light of the different relationships of the baptized and the ordained to the priesthood of Christ—to the extent that orders of blessing that *may* be celebrated by a layperson (such as a parent) *should* be presided over by a member of the clergy if one is present. The rationale is consistent throughout the *BoB*: "The ministry of blessing involves a particular exercise of the priesthood of Christ," which laypeople may exercise in certain prescribed circumstances in virtue of their incorporation into Christ's universal priesthood through their baptism, and yet "whenever a priest or a deacon is present, the office of presiding should be left to him" (*BoB* 18). The practical consequence is that, for blessings pertaining to parents and children, the natural and social incentive to celebrate such rites within the orbit of the relationships of the domestic church assumes a secondary role to the power and interest of the larger church in blessing these relationships at a more official, ecclesial level.[13] The tension between the exercise of priestly power in the name of what most directly impinges on one's own life as a parent and the interests of the church emerges already in the BoB's *Praenotanda*, which situate blessings in the context of salvation history. While God's blessing extends to all of creation, some persons have a preeminent role in mediating God's blessings—particularly "patriarchs, kings, priests, Levites, and parents" (*BoB* 6).[14]

The priority of the hierarchy's power to bless[15] over a parent's could emphasize that blessing rites are *ecclesial* actions with a connection to the church's seven sacraments through the sign value of having ordained clergy (the ordinary ministers of every sacrament but marriage) preside whenever possible. The purpose of outward signs of blessing "is above all to bring to mind God's saving acts, to express a relationship between the present celebration and the Church's sacraments, and in this way to nurture the faith of those present and move them to take part in the rite attentively" (*BoB* 25).[16] Viewing clergy as outward signs by analogy situates them within the rite as ones who exercise sacramental power through making the mediation of God's grace to humanity through the intercession of the church *visible* within Christ's body, the church—which is exactly what a sacrament does.[17] Without careful catechesis, however, participants in the rite may experience the insistence on clerical presidency as an instance of clericalism. Moreover, if the power to bless exercised by the clergy is driven by a model of the church as institution instead of sacrament,[18] questions could inevitably arise as to whether the blessing of children by a priest or deacon is "better" or results in children who are "more blessed" than if their mother had used the same rite.

Fixating on the specific quality or amount of grace given runs counter to the character of blessings as first of all gifts from God—and also to contemporary theological discussions of grace. Karl Rahner's presentation of grace as the free self-communication of the triune God to creatures who have the capacity to receive and actively respond to it, for example, is a far cry from the neo-scholastic emphasis on the causal connection between sacraments and grace.[19] Applying the logic of what postmodern sacramental theologian Louis-Marie Chauvet calls "symbolic exchange" to blessings, the focus turns instead to the reception of the blessing as a gift from God through the prayer of the church, a gift that calls the blessed ones to ongoing conversion and transformation, the fruits of which are manifested in their ethical conduct. The blessing is revealed as fundamentally an act of the church that invokes and engages God's gifts in the past (recounted in the Scripture reading), present (reception of the sacramental blessing), and future (motivation to love and serve God and one's neighbor).[20] Since the future-oriented ethical component begins to be received with the blessing but is only completed in the rest of life, it becomes especially important to consider how the blessing prayers frame the Christian identity of parents and children. What blessings are ascribed to God and asked of God? What does this imply about God's power in relation to family life? How are the recipients envisioned as exercising power?

Parents, Fathers, and Mothers: Realizing Blessing in Potency and Passivity

Jean-Marie Tillard remarked, "It is not possible to say whether the . . . persons for whom a blessing is sought have a special power derived from God . . . but the blessings of the Ritual certainly define and to some extent denote the sphere in which God is asked to make his blessing manifest."[21] Therefore, if the language of blessings has the power to form the spiritual identity of those who engage them, it is noteworthy that blessings for fathers and for parents in general are more precise in articulating how the blessing reflects the power of God at work in those who are blessed and more specific in elaborating how these roles commit one to leadership within the family, the church, and the world than are blessings for either mothers or children.[22]

The *BoB* contains several rites blessing parents, including a blessing of a mother or both parents before childbirth, of parents after a miscarriage, and of parents and an adopted child. The role of parents in family life emerges most strongly in the blessing for adoptive parents: "[G]rant to these parents patience and wisdom, that their lives may show forth the love of Christ as they bring N. up to love all that is good" (*BoB* 319). Note that here the church prays for *specific* gifts—patience and wisdom—and hopes that the parents may actively model Christlike love to their adopted child.

The contrasting portrayal of maternal and paternal roles in blessing prayers is most striking in parallel prayers for mothers and fathers. For example, two of the four options in the concluding blessing of the Rite of Baptism for Children include distinct blessings for mothers and for fathers. The wording for option A is:[23]

God the Father, through his Son, the Virgin Mary's child, has brought joy to all Christian mothers, as they see the hope of eternal life shine on their children. May he bless the mothers of these children. They now thank God for the gift of their children. May they be one with them in thanking him for ever in heaven, in Christ Jesus our Lord.	God is the giver of all life, human and divine. May he bless the fathers of these children. With their wives they will be the first teachers of their children in the ways of faith. May they be also the best of teachers, bearing witness to the faith by what they say and do, in Christ Jesus our Lord.

Observe that God gives joy to Christian mothers, but their maternal vocation is vaguely delineated—to thank God now and (hopefully) forever in heaven. While this prayer does contextualize the human relationship of mothers and children in light of God's claims on the newly baptized, the mother's role of actively caring for her children in myriad ways in *this* life is neglected completely. The contrast becomes clearer when comparing this to how God is asked to bless fathers, who are identified as "the first teachers of their children . . . bearing witness to the faith by what they say and do." While the mothers are also identified as teachers alongside them, fathers are more specifically blessed for their leadership role, giving the overall impression that fathers are called to play a more active part than mothers in modeling faith for their children and that the mother's activity is always subordinated to that of the father.

Blessing Children and Embracing Childhood

Prayers blessing children somewhat ambiguously recognize children as a blessing from God and capable of blessing God while expressing hope that children might come to bless God more robustly when they mature and become capable of adult faith and discipleship. The Order for the Blessing of Baptized Children, as one of the few official liturgies in the Roman Rite focusing explicitly on children, serves as a good test case. The prayer of blessing prayed by an ordained minister begins by blessing God:

> Lord, our God,
> out of the speech of little children
> you have fashioned a hymn of praise.
> Look with kindness on these children
> whom the faith of the Church commends to your
>   tender care.
> Your Son, born of the Virgin Mary, gladly welcomed
>   little children.
> He took them in his arms, blessed them,
> and held them up as an example for all.[24]

Children are presented here as people who are profoundly capable not only of praising God but also of *imaging* God—who was born into the world as a child and grew up to affirm children's desire to approach God. Furthermore, children are set in the midst of the community as a model of the parabolic logic of the kingdom of God; those who have little power or status in the human community and are especially vulnerable to exploitation can effectively invert society's expectations, even by becoming ideal teachers for adults.

The petition section reads:

> We pray that you, Father,
> will also send your blessing on them,
> so that they may grow in Christian maturity
> and, by the power of the Holy Spirit,
> become Christ's witnesses in the world,
> spreading and defending the faith.[25]

The sense of the present agency of children disappears completely in this section of the prayer requesting God's future-oriented blessing. Children will ideally grow in Christian maturity from this point forward, but they seemingly will be empowered by the Spirit to become Christ's witnesses only once that maturity in faith has progressed at least a bit further than it already has. The parameters of the blessing requested from God are also quite nebulous; there is nothing in it specific to baptized *children* that is not common to the vocational calling of all baptized Christians. While there is a certain wisdom to employing broad language when speaking of children's baptismal vocations, there is a real missed opportunity here to bless children for who they are *now* as the "subject and site of divine revelation,"[26] with distinct gifts and responsibilities appropriate to their current developmental stage, as witnesses of a way of being in the world that conveys something important about how *all* Christians are called to relate to God.

The rather static and limited vision of children's faith experience in this blessing prayer coincides with a longstanding neglect of children as a distinct category of Roman Catholic theological concern, especially if moral issues related to procreation and the status of unbaptized children are bracketed.[27] Marcia J. Bunge notes that the result of this tendency is that "theological discourse in many Christian traditions has been dominated by simplistic and ambivalent views of children and young people that diminish their complexity and integrity."[28]

Karl Rahner made substantial contributions toward a more sophisticated discourse in an essay entitled "Ideas for a Theology of Childhood."[29] Especially relevant to the current discussion is Rahner's critique of viewing childhood as a phase of human development that is eventually surpassed and integrated into later, more mature stages of human existence. Rahner observes, "We do not move away from childhood in any definitive sense, but rather move towards the eternity of this childhood, to its definitive and enduring validity in God's sight."[30] Thus, for Rahner, childhood is an enduring part of our eschatological future that we will forever "grow into." Another key Rahnerian insight is that "childhood invokes a mystery . . . the ineffable element in which is God himself."[31] Surrender to the mystery of childhood, therefore, is a potential way to encounter God.[32] The child thus becomes "a sacrament of that radical openness to the future which is a characteristic posture of the Christian believer precisely because the child reveals not only what we once were, but what we will be."[33] The blessing prayer considered above mentions God's childhood in Christ and highlights children's need of the church's care, yet it also presumes that childhood's characteristic immaturity will be surpassed. The dependency of children is perceived as a temporary liability rather than a source of present power.

The *lex orandi* of current Roman Catholic blessing prayers for parents and children affirms that the blessing of family members is an important dimension of the church's liturgical life. Even if these blessings are used infrequently in some cultures, they are nonetheless enshrined among the church's prescribed ritual texts. Blessings prayed by the ordained emphasize well the priestly role of the church's intercession for God's gifts directed toward the needs of family life, but the absolute priority of the presidency of the clergy potentially constrains the reciprocity of the flow of blessings between the *ecclesia* and the family as a miniature *domus ecclesiae*. Furthermore, the characteristically passive portrayal of the power of mothers and children compared to the more active leadership of fathers within the family raises questions about whether those who composed and approved these texts envisioned women and the church's youngest members as equally capable of imaging and manifesting God's potency, albeit in diverse ways.[34]

There is good reason to encourage further theological reflection and adaptations of the typical editions of the church's blessing prayers[35] such that the maternal, paternal, and childlike qualities of God can be celebrated and praised as they are actually manifested in the lives of family members for the building up of the church, the family of God, in service to the family of humanity. For example, could the theology of parental blessings of children be informed by the Catholic Church's theology of the sacrament of matrimony, in which the bride and groom minister the sacrament to one another with the church's official (and ordinarily ordained) ministers serving as witnesses such that parents, at least sometimes, could bless their own children even when clergy are present? Might prayers blessing parents incorporate nurturing imagery for fathers and mightier metaphors for mothers to better reflect the multifaceted roles of both parents within family life? Can the church engage the present and future dynamism of children's vocations and depute older children to bless their parents? There is power in possibilities like these to lead participants to respond to these blessings, in liturgy and life, with a more rousing "Amen."

Notes

[1]Meeting in Vatican City October 4-25, 2015, this Synod's particular topic was "the vocation and mission of the family in the Church and in the contemporary world." For an overview of recent episcopal discussions on the family, see "2014-2015 Synods of Bishops on the Family," United States Conference of Catholic Bishops, http://www.usccb.org.

[2]This theology of blessing is treated in the *Praenotanda* of the 1984 typical edition of *De Benedictionibus* (Vatican City: Libreria Editrice Vaticana, 1993), the Roman ritual that presents an extensive collection of blessings for persons, objects, and needs within the life of the church and its members. See Catholic Church and ICEL, *Book of Blessings: Approved for Use in the Dioceses of the United States of America*, hereafter *BoB* (Collegeville, MN: Liturgical Press, 1989), nos. 1–15. Subsequent references to this edition will be given in parentheses in the body of the text.

[3]On euchology as a theological source, see Kevin W. Irwin, *Context and Text: Method in Liturgical Theology* (Collegeville, MN: Liturgical Press, 1994), 176–218.

[4]See, e.g., the chart in Cipriano Vagaggini, *Theological Dimensions of the Liturgy: A General Treatise on the Theology of the Liturgy*, trans. Leonard J. Doyle and W. A. Jurgens from the 4th Italian ed., rev. and augmented by the author (Collegeville, MN: Liturgical Press, 1976), 118. However, the lived experience of liturgy and devotions, especially after Vatican II, leads some theologians to situate them along a continuum of the church's worship practices rather than confine them to separate categories. For various perspectives on the relationship between liturgy and devotions, see Carl Dehne, "Devotions, Popular," in *The New Dictionary of Sacramental Worship*, vol. 1, ed. Peter E. Fink (Collegeville, MN: Liturgical Press, 1990), 331-340.

[5]"Benedizione," in *Enciclopedia Cattolica* (Vatican City: Ente per l'Enciclopedia Cattolica e per il Libro Cattolico, 1949), vol. 2, col. 1303; quoted in Josep Lligadas, "The Doctrine of Blessing in the New Roman Ritual," trans. Francis McDonagh, in *Blessing and Power*, ed. Mary Collins and David Power (Edinburgh: T & T Clark, 1985), 113.

[6]For some brief but substantial discussions of sacramentals, see Vagaggini, 112–23, and Anscar J. Chupungco, *Liturgical Inculturation: Sacramentals, Religiosity, and Catechesis* (Collegeville, MN: Liturgical Press, 1992), 55–94.

[7]Translation from *Vatican Council II: The Basic Sixteen Documents*, ed. Austin Flannery (Northport, NY: Costello Publishing Company, 1996).

[8]On the importance of this semantic shift, see Anscar J. Chupungco, *What, Then, Is Liturgy?: Musings and Memoir* (Collegeville, MN: Liturgical Press, 2010), 85. The connection between sacraments and sacramentals is further strengthened by the provision of fuller postconciliar liturgical rites for sacramentals, typically including a greeting, introduction, Scripture reading, ritual actions, and blessing prayer.

[9]On the value of nonliturgical blessings, see ibid., 93.

[10]This innovation created considerable controversy, and the precise meaning of "qualified" was left unspecified in SC. See Chupungco, *Liturgical Inculturation*, 69–70.

[11]According to the criteria laid out in *BoB* 18 on the qualification of laypersons to celebrate particular blessings, parents would bless children "in virtue of their office," presuming they have demonstrated "proper pastoral formation and prudence in the apostolate."

[12]See *BoB* 190 for the text of the prayer used by parents and 191 for the alternative prayer to be used by "a minister who is not a parent of the children" (which is identical to the blessing prayer used by a lay minister in the Order for the Blessing of Baptized Children [151]).

[13]Since the blessing of children can be repeated in different contexts (*BoB* 174–78), this directive need not represent an insurmountable obstacle to parents blessing their own children liturgically on at least *some* occasions.

[14]This specification "seems to present a different form of God's presence," suggests Lligadas in "The Doctrine of Blessing," 112.

[15]On the characterization of hierarchy as the "power to bless," see David W. Fagerberg, "Liturgical Theology," in *T & T Clark Companion to Liturgy*, ed. Alcuin Reid (London: Bloomsbury T & T Clark, 2016), 10–11. Fagerberg synthesizes insights from Dionysius the pseudo-Areopagite and Yves Congar.

[16]The signs mentioned involve actions in the rites of blessing such as handlaying, the sign of the cross, sprinkling with holy water, etc.; see *BoB* 26–27.

[17]The importance of visible sacramental mediation is a recurring theme in Edward Schillebeeckx, *Christ the Sacrament of the Encounter with God* (Franklin, WI: Sheed & Ward, 1963).

[18]See Avery Dulles, *Models of the Church*, expanded ed. (New York: Image Books, 2002).

[19]Karl Rahner, *The Trinity* (London: Continuum, 2001), 34-36. For an overview of the intersecting dynamics of the Trinity, God's grace, and the sacraments, see Kimberly Hope Belcher, *Efficacious Engagement: Sacramental Participation in the Trinitarian Mystery* (Collegeville, MN: Liturgical Press, 2011), 1-31.

[20]See Louis-Marie Chauvet, *Symbol and Sacrament: A Sacramental Reinterpretation of Christian Existence*, trans. Patrick Madigan and Madeleine Beaumont (Collegeville, MN: Liturgical Press, 1995), especially 99–109 and 266–89.

[21]J-M. R. Tillard, "Blessing, Sacramentality and Epiclesis," trans. David Smith, in *Blessing and Power*, ed. Mary Collins and David Power (Edinburgh: T & T Clark, 1985), 107–8.

[22]This echoes the observation made by Janet R. Walton after comparing the blessings for mothers and fathers in the Canadian bishops' resource, *A Book of Blessings* (Ottawa: Canadian Conference of Catholic Bishops, 1981), 51–52. See Walton, "Ecclesiastical and Feminist Blessing: Women as Objects and Subjects of the Power of Blessing," in *Blessing and Power*, ed. Mary Collins and David Power (Edinburgh: T & T Clark, 1985), 75–76.

[23]Rite of Baptism for Children, no. 70, in *The Rites of the Catholic*

Church, vol. 1 (Collegeville, MN: Liturgical Press, 1990). Option C also includes separate blessing prayers for mothers and fathers and reflects similar dynamics as option A. This trend continues in the Rite for the Blessing of a Child in the Womb recently developed by the United States Conference of Catholic Bishops (Washington, DC: USCCB, 2012; also available online at http://www.usccb.org).

[24] *BoB* 150. For the sake of intelligibility, the prayer is presented in plural language with singular options omitted.

[25] Ibid. The structure and content of the prayer used by a lay presider is similar; however, the sense of the presider invoking God's blessing is more oblique: "Hear our prayers and, with your [Christ's] unfailing protection, watch over these children whom you have blessed with the grace of baptism" (151).

[26] See Laurence Paul Hemming, "The Liturgical Subject: Introductory Essay," in *The Liturgical Subject: Subject, Subjectivity, and the Human Person in Contemporary Liturgical Discussion and Critique*, ed. James G. Leachman (Notre Dame, IN: University of Notre Dame Press, 2009), 15.

[27] See Todd David Whitmore with Tobias L. Winright, "Children: An Undeveloped Theme in Catholic Teaching," in *The Challenge of Global Stewardship: Roman Catholic Responses*, ed. Maura A. Ryan and Todd David Whitmore (Notre Dame, IN: University of Notre Dame Press, 1997), 161–85. Despite some advances in the intervening years, the general premise still applies.

[28] Marcia J. Bunge, "The Vocation of the Child: Theological Perspectives on the Particular and Paradoxical Roles and Responsibilities of Children," in *The Vocation of the Child*, ed. Patrick McKinley Brennan (Grand Rapids, MI: Eerdmans, 2008), 33.

[29] Karl Rahner, "Ideas for a Theology of Childhood," in *Theological Investigations*, vol. 8, trans. David Bourke (New York: Herder and Herder, 1971), 33–50. Many subsequent treatments of the theology of childhood draw on Rahner's insights.

[30] Ibid., 36.

[31] Ibid., 43; see 43–50 for further exploration of this claim.

[32] Mary Ann Hinsdale, "'Infinite Openness to the Infinite': Karl Rahner's Contribution to Modern Catholic Thought on the Child," in *The Child in Christian Thought*, ed. Marcia J. Bunge (Grand Rapids, MI: Eerdmans, 2001), 418.

[33] Nathan Mitchell, "The Once and Future Child: Towards a Theology of Childhood," *Living Light* 12 (1975): 428.

[34] Cf. Walton, "Ecclesiastical and Feminist Blessing," 75–76.

[35] Bishops' conferences may propose adaptations and prepare alternative texts (see *BoB* 39). The American edition of the *BoB*, for example, includes Orders for the Blessing of Mothers on Mother's Day and Fathers on Father's Day that use parallel (if exceedingly generic) language: "Bless these women [men], that they may be strengthened as Christian mothers [fathers]. Let the example of their faith and love shine forth." See *BoB* 1728 and 1733.

The Power of Virtual Space

Derek C. Hatch and Katherine G. Schmidt

The following essay emerges from the consultation of Evangelical Catholics and Catholic Evangelicals at the 2016 convention of the College Theology Society, which brings together Catholic and Protestant voices concerning a shared topic. In 2016, the theme of liturgy and contemporary social and communications media was in focus. As panelists, we offered complementary papers that have become two sections of this essay. In the first section, Katherine Schmidt provides a theological account of media from a Catholic perspective. Through reflections on the mediatory character of the incarnation, she argues that para-liturgical or extra-liturgical spaces are integral to the Eucharistic assembly and that the internet is at once challenging and cultivating such spaces. In the second section, Derek Hatch provides an historical account of the broader Christian engagement with media, presented through his experience as a Baptist. He argues that, while earlier technological approaches reinforced confessional boundaries, the internet provides new spaces for fruitful ecumenical relationships. Together, we claim that contemporary experience with social media technologies offers a particular cultural and ecclesial moment for engaging with theological difference both within and without our respective traditions and for cultivating renewed vision of the fullness of the church catholic.

Theological Account of Media from a Catholic Perspective
Katherine G. Schmidt

The Christian tradition has a vested interest in technological culture not only because the church is in the world and cannot be otherwise, but also because questions about technology invite questions about mediation. And religion is about mediation. Birgit Meyer reminds us that, "After all, the relation between religion and media is neither as new nor as weird as was suggested by the initial excited attention devoted to electronic mass media such as television and film. Upon deeper reflection, media were found to be intrinsic to religion."[1]

In what follows, I would like to argue two related points. First, I advance the idea that Christian liturgy can be understood as virtual. This is an expansion and concretization of the idea of religion as mediation. Second, I would like to propose that the virtual nature of Christian liturgy—and indeed, the virtual nature of the church itself—turns toward a self-reflective theological analysis of the internet. I propose under this second point that the internet has changed what it means to be social to such a degree that we must now understand its social spaces as ancillary to the liturgical spaces of the tradition.

The following reflection on the relationship of technology and liturgy has an important starting point: what I have to say will only apply to Christian traditions that understand what happens in their sanctuaries and on their altars to be indispensable. That is, the following arguments have no foothold in traditions that understand going to church as optional for the Christian life. What follows is contingent upon the theological import of "being there," be it for mass or sermon, rite or reading. We might debate the finer points of what constitutes liturgy elsewhere, but I will take people at their word, meaning that if they are calling it liturgy, that is what I mean by liturgy here.

I propose we understand the liturgy as "virtual." Virtuality seems like a shiny new thing, as that which belongs properly to a world dominated by computer-mediation. "Virtual" is a word used by the young, the affluent, and the otherwise technologically adept. It might even be one of those words that marks identity; perhaps the world can already be divided into those who use it— who know it intimately and know the world by it—and those who don't. If this is true at all, then "virtual" is a very important word. We should be clear about what it means. It does not mean (only) the new and the shiny. In fact, I contend that virtuality as a mode of cultural production and participation is very, very old. I submit virtuality is a possible hermeneutic for the sacramentality of the church. A broader and more inclusive definition of "virtual" allows us to read different moments of Christian history as performances of mediation that are, essentially, virtual. This understanding of virtual refers not simply to digital contexts but to a much broader dialectic at the heart of mediation.

Because of the incarnational foundation of the Christian tradition, mediation is a central aspect of the church. This becomes more apparent as one wades into sacramental theology, as well as into exploring the role of scripture in the church. Indeed, it may be the case that debates about the sacraments have very similar battle lines, tone, and theological stakes as debates over scripture. But at the heart of both Word and Sacrament is the radical idea that we can experience God in the gift of mediation. The economy of salvation and the sacramental economy speak to the deepest aspects of what it means to be human on precisely this point.

Media scholars Jay David Bolter and Richard Grusin unwittingly touch upon theological anthropology in their exploration of mediation.[2] They argue that the proliferation of modern media reflects a desire for immediacy. Somewhat ironically, a desire for immediacy actually engenders a logic of 'hypermediacy.' They argue that the desire for immediacy motivates and inspires all kinds of media: "In every manifestation, hypermediacy makes us aware of the medium or media and (in sometimes subtle and sometimes obvious ways) reminds us of our desire for immediacy."[3]

Bolter and Grusin argue that this desire is about as old as the Renaissance. While I appreciate Bolter and Grusin's historical sensitivities, I maintain that the desire for immediacy is not an effect of the modern view of nature but is in fact a constitutive part of what it means to be human. This claim is theological. For Christians, the desire for immediacy is the longing for communion with God, the source of all truth and reality itself. In fact, the very dialectic of immediacy and hypermediacy is essential to the Christian imagination: the longing for communion with God and with one another drives us into mediating structures that reflect the desire for immediacy while simultaneously bespeaking the inevitability of (hyper)mediation. When God takes flesh in Jesus Christ, God becomes at once immediate and hypermediate to the human condition. That is, Jesus takes human nature fully while at the same time transforming what it means to be human. This affects the Christian perspective of all materiality and informs the hypermediating practices of the as yet-insatiable human desire for immediacy with our Creator.

The dialectic between immediacy and hypermediacy is not frictionless. We feel it acutely in moments of miscommunication, dropped connections, and imperfect mediations. But it is precisely this friction that constitutes mediation and therefore constitutes religious ritual. We can describe this friction between the desire for immediacy and its hypermediating productivity as an essentially virtual experience.

By describing the sacramental life of the church as virtual I mean to highlight the various ways in which the church lives in the productive space between immediacy and hypermediacy. More precisely, I want to highlight the dialectic of presence and absence upon which these logics rely, a dialectic without which the Church and its liturgy cannot function. Virtuality is the making present of something that is absent. Mediated presence, however, is predicated upon and constantly referring back to absence. Theologically speaking, this tension between presence and absence is just how we have to understand God in the world after the Ascension. As Michel de Certeau describes it, the Church is a protracted experience of Mary Magdalene's question, "Where have you put him?"[4] We are a people with and without a Body. The tension between presence and absence, then, is the creative space in which God invites the church into the mystery of the God-man.

The Christological councils, ancient in their logic and definitive in their teaching, continue to remind us of our own collapsing tendencies with regard to the mystery of the incarnation. The doctrine draws us into the tension between presence and absence (as well as between humanity and divinity) but we are always reaching to resolve it. Sometimes, we are tempted to emphasize Christ in his divinity, carving a space for the divine in a world that no longer has eyes to see it. Other times, we are tempted to emphasize Jesus in his humanity, joining our sufferings and our other distinctly human experiences to his. The teachings of the councils function as the boundary lines for such Christological reflection. This allows us to see the tension between humanity and divinity, between God being present to us and utterly absent and ineffable, as a space of our salvation. This tension functions as a kind of necessary logic for understanding both God and the world.

It is within these doctrinal boundaries that the liturgical game is played. Here I will draw upon the work of sacramental theologian Louis-Marie Chauvet, who builds his sacramental system upon the idea of "symbolic exchange." Chauvet wants to assert the gratuitousness of grace and rescue it from the instrumental causality that has dominated sacramental theology. He does so by means of a contrast between two logics: "that of the marketplace and value, based on objects in themselves, and that of symbolic exchange, before or beyond the realm of worth and based on the relations between subjects as such."[5] According to Chauvet, a symbol is that which "introduces us into a realm to which it itself belongs."[6] It "brings with itself the entire socio-cultural system to which it belongs."[7] A symbol is fundamentally about the relationship between subjects for Chauvet, for it is meant to "join the persons who produce or receive it with their cultural world (social, religious, economic…) and so to identify them as subjects in their relations with other subjects." Symbols are not mere representations of another reality; they are a "function of summons or challenge, of coming-to-presence…of communication between subjects."[8] Contrasted with the logic of market exchange, "the symbol is by its nature outside *the realm of value*. What is important is not the utility of the object, but the exchange that it permits between the subjects."[9]

I want to recapitulate Chauvet's sacramental theology using Genesis 2-3. The Garden reminds us that we possess an objectifying tendency that often eclipses communion with God and each other. Reaching for the fruit is reaching for divinity as an object to be possessed, made in our own image and responding to our demands. The temptation is to dominate by objectification, to respond to our desire for immediacy with divinity by taking it for ourselves and making ourselves little gods. In short, it is to act without regard for our identity as creatures and God's identity as Creator. In tragic irony, our objectifying tendency born out of the desire for immediacy results in a mediated relationship with God, as our expulsion from the Garden means an expulsion from God's unmediated presence.

But in the beauty of God's redemptive creativity, mediation is not just a mark of our sin; it is also the means for our salvation. The sacraments are a symbolic system of actions, words, and objects that evoke both presence and absence. Inasmuch as the sacraments are meant to bring us into the presence of God, they are also meant to remind us of God's absence. Their corporality bespeaks the grace of God in Christ, who takes flesh to redeem us. And their corporality bespeaks God's absence from us by pointing us back to the mediation that marks our humanity and our distance from God after the Garden and this side of the eschaton. It is precisely here that the sacraments reveal themselves as virtual: They are suspended in the uncomfortable and productive tension between presence and absence. To live incarnationally is to live suspended between these two without collapsing one into the other. To emphasize presence over absence is to covet a closure of the distance between creature and Creator; to emphasize absence over presence is to doubt the apostolic witness that God dwelt among us in a real way.

So what does understanding the sacramental economy and its liturgical instantiation as virtual do for the church? Bringing the virtual into a theological mode can begin to expose biases and fears about technological culture that can be harmful to the church's relationship to the historical moment in which it exists. By acknowledging the centrality—and indeed, the theological necessity—of mediation in the church, we are better equipped to evaluate the media ecology in which we live and work. We can acknowledge the anthropological truths at the heart of cultural particularities and trends. Moreover, we can have theologically rigorous conversations about the place of the church in technological culture that neither reduce the church to a pastoral ideal nor oversimplify the culture into an amalgam of corrosive forces.

This rigor is especially important given the sociological challenges currently facing the American church. Christian traditions in the United States are facing the problem of dramatic disaffiliation, sometimes referred to as the rise of the "nones."[10] This is a multifaceted phenomenon for which it would be foolish to propose root causes. Taking the moment for what it is, however, my analysis of this moment is that we live, regardless of geographic location, in a suburbanized economic culture, wherein traditional centers of social life have become simply one aspect among many from which we choose as we construct personal identity. This means that religion, too, is suburbanized, insofar as religious communities no longer function as the center of communities of all kinds, and therefore no longer function as the center of social life.

Given this sociological landscape, understanding the virtual as a theological category can open creative ways to re-engage social life. I propose that we diagnose our current social moment in the church by asking after the theological relationship between the altar or sanctuary and the vestibule or fellowship hall. The latter are liminal ecclesial spaces that can function as strong symbols of the church/world relationship. They are threshold spaces that function extra-liturgically but are still liturgically referential. These are the spaces of sodalities, Bible studies, prayer groups, schools, homeschool co-ops, labor unions, and bowling leagues. American Christian communities have at certain points in their history enjoyed a great variety and robustness of these spaces, extending well beyond the vestibule or hall and into neighborhoods, towns, regions, and cities. To the degree that American religious communities are suburbanized, they can no longer rely on the traditional ancillary social spaces to form the complex network that reinforces, sometimes daily, the church as the center of one's social life. Rendered a choice among many in the logic of market exchange, the church is thrust now into a system with a voluntaristic logic that is alien to the pedagogy of symbolic exchange.

From a Catholic perspective, the sacramental efficacy of the Eucharistic assembly is not affected by these spaces. This is the heart of *ex opere operato*. But this does not exclude a theological relationship between these ancillary social spaces and the sacramental life of the church. The spaces are "ancillary" because they are supportive of the Eucharistic assembly insofar as they are the very spaces that make up the cultural frame of reference for the sacramental rite. They are "social" insofar as they are spaces wherein the members of the Body of Christ have the opportunity to practice the symbolic exchange learned in the powerful pedagogy of the Eucharist. Put more simply, these ancillary social spaces are the spaces of potential acts of Christian charity between the members of the Body. These are the sites for potential communion, a sort of connective tissue between each Eucharist. Therefore, while their successes and failures do not affect the sacrament as such, they do represent an important feature of the viability of the Body of Christ as a eucharistic people.

The dense networks of social communication that sustained a robust liminal space symbolized by the vestibule or hall have become weak, nonexistent, or replaced by new means of connection in this technological paradigm. But we cannot simply name this crisis and double down on doctrine, tempting though it may be. What is before us, I believe, is a moment of great opportunity, wherein the church should pay careful attention to the ancillary social spaces being created and maintained by and among the members of the Body through technology. This does not necessarily mean that we all begin live-tweeting Sunday services. But it may mean that pastors and leaders stop joking about Twitter and start asking the young people who remain in their communities about the role that platforms like Twitter play in their social lives. It means that the church make concerted efforts to produce technologically literate leaders who are open to understanding the ways in which the internet has changed and continues to change what it means to be social. It is a time of possibility, wherein the catholicity of the church can be brought to the fore as consonant with a cultural paradigm of virtuality.

I want to provide two examples of technological changes regarding these ancillary spaces, the first of which is closer to the liturgical life of the church than the second. Both examples demonstrate the importance of ancillary social spaces, as well as the way those spaces have already come to rely upon technology for their initiation and cultivation.

A few years ago, I was part of a group of women who sustained our parish's eucharistic adoration ministry. We each took an hour or two a week to make sure that the Blessed Sacrament was not left alone in a side chapel. While it is not a Mass, adoration ministry is a liturgical act that represents an ancillary space for further eucharistic pedagogy and for potential communion between members of the Body of Christ. This is a commonplace ministry for Catholic parishes the world over and one sustained by many people before me, including my grandmothers. One curious feature of my experience of this ministry, however, is that I only knew what two of the women in the group looked like: the one who had the hour before me and the one who had the hour after me. I knew everyone's name and I'm sure I was at Mass with many of them. I also knew everyone's email address. The entire ministry was sustained over email, which is not altogether unique for many communities today. One reading of this experience is that the network functioned as the newest tool for the logistical realities of parish life. In light of the idea of the church as virtual, however, this email chain becomes another moment of the church's sacramental life that relies on the dialectic of presence and absence. In a sense, the space created by this email list was a microcosm of the church itself: its theological center was the Eucharist, and its members are both present and absent to one another over space and time.

A second anecdote of these ancillary social spaces is less directly liturgical. I recently found myself at the first meeting of a new chapter of Young Catholic Professionals. Young people from all over the diocese had gathered at a local bar to pray, have a drink, network, and plan. Here before me stood the children of suburban Catholicism, isolated in this parish or that, reaching through cyberspace for community. Indeed, the impetus for the entire ministry is to connect young Catholics to older Catholic professionals in order to help them sustain their Catholic identity in non-Catholic work settings. On the one hand, Young Catholic Professionals is the new generation of the ancillary Catholic social spaces of old. On the other, it is inflected with a technological and organizational logic that reflects a tacit response to the erosion of these spaces in a paradigm of fracture, anxiety, and the longing for extra-liturgical communal practices.

We may long for a time in the church when it was simple— when iPhones didn't ring during the consecration and people talked face to face to plan liturgies. But the Incarnation is about mediation—the person Jesus Christ, the church he founded, and the Word inspired by the Spirit to bring us into contact with the living God. As we struggle with media and technology, we may come to realize that our struggle is simply another form of lament over life outside of the Garden. The church is already well-versed in the world of mediation, and the opportunity before us is to bring our rich and ancient traditions of mediation to bear on the mediated world in which the church now lives.

The media ecology within which the church must find a way to thrive often forces Christians to come face to face with the brokenness of the *ekklesia*. Members of various Christian communities and traditions continually run into one another online, often with vitriolic consequences. In what follows, however, we attempt to present the other side of this new experience of old divisions, asking whether online space—as another sort of extra-liturgical social space—can actually function as a paradigm for ecumenical dialogue and even friendship.

Broader Christian Engagement with Media
Derek C. Hatch

While it is worth stating that technology has been with the church from the beginning (consider that even the production of the material elements of the Eucharist requires some form of making), the focus of this consultation is on something more peculiar. It is not hard to find an opinion about technology in the church, whether focused on questions of projector screens (or even flat panel televisions) within the sanctuary (a question that has been going on in evangelical churches for at least the past two decades), the use of online methods for tithing, at least one church's experiment with a holographic projection of the pastor in satellite campuses of his church, not to mention other curiosities even further afield, such as the emergence of churches wholly located online (e.g., Second Life church) and moral deliberations about whether virtual interactions violate physical relationships and commitments. While these questions (and many others) are serious, and some may even be fascinating to examine, I want to focus on the role of technology in ecumenical endeavors. To do so, I will offer a broad overview of the ways in which technology has impacted confessional boundaries in prior historical eras as well as in the more contemporary period (with a particular emphasis on the latter for liturgy). I should state that these observations are very broad and subject to further discussion, nuance, and detail (especially concerning key exceptional cases). Despite the potential overreach of my broader comments, I do think some key differences will come to the fore, differences that might sharpen our understanding of how technology in general (and social communications media in particular) might shape our conception and practice of liturgy as well as the ever-present ecumenical challenges facing the body of Christ today.

As has been discussed by numerous historians, the Protestant Reformation gained traction and perhaps came to fruition because of the invention of the movable type printing press by Johannes Gutenberg in the mid-fifteenth century. While this new technology was initially used for scholarly work, it fueled humanist intellectual interests, including those involving the primary languages of the Bible.[11] After all, once he refined the printing process, Gutenberg's major printed work was completed—a whole edition of the Latin Vulgate around 1455. Several decades later, printing expanded its aim to the wider masses. When the spark of the Reformation was lit in 1517 with Martin Luther's hand-written Ninety-five Theses, it was the printing press that spread that small fire into a blaze. Soon various editions of Protestant texts by Luther, John Calvin, Ulrich Zwingli, Martin Bucer, and others were scattered across Europe. Moreover, while the first Bible produced by Gutenberg's invention was a Catholic version, it was the Protestants who dominated the reproduction of the biblical text. In 1522, Luther completed a German translation of the New Testament from the original Greek, and by 1534, his entire German Bible was in production. Other vernacular translations were created and printed, serving the Reformation's aim to make Scripture more accessible to the laity. So important is the printing press to the events of the Reformation that historian Philip Schaff described its role as providential.[12]

Several centuries later, the energy provided by the printing press to the reform-minded Protestants had not generated reform, but in fact division. One example of such separation is found in the nineteenth-century American context where Catholic school-children were caught between the publicly available schools and their Protestant shape, emblematized by the use of the King James Bible. In Philadelphia, Bishop Francis Patrick Kenrick asked that Catholic schoolchildren in public schools be allowed to recite the Ten Commandments from the authorized Catholic Douay Bible. This request was granted, but the response by anti-Catholic protestors was fierce. Riots broke out, killing several people and injuring many more.[13] Additionally, there was significant damage to property, including several Catholic churches in the city. In Boston in 1859, numerous Catholic children refused to recite the King James version of the Ten Commandments. No riots broke out this time, though it fueled the creation of Catholic parochial schools, in effect further dividing Catholic and Protestant children from one another.[14]

While there were certainly occasions when print books and articles served the uniting impulse of ecumenism, these incidents and others highlight the role of technology in reinforcing divisions within the body of Christ. In short, there were Catholic Bibles and Protestant Bibles, and there were Catholic books and

Protestant books. Within Protestantism, there are even more divisions—Methodist books, Presbyterian books, Baptist books, etc. Someone inhabiting this world was (and occasionally still is) reminded of this state of affairs. Thus, even though accessing intellectual sources from another tradition was possible (and some rare few did such work), it was difficult to do so because the inventory of university libraries and confessional bookstores also operated along these conventional lines. Why would a Baptist bookstore have a Catholic book or Bible? Why would a Catholic school library carry a Lutheran periodical? Moreover, there was a social stigma attached to serious engagement with a neighboring Christian tradition, as though such interest meant a departure from and betrayal of one's present home. With these broad observations in place, we see a steep uphill climb for any efforts at ecumenism.

Turning to the contemporary period, it seems that the internet and its creation of new virtual spaces (as well as new reflections on old virtual spaces) has offered different contributions to the work of ecumenism. Of course, the rise of disaffiliation (mentioned in the first section) and the dissolution of the subcultures that undergirded many traditions are at work in bringing the diversity of Christians into closer proximity. Now Catholics and Baptists have great difficulty speaking solely within their distinct confessional circles. This creates a fertile ground for friendships that transform the most pressing ecumenical questions. As indicated above, indicated, liminal ecclesial spaces (e.g., universities, neighborhoods, labor unions) have become significant for the church/world relationship. Interestingly, they have also become somewhat ecumenical. Insofar as this is the case, liturgical reflections, especially among Protestants, have taken on a more catholic tone and shape. That is, whereas previously confessional boundaries (including their liturgical elements) were reinforced by technology, a different dynamic exists presently, as can be observed in several ways.

First, access to musical resources such as hymnals has certainly increased, but the openness to alternate songs and musical traditions (e.g., Gregorian chant) has been augmented by digital archives and collections.[15] Baptists can borrow Catholic, Lutheran, or Orthodox hymns. Moreover, the space that print books inhabit is different. For instance, I recently purchased an Eastern Orthodox service book for Holy Week and Pascha as well as Dom Gregory

Dix's *The Shape of the Liturgy*, neither of which come from my tradition. Yet not only was the means by which I purchased these books different (a website as opposed to a confessionally affiliated brick-and-mortar store), the purchase carried with it less of the stigma that might have occurred if these texts were purchased in a previous era.

Second, many free-church Protestant traditions have cultivated greater familiarity with the lectionary and the rhythm of the liturgical calendar. Both the Revised Common Lectionary and the Catholic lectionary are openly available in numerous places. Within Baptist life and thought, a great deal of liturgical renewal has come about as a result of preaching according to the lectionary (or at least one of the texts found therein). For free-church Protestants, this new rhythm has prompted an openness to aspects of the calendar that were viewed as off-limits (e.g., Lent). Now, rather than sharp divisions along confessional boundaries (divisions that involve the Bible as well), the shared use of the liturgical calendar brings Christians from different traditions into liturgical proximity (and perhaps even contact) with one another.

Third, numerous liturgical resources are available on the internet. Many of these transcend confessional boundaries. The Taizé community most certainly predates this new context, but the spread and influence of this ecumenical monastic movement has increased as a result of their efforts to share songs and prayers with a community the boundaries of which extend far beyond this small French village. Similarly, other liturgical resources have emerged through crowd-sourcing. One particular blog, which receives and catalogues liturgical elements such as calls to worship, prayers, litanies, and benedictions, is operated by a female Mennonite. Even the Roman Missal—all 1,500 pages of it—can be accessed digitally.

Finally, devotional materials have become more widely available due to social communications media. For instance, the Book of Common Prayer daily office is available on Twitter in several formats. Orthodox icons are visible on Instagram and Pinterest. The presence of these materials on the internet is interesting for several reasons. Not only are they present to people who may not have seen them previously, but they introduce a diachronic element to the virtual space. For example, the use of the daily office on

Twitter issues an invitation to participation – an invite that most certainly has an ecumenical character.

These developments are not exceptional cases; they exist within a deeper trajectory that moves toward something like catholicity. Further, recent treatments of liturgy by evangelicals have not maintained confessional boundaries, but embraced all liturgical resources in hopes of renewing their liturgical shape by engaging all voices within the great tradition.[16] This leads to another question: Are these encounters and their fruits truly ecumenical? To be sure, if they are, then the form of ecumenical engagement seen here is without a doubt more diffuse and hard to track. Unlike more conventional ecumenical approaches (which have sought formal multi-lateral dialogues and high-level meetings), this approach occurs more tacitly, on the parish or congregational level, within worship planning sessions, or in conversations in virtual spaces on social media. On first glance, this might even look like chaos, with the potential to destroy confessional identity (certainly a few Baptists in my part of the world would think so). Yet, the result of this new virtual ecumenism is certainly greater diversity of liturgical practice, but also liturgical encounters that fuel an embrace of the wider catholicity of the church.

In many ways, it seems that this sort of engagement resonates with the ecumenical dialogue discussed in the 1995 encyclical *Ut Unum Sint*. There, John Paul II speaks of dialogue as more than an exchange of ideas, but rather "an exchange of gifts."[17] The ways in which liturgical resources and rhythms have been shared by these new media open up lines of communication that were not previously present or acknowledged. The role of liturgy in ecumenical dialogue was also highlighted. John Paul II stated that liturgical renewal had occurred in the Catholic Church as well as in "certain other Ecclesial Communities." He noted that more frequent Eucharistic celebration and relative synchronization of liturgical readings (i.e., through the lectionaries) are the fruit of this ecumenical effort.[18]

Contemporary ecumenical conversations have focused on what Catholic theologian Paul Murray has called "receptive ecumenism." This strategy shifts the focus from teaching other traditions about one's own ecclesial home. Instead, as was described in an international conference in 2006 on the subject, what is pursued is "a mutual process in which each offers its own gifts as well as receiving from those of others" in which "the primary emphasis is upon learning rather than teaching."[19] This stance, then, does not look for the uncrossable boundaries between traditions, but the gifts that open up space for new life together. Without a doubt, liturgy (and its shape within various ecclesial communities) is one of those gifts. As Peter Leithart states, even though receptive ecumenism is not a smooth path, when pursued, "Christians fall in love with the presence of God in the people, practices, and structures of other Christian traditions."[20]

Insofar as the various forms of social communications media have aided Christians of diverse traditions to not only see their brothers and sisters as such, but also to produce a genuine openness to their liturgical practices, steps toward receptive ecumenism have taken place. As we have noted, for free-church Protestants, something like a liturgical renewal movement has occurred. Yet more than liturgical shape is transformed. In the spirit of the ancient church axiom *lex orandi, lex credendi,* as new liturgical practices give rise to better theological reflections, new horizons are recognized. In other words, a growing Baptist embrace of the rhythm of the liturgical year can prompt reflections on salvation as participation in the pilgrim church on its sojourn toward union with God or the role of saints in deepening this regular pattern. As a result, ecumenical possibilities will emerge as well, and each of these in small yet significant ways will contribute to the realization of the one, holy, catholic, and apostolic church.

The two parts of this essay highlight the role of extra-ecclesial encounters within liminal spaces (e.g., fellowship halls and blogosphere) in deepening the ties that bind together the Body of Christ. These spaces, previously overlooked or relativized, now play a significant part in maintaining and passing on the faith. These spaces (digital or otherwise) are virtual, meaning that they oscillate between presence and absence, both concerning Christ himself and the eschatological *ekklesia.* As such, further reflection is needed in order to fully discover how these extra-liturgical spaces fruitfully support the liturgical life of the church.

This consultation yielded some new directions for future collaboration. The most promising of these is investigating how the confessional differences between Christian traditions affect their distinct approaches to technology. While more consideration is certainly needed along these lines, both of us suspect that the more open approach that Free Church traditions have toward technology in their liturgies owes in large part to the nature of their sacramental theologies and congregational-based ecclesiologies. This only furthers the claims made in this essay that the sacramental life of the church is not merely subject to technological culture, but is instead intimately interwoven with the technological paradigm. It is our hope that future scholarship in subjects such as ecumenism, sacramentalism, and ecclesiology attends to these dynamics.

Notes

[1]Birgit Meyer, "Media and the Senses in the Making of Religious Experience: An Introduction," *Material Religion* 4, no. 2 (July 2008): 127.

[2]Jay David Bolter and Richard Grusin, *Remediation: Understanding New Media* (Cambridge, MA: MIT Press, 1999).

[3]Ibid., 34.

[4]See Michel de Certeau, *The Mystic Fable: The Sixteenth and Seventeenth Centuries*, vol. 1 (Chicago: University of Chicago Press, 1995), 81.

[5]Louis-Marie Chauvet, *Symbol and Sacrament: A Sacramental Reinterpretation of Christian Existence*, trans. Patrick Madigan, S.J. (Collegeville, MN: Liturgical Press, 1995), 111.

[6]Ibid., 113, quoting E. Ortigues, *Le discours et le symbole* (Paris: Aubier-Montaigne, 1962), 65.

[7]Chauvet, *Symbol and Sacrament,* 115.

[8]Ibid., 121.

[9]Ibid., 129.

[10]Pew Research Center, "America's Changing Religious Landscape," http://www.pewforum.org.

[11]See Justo L. Gonzalez, *The Story of Christianity*, vol. 1 (New York: HarperCollins, 1984), 366-67.

[12]Philip Schaff, *History of the Christian Church*, vol. 6 (New York: Charles Scribner's Sons, 1888), 560.

[13]John T. McGreevy, *Catholicism and American Freedom* (New York: W.W. Norton, 2003), 40; Mark A. Noll, *A History of Christianity in the United States and Canada* (Grand Rapids, MI: Eerdmans, 1992), 405.

[14]McGreevy, *Catholicism and American Freedom*, 7-11, 41-42. Similar tensions occurred in Cincinnati in 1869-1870 (ibid., 115).

[15]It is worth noting that some hymnals have displayed some level of ecumenicity since, for example, Baptist hymnals have included hymns from the Wesleyan movement (such as those by Charles Wesley).

[16]See the works of Robert Webber and the essays in Kennedy and Hatch, eds., *Gathering Together: Baptists at Work in Worship* (Eugene, OR: Pickwick, 2013).

[17]Pope John Paul II, *Ut Unum Sint* §28. It is worth pointing out that Chauvet

uses the mechanics of gift giving to depict his model of symbolic exchange (cf. *Symbol and Sacrament*, 102-9).

[18]Pope John Paul II, *Ut Unum Sint* §45.

[19]Quoted in Walter Kasper, foreword to *Receptive Ecumenism and the Call to Catholic Learning: Exploring a Way for Contemporary Ecumenism*, ed. Paul D. Murray (New York: Oxford University Press, 2008), vii.

[20]Peter Leithart, "Receptive Ecumenism," *First Things*, online, http://www.firstthings.com/web-exclusives/2015/02/receptive-ecumenism.

Contributors

Cynthia L. Cameron is a PhD candidate in theology and education at Boston College. Her research looks at adolescent girls through the lenses of theological anthropology, developmental psychology, and Catholic schooling. She is also actively working on projects bringing theology into conversation with the phenomenon of self-injury in adolescent girls.

Anne M. Clifford, Msgr. James A. Supple Chair of Catholic Studies at Iowa State University, has held the Walter and Mary Tuohy Chair at John Carroll University and taught at Duquesne University. Active in CTS for thirty years, she served as president (2007-2008) and co-edited the 2003 volume on Christology with Anthony J. Godzieba. In the past decade she presented twelve public lectures on ecological theology at U.S. colleges and universities, including the plenary at "*Laudato Si'* and Northern Appalachia: A Conference on the Environment and Catholic Social Teaching," held at St. Vincent College in Latrobe, PA, in October 2016.

Brian P. Flanagan is associate professor of theology at Marymount University in Arlington, Virginia. He is the author of articles on ecclesiology, ecumenism, and liturgy, and of the book *Communion, Diversity, and Salvation: The Contribution of Jean-Marie Tillard to Systematic Ecclesiology*. He has served the CTS as its treasurer and is a contributor to *Daily Theology* (https://dailytheology.org).

Derek C. Hatch is associate professor of christian studies at Howard Payne University in Brownwood, Texas. He received his PhD in theology from the University of Dayton. He is the co-editor of *Gathering Together: Baptists at Work in Worship* (2013), and the author of *Thinking with the Church: Toward a Renewal of Baptist Theology* (forthcoming). Additionally, he has published articles related to *nouvelle théologie*, theology and literature, and Baptist life and thought.

Ricky Manalo, CSP, is a Paulist priest and a liturgical composer, currently teaching at Santa Clara University. He also serves as the main facilitator of the Cultural Orientation Program for International Ministers/Priests (COPIM) of Loyola Marymount University. He has written numerous articles and books on liturgy, culture, liturgical music, and intercultural communication. His book *The Liturgy of Life: The Interrelationship of Sunday Eucharist and Everyday Worship Practices* (2014) was published by Liturgical Press.

Anne McGowan is assistant professor of liturgy at Catholic Theological Union in Chicago. Her research and teaching interests focus on the theological, historical, and ritual development of Christian worship practices and on sacramental theology in Roman Catholic and ecumenical contexts. She is the author of *Eucharistic Epicleses, Ancient and Modern: Speaking of the Spirit in Eucharistic Prayer* (S.P.C.K. / Liturgical Press, 2014).

Marcus Mescher is assistant professor of Christian ethics at Xavier University in Cincinnati, Ohio. In his graduate studies at Boston College, he received an MTS in theological ethics and a PhD in theology and education that focused on moral formation. He specializes in Catholic social teaching, and his research and writing concentrate on ecology, the common good, and solidarity. Some of his publications include the chapter "Neighbor to Nature" in the edited volume *Green Discipleship* (2011), the article "Beyond Slacktivism" in *Journal of Catholic Social Thought* (2016), and several articles featured in *Millennial Journal* and *Justice Magazine* (UK).

Bruce T. Morrill, SJ, is Edward A. Malloy Professor of Catholic Studies at Vanderbilt University. Noted for his work in sacramental-liturgical theology, he lectures and has held visiting chairs and fellowships in the USA, Europe, and Australia, and has published numerous articles, chapters, and reviews in addition to several books. His most recent books are *The Essential Writings of Bernard Cooke: A Narrative Theology of Church, Sacrament, and Ministry* (Paulist, 2016) and *Encountering Christ in the Eucharist: The Paschal Mystery in People, Word, and Sacrament* (Paulist, 2012).

Susan Bigelow Reynolds is a PhD student in theology and education at Boston College. Her research focuses on ecclesiological and pedagogical dimensions of religious practices in parishes that serve multiple cultural, ethnic, or linguistic communities. She has also done extensive work in the area of theology and prenatal loss.

Susan A. Ross is professor of theology and a faculty scholar at Loyola University Chicago. She is a past president of the Catholic Theological Society of America. She is past vice-president and member of the Board of Editors of *Concilium: International Journal for Theology*, and co-edited three of its recent issues; she has also written numerous journal articles and book chapters. Her most recent book is *Anthropology: Seeking Light and Beauty* (Liturgical Press, 2012).

Michael Rubbelke is a PhD candidate in systematic theology at the University of Notre Dame. His dissertation examines the development of Karl Rahner's mystical theology, its mystical sources, and its Christological and charismatic contours in light of contemporary discussions on mysticism. His other research interests include the relation of spiritual practices to theology, twentieth-century Trinitarian theology, and the spiritual senses of Scripture. He is a contributor to *Daily Theology* (https://dailytheology.org).

Katherine G. Schmidt is assistant professor of theology and religious studies at Molloy College, Long Island, New York. She received her BA in theology from Mount St. Mary's University (Emmitsburg) in 2007, her MA in theological studies from the University of Dayton in 2010, and her PhD in theology from the University of Dayton in 2016. Her research interests include American Catholicism and religion and culture.

Paul J. Schutz is a doctoral candidate and senior teaching fellow at Fordham University. His current research, on the writings of Jesuit astrophysicist William Stoeger, aims to construct a robust ecological theology that interprets the Christian tradition in dialogue with contemporary science on the basis of its promotion of the full flourishing of all life in relationships of love and fulfillment.

Annie Selak is a doctoral student in systematic theology at Boston College. Her current research is located at the intersection of ecclesiology and theological anthropology, examining how images of church inform and are shaped by understandings of the body. Maintaining a commitment to Catholic higher education from her experience as a student affairs professional, Selak also researches issues of race in the university setting and theological implications of sexual assault on college campuses.

Krista Stevens is visiting assistant professor of ethics in the department of theology at Marquette University. She specializes in Catholic social ethics, with particular attention given to radical solidarity as a response to racism, racial justice, and white privilege. In addition to social ethics, she focuses on U.S. Catholic history, black Catholic history, and the U.S. Catholic Church's response to racism from the 1700s to the present.

Johann M. Vento, PhD, is professor of religious studies and theology at Georgian Court University in Lakewood, NJ. Her primary research interests are political theology and mercy; praxis theory and spiritual formation; violence, trauma, and healing; and inter-religious dialogue. She has published articles in *Horizons, Teaching Theology and Religion, Jnanadeepa: Pune Journal of Religious Studies*, and in several edited volumes.

Todd Whitmore is associate professor in the department of theology and concurrent associate professor in the department of anthropology at the University of Notre Dame. His articles include, "Crossing the Road: The Case for Ethnographic Fieldwork in Christian Ethics" (*Journal of the Society of Christian Ethics*) and "'If They Kill Us, at Least the Others Will Have More Time to Get Away': The Ethics of Risk in Ethnographic Practice" (*Practical Matters*).